WOMEN OF SPIRIT
share
RITUALS DIVINE

Diverse, Personal, and Evolution-Empowering
Stories of our Connection to the Divine

Inspired By
DR. ANGELES ARRIEN

Edited By
AMSHATAR H. MONROE

Section 1: In the Stillness
"Spirit Speaks—Alle-alleluia!" copyright © 2015 by Rickie Byars.
"Remembrance: The Sufi Ritual of Zikr" copyright © 2015 by Diane W. Elliot.
"Transform Your Life: Affirmations and How to Use Them" copyright © 2015 by Rev. Dr. Barbara King.
"My Mother's Gift: The Sustaining Ritual of Prayer" copyright © 2015 by Rev. Linda Vanessa Boyd.
"Transforming Days and Spaces: Using Triangles of Light and Buddhic Column Rituals" copyright © 2015 by Judith Kravitz.
"Preparing for Sacred Time: Rituals for Greeting the Divine" copyright © 2015 by Baiyina Abadey.
"Simplified Water Practice" copyright © 2015 by The Venerable Dhyani Ywahoo.
"I Give Thanks" copyright © 2015 by Barbara Daniel Cox.

Section 2: The Voice of God
"Morning Light: Assessing Intuition at Dawn" copyright © 2015 by Sharon Franquemont.
"Dream World: A Prose Poem" copyright © 2015 by Margaret "Meg" Wheatley.
"Women of Craft: Art as Ritual" copyright © 2015 by Carole Schwinn.
"Beginning with the End in Mind… The Evolving Self" copyright © 2020 by Queen Mother Osunnike Anke.
"Tapping Into the Oneness: Co-creating Your Life with Intentional Rituals" copyright © 2015 by Rhonda Anderson.
"Listening for God Within: Achieving Balance and Guidance with a Variety of Practices" copyright © 2015 by Patricia Moore Harbour.
"The Smoke Always Tells the Truth" copyright © 2015 by Adelia Sandoval.
"Journeying Into the World of Spirit: The Mourning Process" copyright © 2015 by Iya N'Ifa Farinola Efunyale (Mother Pamela Taylor).

SECTION 3 ~ Sankofa
"Ritual: Food for the Soul" copyright © 2015 by Sobonfu Somé.
"Honoring the Past, Embracing the Future: Healing and Prospering with the Ancestors' Blessings" copyright © 2015 by Michelle Coghill Chatman.
"From Seeker to Finder: Co-creating Your Life with Spirit" copyright © 2015 by Gabriella.
"Cool Revolution" from NOW IS THE TIME TO OPEN YOUR HEART: A NOVEL by Alice Walker, copyright © 2004 by Alice Walker. Used by permission of Random House, an imprint and division of Penguin Random House LLC. All rights reserved.
"Becoming an Ideal Woman: Rituals for Developing Clarity and Spiritual Connection" copyright © 2015 by Nana Yaa Densua.
"The Ritual of Retreat: Restoring Balance" copyright © 2015 by Pamela Ramadei.
"Weaving in Ritual: A Weaver's Tale of Basket Making, Biodynamic Cranialsacral Therapy, and Conscious Dying" copyright © 2015 by Janet Evergreen.
"Ceremony for Maggie" copyright © 2015 by Rev. IONE.

In Dedication to the SPIRIT, JOY and WISDOM
of our Beloved

DR. ANGELES ARRIEN

1940–2014

Angie, the awesome Basque-American cultural anthropologist, was an award-winning author, educator and corporate consultant to many organizations and businesses. Though Angeles has moved on from this mortal body, her spirit NO DOUBT continues to spread her incredible and extraordinary wisdom, loving-kindness, guidance, vision and encouragement, she lives on in the hearts and minds of so *many* who have been touched and changed by Angie's presence.

Angeles inspired, midwifed, called forth, continued… and continues… to breathe life into this Collective Volume, **WOMEN of SPIRIT share RITUALS DIVINE**. Interestingly, Angie's transition sparked its rebirth!

Rituals Divine Foreword

By

Linda Lantieri and Michelle C. Chatman

Who would have thought a decade ago when this project began that it would actually be birthed during the time of global pandemic; a time when turning to the sacredness of ritual was, in many ways, the only thing that made sense? As the indigenous grandmothers warned in 2010 the time for a shift was approaching. A new prophecy was needing to emerge to balance and correct centuries-old ways of operating that put profit and exploitation, competition and greed over people and the environment. That time is now upon us. As we write this, the entire world is gripped with COVID-19, the novel coronavirus that has claimed the lives of hundreds of thousands of people across the globe—people on the margins, poor people, wealthy people, old people, young people and those in between; people with compromised immune systems; people who are food, safety, and income insecure. We have seen literary and business icons succumb to this illness and we have lost many public servants on the front lines who are working to save our lives—nurses, doctors, delivery people, clerks, teachers, and essential workers. The experts tell us that if "we find purpose and meaning" in what is happening, our psychological well-being can benefit. Yet many of us are having a hard time doing that.

This pandemic and the global shift it is creating through historic acts–the cancellation of international sporting events, shelter in place orders on all seven continents, massive school and business closings–makes the suffering that has always been with us now impossible to ignore.

Healers, activists, and scholars are urging us to be still now. They are imploring us to not transfer the madness that brought us to this place into the new world we are imagining and have the once-in-several lifetimes opportunity to create. We hope the rituals contained in this book and others, will serve our collective soul's yearning to recreate something new that works for all of humanity and all of the living.

The paradox of this moment is that we are being called to hold two powerful but equally vital truths. In the midst of tremendous suffering, death and uncertainty we are being called to ask, What is my deepest truth? What is my soul's work? What am I here to do? How can I help heal the world? The answers demand vision, hope, and wisdom from the unseen realm. These questions are even more salient now, perhaps, because of this global moment of pause.

What now? Ritual and Recreation

This offering of rituals by women of varied traditions, ages, ethnicities, and backgrounds, is actually being born at the most perfect time. It is actually happening at a time when all of us worldwide have experienced the loss of common rituals most of us celebrate–birthdays, holidays, graduations, etc. Perhaps the aim of this collection of writings is to convey to us that now, more than ever, the deeper urgings that invite us into sacred space must be our primary focus. Our deeper needs for connection, sacred presence, healing, and communal, interdependent existence must be the value upon which we form our new world. They must be the leading questions in the forefront of our consciousness. The Divinity within each of us yearns to express itself more fully. Rituals can fuel our souls and our external work, whether that work is delivering mail, healing the sick, preparing meals, teaching, or farming. Our internal and external selves are not so distinct, yet we have made them so. Ritual is an invitation to dismantle the false barriers we have created to protect ourselves. They invite us out of hiding and into the glorious vulnerability of our shared destiny and deep interconnectedness and interdependence. Interestingly enough, during the COVID-19 pandemic, people from all walks of life have begun to create new rituals and open up to the power and healing they hold and offer.

We invite you to follow your soul's yearning as you explore the pages in this book. In these pages, are reminders of what the deepest parts of ourselves already know–that we are divine, we are of the Earth, water, and the stars. It is a gift to offer this Foreword in honor of a woman, now an ancestor, who knew this deeply and lived it fearlessly, our beloved Angeles Arrien, a cultural anthropologist who both studied and lived with many indigenous cultures on all of the continents. She guided this project every step of the way. Linda recalls when one of her students got very upset at the thought of her death, Angeles said, "Not to worry, then I can be available to you 24-7!" We certainly felt her steadfast presence as we were moving this project to completion. Angeles reminded us that "ritual is the oldest way to support change because it functions as a bridge between the inner world and the outer world." She often would say that ritual is a way of honoring "sacred intention". She believed that the more we brought ritual into our lives, the more balanced our inner and outer worlds would become.

Yet, even with ritual there is the risk of approaching it from a mechanistic way. But it's so much more than that. It's so much deeper. It is our soul's yearning, our soul's calling. Rituals need not be elaborate or shrouded in ancient mystery, although many are. We can also ground ourselves in simple rituals for they too, hold great potency when entered into with humility and reverence for the transformation they catalyze.

An essential message of this book is that we can center the sacred in our lives at any time, not just on special occasions, but in our everyday walk. We need this lesson now. The birth of this book in print was waiting for the time in human history where making sense out of it will depend on a very deep dive into our souls–and rituals are one of the strongest vehicles for going there. May you find the inspiration, love, and belonging both of us feel because of the presence of rituals as a regular part of our lives.

TABLE OF CONTENTS

 INTRODUCTION

May this offering to the Divine also be an invitation and inspiration to Its readers.

We offer this invitation to see ritual as a tool to further cultivate and personalize an active relationship with the Divine that we might actualize our innate and eternal desire to be the very best spiritual expression that we can be!

This Rituals project is intended to soften the lines of difference (right/ wrong, good/bad, ageless wisdom/new age) to create an openness and space for each of us to imagine and explore simple, diverse, creative, and time-honored ways to connect with the Divine in our everyday lives.

The once highly respected ancient and contemporary, daily, and seasonal rituals that were widely practiced with honor and religiosity among most spiritual practitioners have seemingly been demoted to rare, occasional, misunderstood and/or clandestine use. Today, as more people deeply consider and cultivate their personal and spiritual development, many are restructuring ritual into the fabric of their spiritual practice.

Unfortunately, however, the word *ritual* means something different to most everybody.

For many, it conjures up less than positive images and thoughts of witch-craft, sorcery, paganism, animism, etc. It is these kinds of knee-jerk, often misunderstood, out-of-context and over-dramatized associations and divides that this collection of personal stories seeks to bridge and offer new context and perspective.

Interestingly, even among the seasoned women contributing to this work, all of whom live ritually- and spiritually-rich lives of activism and service, many paused at the thought of how their voice would fit into a Collective Volume about "ritual." Serving as a consultant to this project, noted cultural anthropologist, cross-cultural educator and researcher, and award-winning author, Dr. Angeles Arrien made the brilliant suggestion that the contri-butions could come in the form of story or poem. This simple suggestion provided space for creative, uniquely individual expression and more authentic and comfortable sharing. It invited the "spirit" of the participant to show up, and created a warmer welcome and greater ease for the reader.

Additionally, this approach invites a wider audience AND helps to demys-tify the term "ritual." Authentic creative expression supports a broader and more diverse outlook that makes for a more relevant definition for ritual. It provides a way to elicit more interaction with the experience of ritual in our everyday life.

Our shared stories are offered through a broad and inclusive definition of ritual as **that which strengthens and sustains one's connection to the Divine in our everyday life!**

This Collective work presents the personal ritual stories, experiences and/or perspectives of forty women from diverse backgrounds, from five different continents and all four directions of the globe, who embrace a wide array of spiritual and religious practices including Christianity, Judaism, Islam,

Sufism, Buddhism, Hinduism, African (Akan, Yoruba), Native American (Acjachemena, Cherokee, Dakota) and other traditional and indigenous Earth- and Nature-based practices as well. All of the contributors are widely known and celebrated for their life of service and for the spiritual integrity from which they live their lives. Many of the contributors are renowned authors, several are scholars, recording artists, sound healers and visionaries, others are community and global leaders, spiritual activists, traditional healers, ministers, and spiritual teachers… they are all women who value the profound difference that *ritual* makes in their life and in their work of service in the world. As do their varied and unique walks in life, their compilation of stories interestingly convey and demonstrate the unique, expansive, chameleon-like nature of *ritual*.

The offerings are presented in five distinct sections. Though the individuality of each story is strong, clear, and uncompromised, there is an underlying relatedness that is held among the stories within each section. Each section mirrors one of five stages of manifestation—from the point of contemplation *(In the Stillness)*… to the spoken intention *(The Voice of God)*… to retrospective reflection *(Sankofa)*… to creation *(Love in Action)*… and to co-creation *(The Braided Path)*!

You may choose to read this book from cover to cover, or to allow the book to "read you"—as you randomly open the book—that it might offer *just the right story* for you at that particular moment. You may choose to make this a 40-day ritual of your own and read a different story each day. However you choose to proceed, we trust that you will have a joyful and inspiring journey, replete with interesting twists and turns, subtle profundity, surprise, great reminders, some eye-openers, sweetness, encouragement, and at least a few perspective-broadening encounters.

 WOMBSPACE

How This Book Came to Be

During much of my adult life I was consumed with an inner-personal battle between love, hate, acceptance, fear, and forgiveness. I had not yet developed the skillful use of the tools that could liberate me from the socio-political, racial, and religious anger that had taken up residence in and with me. The unattended anger turned to suppressed rage—I was diagnosed with lupus. A dear sister-friend gave me a note-card with a powerful African Proverb printed on front, "The bitter heart eats its owner!" She said, "*This* is what lupus is."

Very shortly after the proverbial clarity of my medically diagnosed lupus, while participating in a very sacred and ancient ritual, it was made clear to me that my work of service was to gather people from different ethnic/social/cultural/spiritual backgrounds together to find the common-unity in the Sacred Space of our likeness. This "gathering and bridging" work unfolded as *SACRED SPACE: Where Indigenous Paths Meet*, a non-profit organization that I founded in 1996 primarily to facilitate ethnic, cultural, and spiritual reconciliation through community gatherings designed to re-introduce us to the Sacred Space in the "center" where we are all more alike than we are different.

It was with the work of SACRED SPACE that I saw how many people had an initial, impulsive hesitance to anything that outwardly referenced ritual or ceremony and would energetically and sometimes physically "step back" if words like *invocation* or *libation* were mentioned, or if prayers began in words that were unfamiliar to them, or if the altar had objects that reflected other religious or spiritual paths different from their own. I sought to find unobtrusive ways to get people comfortable with the presence of "difference" in spiritual settings and to even dare to find our sameness and our ONE God in it!

I learned to rely more on ritual and ceremony than dialogue to facilitate healing, reconciliation, and peace- and community-building work. It was in the cross-cultural community gatherings and rituals of SACRED SPACE that I witnessed and experienced the profound power of the simplest rituals—song, riverside prayer, hand-holding or open-heart circles, silence, fire-keeping, tobacco offerings, labyrinth walks, round-dances, sacred art, collective altar creation, and countless other forms of witnessing and experiencing the Divine in oneself and in the "other."

Shortly after beginning the work of SACRED SPACE, the hand of Grace extended itself to me yet again, and I was awarded a Fellowship with the Fetzer Institute. The express purpose of the fellowship award was to cultivate and balance the recipients' inner work of spirit and outer work of service. For the next three years I met regularly with the Fetzer Fellows, the most diverse group of people I had ever been involved with. We gathered at least once each quarter under the wise, skillful, intuitive, and ritualized facilitation of Angeles Arrien. This became the cocoon that provided the "safe space" for me to heal my Lupus, to transform and transcend huge amounts of pain and anger, to allow my heart to be broken open, to embrace *difference* beyond what had previously been known or familiar to me, and to begin to truly walk the talk and do the inner and outer work of Community that my soul longed for. It was through ritual that Grace had entered my life to heal my broken heart, to quiet and transmute my rage, and it was through the community ritual work of SACRED SPACE that I witnessed Grace heal the pain and brokenness of others and gently invite us into our individual and collective healing.

Angeles encouraged me then, now more than a decade ago, to write a book about rituals, but I was intimidated by the idea of "putting myself out there" like that. Admittedly, I was uncomfortable with boldly associating myself with *ritual*, even though, at the time, inviting people into community ritual as a means of transcending differences and finding commonality was my primary work of service and the greatest joy of my heart.

THE BIRTHING

Why Now?

All Things in the Fullness of God's Time,
In All Times there is the Fullness of God's Grace!

There seems to be little disagreement around the fact that a major shift toward spirituality is taking place. With this heightened spirituality there appears to be a corresponding, accelerated front-and-center positioning of the Divine Feminine. With the reemergence of the feminine aspect of God that is taking place, there is an inextricable call for and a corresponding ease and abundance of collaboration, cooperation, acceptance, receptivity… more full- and open-heartedness. There seems to be a wonderful and heightened "knowing" among a growing number of us that oneness is a clear pathway to the Divine!

In the Evocation of *A New Earth*, Eckhart Tolle advances the concept that the emergence of the first colorful and fragrant flower in the (theretofore all green) plant kingdom, the first crystal and precious stone in the rock/mineral kingdom, and the first bird in the (previously earth-bound) animal kingdom indicate points of *major* transformation in each kingdom's evolution. Tolle postulates it as a leap in the evolutionary consciousness of the kingdom. Tolle further offers for our consideration the fact that we, the human kingdom, could now very well be poised for a significant transcendence in consciousness, an evolutionary leap, when the "new human" will have evolved—beyond ego. From this new state of evolutionary consciousness that Tolle invites us to consider and embrace (one surely full of greater love, peace, beauty, joy, spiritual wisdom, and oneness) we would, no doubt, create a "new earth." *That idea excites me!*

Like Tolle and a myriad of great spiritual and evolutionary minds, more of us are increasingly aware that "*something* is up," we sense the shift, we sense that things are changing, and we *feel* the evolutionary impulse! More of us are actively involved in the deep inner work of creating richer spiritual lives and are enthusiastically willing to serve the cause of our great evolutionary awakening and transformation of consciousness. Many contend this to be particularly true of women.

As we begin this far-bigger-than-life transformational trek, at critical points along the journey the question of *how* to continue arises. Reflection on the question of how to continue reminds me of Sankofa, an ageless-wisdom word and symbol of the Akan people of Ghana (West Africa). Sankofa speaks to the wisdom of "looking back before going forward... learning from the past to build for the future." As we prepare to "flower" into the next stage of evolutionary consciousness as the "new human" of the "new earth" that we are co-creating, we might contemplate what it is of this soon to be past "now," containing the seed of ageless wisdom that could continue to be useful and beneficial as we evolve. During other major evolutionary change points there was both significant change as well as significant car-ry-over (i.e., even with the advent of colors and fragrances, the flower was and is still a plant; be they amethyst or quartz, crystals are still mineral). So too, albeit extant, Homosapiens are still part of the hominid family.

Might we, at this critical moment in time, dare to ask not what God (the Divine) can do for us, but what we can do for the Divine (God)! Many have said that the Divine needs our "hands and feet" perhaps more now than ever before. I recently heard someone paraphrase the words of the for-ward thinking author, Ken Wilber, who said that in every *individual* action we are casting our vote for what we want to see manifest as our *collective* highest potential. This could very well be the optimal time to gather the daughters and sons of the Divine to join our heads, hearts, hands, and feet in service to the "shift" that is upon us.

If we take a Sankofa-look back at what has sustained and inspired us, as we consider what we might continue to benefit as we evolve, we might be sur-prised at what we find. We might find those *simple* yet fundamental things that nourish, edify, transform, and evolve us *spiritually*. We might find that *ritual,* as demonstrated in countless ways, is a constant tool for spiritual development that qualifies as one such thing. We might find the subtle but certain evolutionary power of ritual!

During my work with SACRED SPACE and the primary work that evolved from it—*Women of Spirit*—I have met some phenomenally wonderful, powerful, spiritually rich women of various backgrounds, professions, and interests who live lives that embrace and rely on *ritual* to inform and improve their work of service in the world and the quality of their spiritual evolution.

Now feels like the time to collaborate with some of these women stewards of the Divine to put forth a heartfelt offering, an invitation to ritual in response to the "all-hands-on-deck" Call of the Divine and our deep desire to serve this sacred moment in time… NOW *is* the time!

 WHAT *IS* RITUAL?

That Which Strengthens and Sustains One's Connection to the Divine in our Everyday Life!

To remove any ambiguity, dissolve any possible unfounded resistance and to invite the most broad and diverse participation both for our writers and readers the "that" in our working definition for ritual can be expanded or limited to whatever is comfortable for the practitioner. We invite you, for the reading of this anthology, to consider and embrace this evolutionary definition of ritual: "that" (any that!) which strengthens and sustains one's connection to the Divine (God, the Creator) in our everyday life. The personal stories shared in this Collective Volume demonstrate the breadth, depth, variety, and range of perspectives that ritual can cover and just how personal, unique, and diverse ritual can be to every individual—meditation, song, dance, spiritual cleansing, walking, writing, ancestral remembrance and reverence, silence, bathing, affirmation, giving, gratitude, weaving, grieving, drumming, caring, and social and/or spiritual activism.

We offer these stories as both a gift and an invitation in hopes that you will find personal connection and inspiration in the stories and that you will embrace the use of ritual in your life, perhaps from a broader and deeper perspective. We offer these stories that you might re-consider the importance, the ease, and the personal and universal value of ritual. We offer these stories that you might tap into a renewed sustained and strengthened connection to the Divine and release your personal, authentic creative expression into the evolutionary process, not only for yourself but for all of creation!

SPIRIT MOVES

How Ritual Shows Up—From the Mundane to the Astonishing

In addition to, or maybe because of, the fact that rituals can be such direct portals to the Divine, another by-product that makes ritual a tool worthy of consideration for this evolutionary phase is its positive impact beyond the individual. As we have conscious connection with the Divine (Love Itself), we are more open to our own loving kindness, toward self and others, and our very oneness with All and all others. When consciously connected to the Divine, what we might otherwise have perceived as "troublesome differences" can easily and quickly shape-shift into "unique variances" that enhance the texture of the fabric and add sparkle to the kaleidoscope of life. Yes, we believe, and have experienced and witnessed, that ritual—a song, meditation, a gift, time in Nature, gratitude, etc.—can be that transforming!

A member of the SACRED SPACE Council of Elders, Mountain Eagle Woman, now an honored ancestor, once told me that she had very much wanted an eagle feather; however, she wanted to receive it in a "good way." She used to see an eagle fly over her property with some regularity. One morning after her ritual greeting of the day with prayers to the four directions, sage and/or tobacco offerings of gratitude to the elements and a sweet morning song from her heart… as she finished her ritual and prepared to go back inside her house, there in front of her was the gift of a beautiful eagle feather. Mountain Eagle Woman knew that her morning ritual had called her feather to her… in a good way.

Admittedly, my personal journey to the heart-opening space of greater love, acceptance of difference, and the desire to embrace universal oneness was neither quick nor straight and narrow and certainly was not "no crystal stair." Many of us grew up with a strong, yet mostly "invisible" foundation of rituals that we took for granted and failed to recognize their deeper purpose and transforming power (daily blessing of food at every meal, on-your-knees prayers of gratitude and protection every night, going to church every Sunday, honorable and kind speech—"please," "thank you," "yes ma'am," "no sir," "excuse me"—and utmost respect to every adult and elder). The strong childhood foundational "ritual instruction" that many of us received notwithstanding, it took a lot of river walks, tree-hugging, full-moon singing, prayers, sweat-lodge ceremonies, healing circles, and various other rituals to even begin to heal and hollow out this ole reed (and countless others, no doubt). However, through the Grace of God, many of us are far better for the journey and pray that the perfecting hollowing of ritual continues to make for ever-increasing useful reeds.

Again, we are pleased that you have responded to our personal invitation (witnessed by your reading of these words) and we hope you will enjoy the personal stories of these phenomenal Women of Spirit who lovingly share their stories, perspectives and everyday ritual practices and experiences. I suspect that you will find your own stories on many of these pages. I pray that you will be inspired to more fully embrace ritual in your life, in your own unique and fulfilling way. May you be encouraged to invite or facilitate others to do the same. More ritual means more connection to the Divine! What better time in our evolutionary trajectory than Now?

INVOCATION

All Are Present… In One Accord… Let Us Begin!

As is the *SACRED SPACE* and *WOMEN OF SPIRIT* tradition… we begin all Circles or Gatherings of significance with an Invocation, acknowledging and inviting the Spiritual Presence of the forces within and around us that support us in showing up in life as the best of who we are. Please join us in this invocation!

BEFORE YOU ENTER THIS *SANCTUARY…*
We invite you to prepare for the journey.
Take a few calming breaths… inhale deeply and exhale slowly.

Now take a moment to
CONNECT WITH THE ONE,
Universal, Creative Force of Love by whatever name You call It:
GOD, Creator, Olodumare, Krishna, Neter, Allah, Buddha, Jesus,
Great Spirit, DIVINE.

GIVE THANKS
for the Presence of Spirit in Your Life with You Now and Always!

Now Connect with
THE CREATOR'S SPIRITUAL HELPERS:
Angels, Saints, Orisa, Neteru, Adawee, Bodhisattvas, Nature Spirits of
Light, Spiritual Guides, by whatever name YOU resonate with.

GIVE THANKS
for their Loving Presence in Your Life with You Now… With You Always!

Take a moment to
REMEMBER YOUR ANCESTORS WITH LOVE AND HONOR,
perhaps Your Great-Grandmother or Grandfather, and to Acknowledge
YOUR SPIRITUAL TEACHERS.

GIVE THANKS
for the Foundation of Light and Love on which You Stand!
Surround Those Who Have Preceded You With GRATITUDE.

Recognizing that
YOU ARE NOT ALONE;
not on an Island unto Yourself.

Take a Moment to
ACKNOWLEDGE THOSE WHO HAVE HELPED
to Guide or Assist You to the Spiritual Consciousness
You are Now Experiencing.

Offer Each of Them Your
HEARTFELT LOVE and GRATITUDE.

NOW… LET US BEGIN!
ENTER… EXPLORE… ENJOY

SECTION ONE

IN THE STILLNESS

 IN THE STILLNESS

As in the stillness, in the silence, before the Beginning!

Once while attending a retreat in the desert near Sedona, Arizona, I woke up very early in the morning… my body was still on East Coast time. As I lay in the bed… in the stillness… in the silence, I was reminded of two things. I remembered that I had been told during the final divination of an initiation ceremony that my optimal time for prayer was 5:00 a.m. I had really been struggling with getting up at that hour and rarely did. I also remembered that we had been instructed by the retreat facilitator to write a haiku. The haiku was to be in the traditional Japanese format of three unrhymed lines, with five syllables in the first and third lines and seven syllables in the second line. I realized, as I lay there wide awake in bed, that nothing had come to me in that format and that we may be asked to share our haiku with the rest of the group this morning.

Unable to sleep, I got up and decided to go outside in the dark and gaze at the heavens while offering my morning prayers. As I stood in absolute awe of the beauty and the profundity of the desert's pre-dawn silence, absolute stillness, and heavenly bliss, an Inner Voice said:

Come, stand before me
As darkness turns into Light
See your Self unfold

Awesome! Out of the stillness and the silence came the affirming message from the Highest Self of the importance that pre-dawn prayer held for me… and it was the haiku that had yet to come!

If each day and each of its moments could be birthed out of the perfection of the silence and the stillness… how much more purposeful, powerful, and joyful might each day be if we first immersed and bathed in the depth of invitation to the lyrics of Paulette Pipe's, "In the Stillness":

There is Peace… There is Quiet
When we touch, the Stillness

There is Light… There is Healing
When we touch, the Stillness

There is Love… There is Knowing
When we touch, the Stillness

There is Hope… There is Growing
When we touch, the Stillness

May you Rest… May it Flow
Weaving in… Letting go… In the Stillness

There is Peace… There is Quiet
When we touch, the Stillness

I invite you to listen-in to the depth of simplicity found in stillness and silence as offered by these phenomenal women, as they share their stories of the power of prayer, meditation, gratitude, purifying rituals, remembrance, and song to ground, uplift, and solidify our relationship with the Divine.

During Meditation: Spirit Speaks—Alle-Alleluia!
Rickie Byars

Rickie Byars is a multidimensional artist: she is a singer, composer, performer, arranger, recording artist, and founding director of the more-than-200-voice multicultural Agape International Choir. An intuitive channel of healing music, her compositions give rise to a profound experience that opens the heart, touches the soul, and lifts the spirit. Acclaimed as a pioneer in alternative spiritual music and recognized with an honorary doctorate in music and numerous awards, Rickie loves to collaborate! Rickie's sound crosses all musical boundaries, including gospel, rhythm and blues, jazz, and world beat. Before her introduction to Agape, she was lead singer with the New York Jazz Quartet, the Pharoah Sanders Ensemble and the Ronald Muldrow Ensemble. "I have found my niche and my divine vocation," she says! For more information on Rickie Byars, visit her at www.rickiebyars.org.

Prelude

I hit the pavement running, intent on making my dream of getting a re-cording contract come true in 30 days. Sure enough, in about three weeks' time, I landed a record deal and just knew, along with my family and friends back home, that I was on my way to stardom and success. The year was 1975. I was in my early twenties, experiencing the trials and triumphs of life as a budding artist who had left Atlanta on a midnight plane to New York. Undeniably talented, but not yet experienced in the business of music, I signed on with an indie jazz label in hopes that my talent would triumph in a successful project. But any artist who has ever signed a medio-cre recording contract discovers all too soon that what appeared to be gold was not even copper. I spent many days wondering about the intentions of the record label and even more about how to make ends meet. Over the next year, the time I spent on actual stage performance or studio recording was far less than I'd imagined it might be. Yet with the assistance of my brother, Xavier, his wife, my uncles and aunts, and a host of newly made New York friends, I began to understand the value of investing all that extra time in the discovery of my true self.

The call to stardom was still there, but the journey to discover my purpose and the potential within my soul spoke to me in a more powerful voice. Destiny designed me into a more-than-willing student, eager to be a better person for the new life ahead of me. One day, while searching the radio for alternative music, I stumbled on the perfect teacher for that time in my life. His syndicated program aired on Tuesday afternoons on a public broadcast station. The subject was meditation.

Listening to the calm and distinct voice of Roy Masters provided relief from my thoughts of fame and fading cash, and a respite from the street sounds of Brooklyn's Bedford-Stuyvesant. The commentator, an author of several books on the subject of meditation, impressed upon his listeners the necessity of learning to control our emotions. He said that to gain the ability to pull one's self out from states of depression or really high states of excitement we need to strengthen our connection with the "observer" inside of us. With the assistance of his tapes and books, I was able to cultivate a practice of meditation that served me well on my journey through young adulthood. When I had little other spiritual or ritual practice, meditation provided me with just that—a ritual I could perform every day that helped keep me grounded and connected to my spirit.

Nowadays, not only do I try to meditate at least once a day, I also participate at least three times a year in silent meditation retreats led by my former husband and teacher, Michael Bernard Beckwith. Although many believe that those of us who meditate regularly have quiet minds, that isn't always true. The following story is one of scores of hilarious ones that describe what goes on inside my mind when the rest of the room—and everyone else's mind—appears to be completely still. Plus, it illustrates the benefit I get out of the ritual of meditation—even when my mind is far from quiet.

Meditation

With a mind full of thoughts, I began to observe my breaths, one at a time. With each breath I became more aware of my body itching and of not being able to scratch the itchy spots. The body itching is the worst part of meditation. Why not scratch the darned itches and get it over with rather than suffer through the frustration of itching?

There I was again, fighting my ego at another meditation retreat. "HE's not itching," my monkey-mind spoke to me. (That HE would be my husband, the meditation teacher.) "HE's cool and calm, surfing the benefits of mental sobriety one mystical wave at a time." Somehow it just didn't seem fair that he was so full of the Spirit and I so full of myself.

My ego challenged that in the two hours I had sat there watching my breath I could have fed at least 40 starving people. Or I could have sung to an audience of folks who love my music and could have ushered that audience into a state of meditation by just singing from the joy within my heart. I also could have taken a flight half the way to North Carolina to visit my nieces, nephews, sisters, and brothers, whom I missed dearly. Hmm. Hmm. Hmm.

I was a pitiful mess, itching high in the hills of picturesque Palos Verdes, California, at a meditation retreat. My mind was making noise that only I could hear, but I noticed it was not as loud as the snoring of the fellow stretched out on the floor just inches past my feet. His pathetic condition made me feel better about my own meditation failure.

I continued to sit anyway, because I was convinced that I needed to sit and do "nothing" to be more effective at doing "something." I needed to "plug in," so to speak, which presupposed to my ego that I was "unplugged." Anyway, I sat for three hours through the first Friday-night session with breaks in between. At these retreats, I am invited intermittently to sing a song or chant to soothe the soul. The night ended with no apparent success except that I had tried to meditate and I was asked to sing. And sing I did.

Even though we are taught there is no place to go in meditation, and that any meditation constitutes a good one, a point comes when you know you have connected with something greater within you. For sure, I had not felt such connection during the times of silence that day, but when I sang, I was blissfully full of the Spirit every time. So that evening, I released myself from judgment and gave thanks that in this life I get to sing healing music, healing myself in the process of sharing it. Then I returned to my room for a short night of delicious, well-earned sleep.

The next morning's session began promptly at 6:00 and was a little easier. After yoga class and a little breakfast, I treated myself to an early morning walk around the pristine retreat grounds, resplendent with live peacocks that know nothing of quietude and could care less. Then, I was back to another session of Vipassana, an insight meditation that assists one in maintaining awareness.

This time my mind was more surrendered to the ritual of sitting, and I felt better in all ways. Preparing for a long session by positioning myself comfortably in my chair, I scratched all the usual itchy places and listened to my teacher as I began to watch my breathing. The usual fare of monkey-mind came upon me again, but this time the thoughts of serving the world didn't appear. Instead, a curious melody of celebration seemed to erupt within me, and all I could hear was a chant—the sound of the Earth.

The music peeked through me like the sun in a rain forest after a storm has passed. It began to reveal the sound of happy children, dancing and singing. Something was happening. A song was coming to me, through me, and rather than act like it didn't exist or attempt to breathe it away, I arose from my chair, slipped quietly out of the room, and journeyed across the courtyard to a lovely little chapel just 50 paces from the meditation room.

Many days of my youth were spent at Mass in a church slightly bigger than this little chapel. Childhood memories of African-American nuns, Italian priests, jazz Masses, and great talent shows began to stir in my mind as I opened the door. I allowed these thoughts to visit for a few minutes, and then I paid homage to the prayerful spirit of the chapel, a place where previously I had given birth to so many chants now sung by thousands of people all over the world. At a little spinet piano nestled against the wall in the back of the room, I took my place as I had so many times before, and the song that had begun in the meditation room flowed joyfully from my voice and through my fingers.

In what seemed like an eternal moment, I hammered out "Alle-Alleluia" in what would measure about 12 minutes in human time. My soul was satisfied and fulfilled as I returned to the meditation room with a new song, a quieter mind, and practically no itching in my body. With ease I entered a zone of gratitude and stillness. A new song to be shared with the people in that room, the people at church, and the millions of people all over the world had emerged from my heart. My soul was fulfilled, and it all began with meditation.

After Thoughts…

Meditation is the doorkeeper of my soul. A ritual of observing the thoughts and opinions that shape the way we think and live is the most important aspect of spiritual practice. For a long time, I thought the purpose of meditation was to quiet the mind or to shut out the world. But what it has done for me is to open me up to the most creative aspect of my being so that the real ritual of composing can take place. In the space of no thought, the universe reveals itself and I listen. I go to the piano, sit down, and release my soul to music. This is a ritual I have done for years, which allows me to give music to the world. When Spirit speaks, even during meditation, I know it's time to get up and go meet the sun with a song. Alle-Alleluia.

Alle-Alleluia

Surrounded by the presence, surrounded by a friend
The source of all creation allows me to begin
The source of all creation allows me to begin again

Chorus:

Alle-Alleluia, Alle-Alleluia
Alle-Alleluia Alle-Alleluia Alle-Alleluia
Alle-Alleluia

Surrounded by a presence, surrounded by a friend
The source of all creation allows me to forgive
The source of all creation allows me to forgive again

Alle-Alleluia… (Chorus)

Surrounded by a presence, surrounded by a friend
The source of all creation allows my heart to sing
The source of all creation allows my heart to sing again

Alle-Alleluia… (Chorus)

Un mundo, una pas, una allegria
Un mundo, una pas, una allegria
Un mundo, una amor, una allegria
One world, one love, one joy
That's what it is! Alle-Alleluia
Alle-Alleluia

Remembrance: The Sufi Ritual of Zikr

Diane W. Elliot

Diane Miller Wiles Elliot grew up Presbyterian, in Indianapolis, Indiana, graduating in the last all-female class, 1969, Vassar College, Poughkeepsie, NY. She is, or has been, a certified childbirth educator, community volunteer in health, education, and social issues; competitive swimmer, gardener, restaurateur, wife, mother of three. She had no discernible early life indication she would become a leader of Zikr-Sufi Ceremony of Remembrance; a Cheraga (licensed Universal Sufism minister);energy healer; Dances of Universal Peace leader; facilitator of spiritual exploration classes; storyteller, owner of Local Roots, a Farm to Table Restaurant, or connect to her Cherokee heritage. Diane lives in Roanoke, Virginia, with her husband, two cats, a dog and many living green beings. www.localrootsrestaurant.com

Come, come, whoever you are, wanderers, worshipers, lovers of leaving, it doesn't matter; ours is not a caravan of despair. Even though you've broken your vows a thousand times, come, come again.

—Jelaluddin Rumi

Ritual is about experiencing the threshold between the worlds of Seen and Unseen, where our vision and understanding of life on this Earth can deepen and broaden. Standing on this threshold gives us a view of the Limitless that invites us to remember, as the Sufis do at the Ceremony of Remembrance called Zikr. The phrase of Zikr is chanted, repeated over and over in changing cadences and phrases of the main, original phrase: La illaha illa'llah hu. There is only God, nothing else.

My first Zikr is forever engraved in my heart and my being. Late in the summer of 1988, my good friend and sister in spiritual exploration, Rosemary, and I made the journey in my 10-year-old red Volvo station wagon from Roanoke, Virginia, to the Omega Institute near Woodstock, New York. We were signed up for a week of Tai Chi, which was the least-weird offering I could find in the Omega catalogue that year.

The year before I had quickly tossed away, as being too strange, the catalogue—which was filled with such week-long class offerings as mysticism, working with nature spirits, even self-loving. Plus, they served vegetarian meals! At the time, I wasn't sure how the catalogue had even made its way to my mailbox. My family and I were living in southwest Virginia as fine, upstanding Episcopalian members of the community. Twenty years ago, I was attempting to live in an acceptable box.

When the Omega catalogue arrived in 1988, however, I held it in my hands and studied it. "Hmm, the Tai Chi class the last week in August looks like a possibility," I thought. I had at least heard of Tai Chi. After a moment and a breath: "Yep. It is a go," I said to myself, feeling the inner flutter of excitement that told me this decision was on target.

Something had happened in the intervening year that had opened me to this adventure of jumping off a spiritual cliff. Maybe it was learning by osmosis from my young teenage daughter, Emily, who was at a boarding school in Ojai, California, a place where whole wheat bread was standard and spiritual bookstores beckoned with a vast array of possibilities to all who entered. Maybe it was the books on reincarnation and out-of-body experiences that I had taken to reading secretly in my closet. Maybe it was the opening bars of the Symphony of Awakening, which I could not yet hear on a conscious level but was receiving on some level. I don't know.

In any event, commencing to live a double life, Rosemary and I set off for whatever it was that lay before us, sisters in whatever we would find. What we found upon arrival at the Omega Institute's parking lot was at least several worlds away from our southwestern Virginia worldview, but we had paid our money and arranged for the children, and our husbands were resigned to our week away. So we pressed on, with big eyes taking in the panoply of those gathering, all of whom seemed to have some idea of what they were doing there. I could not say the same for myself.

Was I out of my comfort zone? Yes. Was I willing to turn back? No.

Rosemary and I worked with the flow of energy—chi—through our bodies via Tai Chi classes mornings and afternoons, and we took advantage of various lectures and offerings in the evenings. Naturally this led to feeling calm, integrated, and harmonious, as well as to a few sore muscles, but no matter. The real adventure was in the large community dining hall, a relic of the Jewish culture camp that preceded Omega. Such a colorful variety of spiritual seekers—Tibetan Buddhists, Jews, Christian mystics, deep ecologists, meditators, and other categories that slip my mind now—each stream of people there for a week of retreat. Some did not even speak (on purpose) for a couple of days!

Having weathered the initial shock of being at Omega, I became wide open to the entire adventure. Each meal was another opportunity to sit with fascinating human doorways into unexplored realms. I found myself particularly intrigued by a flock that surrounded a magnetic man with black, curly hair pulled back into a ponytail. They would waft across the dining hall, with their leader indicating the way to their table. "Who are these beings? Who is this man?" I wondered.

The energy flowing through me from my Tai Chi classes must have made me bold, for the next thing I knew, on the second day there, I had plunked myself down at the table with them and begun asking them all sorts of questions. They all seemed to know each other; they were friendly and endured my curiosity with a genuine desire to satisfy my queries and to welcome me into their group. I found out that they called themselves "Sufis," a word I had heard about a year before but for which I had never managed to find a definition. At last I could ask them what it meant, and I did. I learned that Sufis are spiritual seekers who follow the path of the heart, living in the world but not of it. To me, they seemed like normal people with families and jobs, yet different from the people I knew and with whom I tried to fit in back home. They were open about their desire for spiritual knowledge and experience. These were people who had answered the Divine invitation to go deeper and deeper into their own beings. They knew something of the Mystery and had a guide, the magnetic man with the black curly ponytail, to help shepherd them along the way. I wanted to know more.

The next day at lunch, a particularly knowledgeable Sufi woman with whom I had made a connection asked if I was coming to the Zikr ceremony the next morning (at 4:00 a.m., which I considered the middle of the night). I knew nothing about it, had never heard the word Zikr, but was definitely intrigued. She told me only Sufi initiates were supposed to attend, but she felt it would be all right if I showed up. "Just don't say anything to anybody," she said, increasing the mystery surrounding the event. I had asked to know more and had just received my invitation from the Divine to sit at the table of the Great Mystery, though I did not quite understand that at the time. In reply to the request for an RSVP, I replied "Yes" emphatically, even though I had no idea at all what would be served. Before going to bed, I set my alarm for 3:45 a.m., donned my red sweat suit (my garb for the Zikr), and turned out my light. Rinnnngg! It was time to wake up—on more than one level.

The nights can be chilly in upstate New York in late August, so I ran across campus to the appointed meeting place to keep warm. "Is this really the right place?" I asked myself. There were no lights to be seen. I opened the door anyway and found myself immediately transported into another time and another dimension both ancient and mysterious. As my eyes adjusted to the one candle burning in the middle of the room, I detected a group of men and women, wrapped in lovely, exotic shawls, sitting motionless in a circle on the floor. Two of them opened up a space for me. The cloak of darkness made me feel safe and anonymous. The stillness was palpable, yet my being felt alert. Presently, the dark-haired man with the ponytail began to lead the group in chanting and head movement. What were they saying? Doing? I did my best to imitate the foreign-sounding syllables, but the head movement eluded me.

La illaha illa'llah hu. Just as my mouth would gain some comprehension of the sounds, they would change. Illa hu, then Hu, Hu, Hu. I did not realize the varying syllables were all from the long phrase. I sat at full attention of body, mind, and spirit, chanting sounds totally foreign to me as I felt ecstasy begin to move through me.

Then it happened. The sky opened up, lights began blazing off and on and showering down upon me, and my being expanded as if my body was not really there. I felt as if I had become a part of the cosmos as I merged with the sounds swirling around and through me. Wow!

Eventually, the sounds of chanting tapered down to softness and then to silence, and the movements to stillness. Gradually bodies, remaining silent, raised themselves to standing and majestically exited the darkened room. My red sweat suit–clad body did the same, then ran, skipped, jumped, and leaped all the way back to our little cabin. "So, that's what a Zikr is! I want more!" I lay awake and waited for daylight. Maybe someone could explain to me what I had experienced.

Maybe they could have explained if I had queried, but I did not know how to articulate my experience. I had no vocabulary for this ritual. My church vocabulary was "Let us pray."

My Journey of Remembering

Eventually, sticking with this unanchored voyage into uncharted waters, I began to gain some earthly comprehension of the Ceremony of Remembrance. Immersing myself in this Path of the Heart, I learned of an ancient way of living in which Zikr—Remembrance—is central. In this ancient way, breath, sound, music, and movement are proven vibrational pathways to waking up, to remembering. I discovered pages and pages and book after book that described endless layers of meaning of the Arabic phrase, La illaha illa'llah hu. The real teaching lay not in figuring out the meaning of the words but in opening to one's own experience of them.

Like an addict wanting to re-create that first high, I sought out settings offering Zikr. The invitations to sit with the Divine kept coming, and I kept answering, "Yes." Each Zikr was different and the same. Each was an invitation, a cry, to the Beloved, to let me drop my small self, at least for a while, and remember what I, what we humans, inherently know. Remember what is already inside me and all of us; remember who I really am and who you really are; and remember that in reality there is no separation between you and me. It is all One. La illaha illa'llah hu over and over and over. There is nothing that is not God. There is no outside of God, no inside of God, and no boundaries of God. It is all God. Whatever it looks like—dark, light, sad, ecstatic, ugly, beautiful, dying, birthing, it is all God. There is no separation, even if we want there to be.

We carry this Knowing in our beings but are forgetful. We need reminding; we need times and places to remember to Remember, that allow us to come to that place where the conscious and the unconscious come together, where the Seen and the Unseen meld. This feeds our souls and reminds us of what is real. Hu, Hu, Hu, Hu, Hu, Hu, Hu, Hu, Hu, Hu, Hu: the sound and feeling of the Divine beyond all form.

The night before last, I led a Zikr in the living room of our house in Roanoke. I was struck by the timing of the Zikr and the writing of this essay. Twenty years had passed since my first experience at Omega. I realized I had not been able to finish this essay because I needed the immediacy of Zikr, of leading Zikr, to give me perspective on where I have been in my Journey of Remembering.

Each of us removed our shoes and entered the dimmed room, which was lit only by a candle. We found our places on large Turkish rug–covered floor pillows or in chairs, pillows and chairs set in a circle. I placed a simple, woven shawl of yellow-orange around my shoulders, connecting with generations of Sufis who have led Zikr and with the Sufi Order International, the order in which I am initiated.

From the darkened silence, we began with an invocation: "Toward the One, the Perfection of Love, Harmony, and Beauty, the Only Being, united with all the Illuminated Souls who form the Embodiment of the Master, the Spirit of Guidance." Then began the chant and head motions so familiar after years of practice: La illaha illa'llah hu… Illa'llah hu… Allah hu… Hu. Each phrase over and over in its turn, moving to a crescendo, then softening to a whisper, then with more speed, and then slowing to a pause—silence—breathing—a new phrase—being moved to stand and turn round and round like dervishes, buoyed in the turning by the synchronous hearts chanting the sacred phrase and the drum beat of the Tar—no thinking—each remembering—the veils of our limited selves dropping to the floor—naked before and with God and all of creation—stopping the turning—stillness—being breathed—Oneness… gradually lowering ourselves to sitting… each transformed into something more real, more of who we truly are.

Ya Shaffee, Ya Kaffee (O Healer, O Remedy), we chant for all those in need of healing of body, mind, and spirit. Ya Shalom, Ya Salaam, we chant for peace in our own hearts, that we may be vehicles for peace on this Earth. Then together we pray the Prayer for Peace: "Send Thy Peace, O Lord, that our souls may radiate Peace. Send Thy Peace, O Lord, that we may think, act, and speak harmoniously. Send Thy Peace, O Lord, that we, Thy Children on Earth, may all unite in one single family." Lastly, we stand in a circle holding hands. Each person in turn kisses the back of the hand of the person next to him or her, each person being the Beloved, one by one, around the circle. We embrace, lingering in love, Remembering.

In the next room, gifts of love are spread before us on the dining room table: nuts, fruit, cookies, tea, and water. We speak with each other from opened hearts. Zikr dances in our cells. It is possible to Remember while engaging in refreshments and conversations with others; we all are doing it. This is our natural state. No effort. Ease.

Gradually the earth-reality of time reappears, and those gathered leave through the door by which they entered, knowing they have answered the Divine invitation to sit at the table of The Great Mystery and having found that what is served is Love.

Through the ancient ritual of Zikr we have, together, made a space within our hearts for Remembering, a space for God to reside within us. The ritual has merged the physical and the metaphysical, the conscious and the un-conscious parts of ourselves. A piece of our limited selves has fallen away as we re-enter the world of time and space and jobs and budgets. We think we have invited God to sit with us, but really it is God who has invited each of us to sit in Remembrance. "Come, come again… ."

Affirmations and How to Use Them

Rev. Dr. Barbara King

Rev. Dr. Barbara King is the Founding Minister of the Hillside Chapel and Truth Center, Inc., in Atlanta, Georgia. She began this nondenominational, ecumenical ministry in 1971 with twelve members in her living room. The Hillside complex, where Dr. King, affectionately called Dr. Barbara by her members, covers nearly twelve acres with a growing congregation numbering more than 10,000. A native of Houston, Texas, Dr. Barbara was raised as a member of the legendary Antioch Baptist Church where she received a very early spiritual orientation, her ministry now extends throughout the world and is regularly featured on national media broadcast. Through elaborate ceremonies, rituals and prayers, in 2001 Dr. Barbara became the first female to be enstooled as a Chief at Assin Nsuta, Ghana, West Africa; her stool name is Nana Yaa Twunmwaa I. Dr. King is the author of seven books and monologues. www.hillsidechapel.org

An affirmation is a positive statement of truth. To affirm is to make firm in your mind. It is stating something to be true regardless of all evidence to the contrary. It is a type of mind activity used for building consciousness (awareness). It lifts you out of false thinking. An affirmation contains the elements of your belief, attitude, and motivation. An affirmation is made up of words. Words charged with power, conviction, and faith will produce after their kind. Every time you speak, the atoms in your body are affected, and the rate of their vibration is either raised or lowered.

God has given us the power of the word to use. We should be selective in the choice of words we use, for they will become our experience.

The purpose of an affirmation is to impress the subconscious mind, for what is impressed is expressed. This is done by repetition, feeling, and imaging. Repeat over and over as often as possible the affirmation with conviction and authority, believing every word you say, and see it taking shape and form. Repeat it until it becomes a part of you. In conclusion always give thanks.

It is also a good idea to give thanks before using an affirmation to prepare your subconscious to accept the truth of the affirmation.

Many people think that affirmations cannot bring about changes because the act of affirming is so simple in comparison to the difficulty of the problem they face. If that is your feeling, it may be that you have given so much power to the problem that it now appears overwhelming and unconquerable. The first thing you must do, then, is to change the way you think about your problem.

Instead of focusing on the problem, focus on the Truths of God. State your desired outcome and then say, "Thank you, God, for answered prayer." Then every time you think about the situation, substitute confidence for the fear thought. Act as though what you desire already is, and so it shall be.

Prepare a Mental Field

Suppose you have been using an affirmation over and over and find that it is not "working." Perhaps your failure to bring about results comes from the fact that you have not done the necessary work to prepare a proper mental planting field for the affirmation. An affirmation, like any thought, is a seed that takes root and grows. However, it must have the proper firmament to grow into what you intend it to be, and it must be sown in the right way at the right time in order to flourish. This is something Jesus knew well, as we can tell from the Book of Matthew, in which He talks at length about the sowing and reaping of seeds.

There is, for instance, the parable of the sower. Some of the sower's seeds fell on the path and were eaten by the birds. Others of his seeds fell on rocky ground, sprang up immediately, and were scorched by the sun. Still other seeds fell among the thorns and were choked. Finally, there were those seeds that fell on good soil and multiplied thirty, sixty, or a hundred times (Matthew 13:3-8).

Jesus gave the disciples an explanation of what this parable meant in terms of the word of the Kingdom of God (see Matthew 13:18-23). There is another way of looking at this parable as it applies to the use of affirmations.

Seeds on the Path

Let us say, for example, that you have written an affirmation that you intend to use as a healing treatment. Suppose you have given yourself the treatment over and over but see no results. Did you, perhaps, sow the affirmation on the "path," the edges of your consciousness, rather than let it sink into the depths of your subconscious where it could take root? How can you tell if the affirmation is falling on the path and not in the depths of your subconscious where you intended it to be? Well, you might find yourself thinking of other, unrelated matters while you are giving the healing treatment. In that case, the affirmation has been crowded out, so to speak, pushed to the edges of your consciousness while the other matters occupied the area of your mind where the real work is done.

Seeds on Rocky Ground

What about the affirmation that falls on rocky ground? Your rocky mental ground might consist of worry, fear, or doubt about the outcome of what you are treating. If this is your state of mind, you are like the disciples, despairing because while crossing the sea—with Jesus right there in the boat with them!—they had only one loaf of bread (Mark 8:13-16). Can you imagine being in a boat with Jesus and worrying because you have only one loaf of bread? If that is your state of mind, you haven't yet accepted the power of Jesus to heal every condition, to fill every need, to comfort every sorrow. "Why do you discuss the fact that you have no bread?" Jesus asked the disciples on this occasion. "Do you not yet perceive or understand? Are your hearts hardened?" (Mark 8:17).

Seeds Among Thorns

There are also affirmations that seem to take root but are smothered by thorns—negative thoughts. These thorns didn't "just come from nowhere." No, they were there all along. Mental thorns are feelings of resentment, bitterness, jealousy, malice, hatred—all the twisted, loveless feelings that eat at one's insides and destroy the person who holds them. An affirmation, on the other hand, by its very nature says, "I want my highest good and that of everyone I encounter." You can't make such a statement and mean it while you are a breeding ground for mental thorns.

Seeds on Good Soil

In other words, it is only those affirmations that fall on good soil which will manifest in your life and have lasting results. An affirmation sown on rocky ground might sprout a little, like the sower's seed that sprang up very quickly after falling on rocky ground. You might see some quick changes in your life, but they may not last because they were not planted in the soil of deep faith and thanksgiving. You might experience these same quick and short-lived results from affirmations sown on the path of your consciousness or in the midst of thorns. The parable, after all, did not say that the seeds sown in the unfavorable places did not grow at all. No, except for the seeds the birds ate all the others grew. This is why people who don't seem to "deserve" something good often get it. But don't be deceived by appearances, now that you know what happens to seeds improperly sown.

Only you know what kind of mental gardening you must do before you sow your affirmations. Only you know where you are in consciousness. But wherever you are when a message is given, a healing treatment is expressed, a song is sung, or an affirmation is offered, there will be that in you which will reach you at your level of awareness. Wherever you are, give thanks and go from there. You don't have to be like your neighbor. You only have to be aware of where you are, of how much you are seeking to further understand yourself and what you are. Once you achieve this awareness and work with it, the achievement of your affirmation is on the way.

AFFIRMATIONS

1. *God is the potential that expresses through me.*

2. *Today is my day to put aside all that worried me yesterday.*

3. *I express love on every level, with God, myself, and my fellow human beings.*

4. *I am in divine order in my thinking and in my relationships.*

5. *The love of Jesus Christ within me gives me the ability to forgive fully and freely.*

6. *I am divinely protected at all times, in all places, and under all circumstances.*

7. *Prosperity is my divine birthright,*

8. *I deserve the best as a Child of God.*

9. *I have faith in God in me to heal my condition.*

10. *I am a unique, unrepeatable miracle!*

11. *I do not look to things, outer conditions, and people to bring me peace and happiness.*

12. *I open my consciousness of love for my business, producing overflowing profits.*

My Mother's Gift: The Sustaining Ritual of Prayer

Rev. Linda Vanessa Boyd

Rev. Linda Vanessa Boyd, a Reiki Healing Master Teacher, founded Reiki by La and facilitates attunement workshops, which provide tools for those open to the healing gifts with which we each are born. Born in Brooklyn, New York, Boyd is a resident of Atlanta, Georgia, and has been a healing practitioner for over 10 years. She was ordained into the Madonna Ministry, a global, mobile, non-denominational church without walls, and co-founded Circles of Sisters Global Link, Inc. and Village Keepers, Inc., two organizations that focus on the needs of the human spirit. For more information on Boyd, please visit her website at www.reikibyla.com

My mother passed away more than 15 years ago, but every day I remember her. I do this not only because of my memories of her but because I possess a wonderful gift she gave to me before she died. It's a gift I use every day and that she gave to me every day from the time I was born until her last day on Earth. It's the gift of prayer. However, her use of prayer—and the lessons she taught my family and me (indeed, everyone who spent any time with her) about the use of prayer went far beyond what most people think of as daily prayer. For her—and now for me—prayer represents an integral part of life, a sustaining ritual that uplifts me and keeps me connected not only to God, but to my inner core and strength.

I come from a family of 11 children—seven girls and four boys. However, our family often included cousins, foster children, and whoever else needed a place to stay. (The pastor at our church would actually announce that our home was available for those in need.) We lived in the Cooper Park Projects, located in the Greenpoint section of Brooklyn. My father, Troy B. Boyd, Sr., was a radio and television technician who, with only a sixth-grade education, founded and owned his business. My mother, Ardrie I. Boyd, was a homemaker for over 15 years, until my youngest brother became of school age. She then became a teacher's aide at our elementary school and kept an eye and ear on us both at home and at school, while also working to earn an associate degree in urban studies.

Our family followed numerous rituals daily. First, we came together for family prayer each morning. We would gather as early as the oldest child was scheduled to leave for school. While we stood in a circle by the door, my mother prayed for our safety throughout the day. When I was 15 years old, we moved from the projects into a home in the Bedford-Stuyvesant section of Brooklyn. My sista-girlfriend Tayari/Danielle reminds me that even when we got together to go to the beach or to go partying at Brown's Guest House on Friday or Saturday night, our mother would call us all together for prayer (friends and family alike) before we could slip out of that door.

On Sunday mornings during family breakfast, we each had to say a Bible verse; this was the "children's" ritual before my mother's long grace. Of course everyone was hungry, and smelling the eggs, grits, and biscuits while suffering through this ritual, waiting for it all to be over so we could eat, was difficult. But we knew not to mumble a word or to be too fidgety.

On school nights, some of us would spend time in our rooms or in the kitchen doing homework; we might be braiding or rolling hair or listening to the radio, since television was not allowed during the week. No matter where you were in the house or what you were in the midst of doing, when my mother sent the call out, "Everyone come to the living room for prayer," we would all come, including those who had already gone to bed. Each would find a space at the couch, the coffee table, or a chair. You had to be on your knees for nightly prayer.

WOMEN OF SPIRIT share RITUALS DIVINE

I eventually left home for college and found the need to develop my own ritual of prayer; there surely was constant need for it while trying to grow into a responsible adult. Once I joined the University Gospel Choir, the music helped raise my spiritual energy to another level. Upon my return home, I would find my mother in the bathroom reading her Bible and talking to God very early every morning, just as she did throughout my childhood. This constituted the start of her day, her quiet and sacred time, and her morning ritual. Morning prayer and Bible study were when and how she fueled up for all the energy she needed daily. This was Mommy and God's time, and it provided the foundation of ritual prayer that sustained her. Not only that, it has sustained her children. This ritual lives on through the daily practice of her children, as well as my cousins, foster sisters, play sons and daughters, and whoever stayed in our home for any length of time.

Since my mother's transition, her gentle spirit is ever-present in my life and my daily rituals of prayer, as well as in my other sacred practices, all of which were born of the foundation she provided and that continues to shape and sustain me. Now, in my circle of family, extended family, friends, clients, and colleagues, I carry on the tradition of prayer in any and all of the various settings in which I find myself. Everybody knows I will raise a prayer in a heartbeat; prayers of thanks, guidance, and protection before and after any gathering, meditation, attunement workshop, or healing session, before starting the car, and again upon arrival at the destination. I have to connect with the Source. I know I have no power, God is the power and I have no problem calling Her forth!

I am so grateful for the spirit and ritual of prayer gifted to me from my mother—and, no doubt, from her mother and her mother's mother. I find myself reminding folks how easy it is to talk to God—you don't have to be formal, just affirm that the good is already done. Mommy was a "Prayer Warrior," and more than 12 years ago, Spirit led me to fashion a monthly meditation circle much like the prayer band she led in Brooklyn. Oh, yes, her spirit and powerful energy lives on in my daily life through the sustaining ritual of prayer. For this, I give thanks!

Transforming Days and Spaces: Using Triangles of Light and Buddhic Column Rituals

Judith Kravitz

Judith Kravitz, an ordained minister and doctor of metaphysics, was diagnosed with throat cancer in 1976. Refusing drugs and surgery, she relied upon the power of conscious breathing and affirmative prayer to heal herself. From that experience, she developed a unique brand of breath therapy, Transformational Breath™. She has "breathed" more than 100,000 people and professionally trained and certified more than 3,000 facilitators and trainers in her therapy methodology over the past 25 years. Author of *Breathe Deep, Laugh Loudly*, Kravitz founded and directs the Transformational Breath Foundation, which now has therapists and programs in more than 20 countries. To learn more about Kravitz and her work, visit www.breathe2000.com.

I had no solid religious background; my early spiritual training was virtually void of consistent practices and rituals. However, as time went on, I discovered pieces that came together to create my existing fulfilling morning practice. This morning practice is so clear and automatic, it seems as if it did not come from me, and my desire to be faithful to it each day is fueled by something deep within me. In fact, I do not feel complete without having performed this ritual faithfully each day. Afterwards, I feel empowered in my ability to make a difference in my world. I greet each day knowing I have utilized and extended a high and loving consciousness to use the universal creative forces to alter and touch the One Life, or that which others call God. Each morning I begin my day with this powerful and spiritually satisfying ritual. Upon finishing, I feel like I am starting my day with a big advantage and the ability to extend my light and vision to many.

Several years ago, two sisters in Italy gave me a pair of off-white, round, tangerine-sized stones reputed to be meteorites from Saturn. These very interesting stones possess a somewhat lumpy surface and they have dark creases that look like the outlines of mountains. Before actually handing them to me, the ladies impressed upon me the uniqueness of these stones, first, by driving all night to give them to me and, second, by spending quite some time telling me how rare and special they were and how they possessed special energy to do healing work.

I began meditating with these stones and could feel them growing warm—almost hot—while holding one in each hand. I also could sense some information coming through while doing this. Soon I got the distinct image of myself and the two Italian ladies holding the stones and forming a triangle of light, with each of us in one corner of the triangle.

As time went on, I received an extended vision of the ladies, myself, and the stones. This became my morning ritual. The visualization begins with the three of us forming a triangle of light that is connected to all other triangles of light in the universe. The light from these triangles combines and magnifies, so that anyone placed in the triangle of light (the composite triangle that consists of everything) is automatically restored to her original template of Divine perfection, wholeness, oneness with her God Presence, abundance, fulfillment of her true desires, and purpose. They become a perfect expression of love, peace, harmony, and light.

I then begin to see all the people in my life—family, friends, and colleagues—as well as the world and its spiritual leaders, being placed one by one in the Ultimate Triangle of Light and restored to their matrices of perfect light essence. As I envision people in the triangle, I get a sense as to whether they require any special energies or healing for that day, and I tune into what is needed and envision it for them.

After a short while I feel complete. I then recite the Great Now Invocation, a revised version of the Great Invocation, a traditional prayer said by many all over the world to invoke world peace and healing. When said the original way—asking for things to change as opposed to affirming that the desired positive change has already been manifested—some people felt the prayer didn't create change but, rather, maintained the status quo. Additionally, originally it was focused on "mankind" as opposed to "humankind," so it was revised.

The Great Now Invocation says:

From the point of Light within the mind of God, Light streams forth into the minds of all, Light emerges on Earth.
From the point of Love within the heart of God, Love streams forth into the hearts of all, Divine Love manifests on Earth.
From the center where the will of God is known, Purpose guides the wills of humankind, the Purpose which the masters know and serve.
From the center where the race of humankind exists, the Plan of Love and Light works out and opens the door where Power dwells. Love, Light, and Power, fulfill the Plan on Earth.

Although I personally received the visualization I use for my morning ritual, anyone can adapt it for her or his own use. You don't need to have the stones I held when I received it (or that I hold while meditating). You can hold stones or crystals of your own choosing, if you like. And you can imagine yourself creating the triangle with two other people. You may find this morning ritual just as powerful a way to start your days as do I.

Working with a Buddhic Column

Whenever I go to a new place, I use another powerful ritual, or ceremony, to clear and to establish a powerful and permanent beam of light. This lifts and heals any negative energy and creates a more positive, lighter space. This ritual is called setting up a Buddhic Column, and it was shared with me by my sister and niece, who both have done extensive work with the energies of the Earth. There are three steps:

1. Connection with Father/Mother God

Feel the love you have in your heart for the Mother, our Earth, and all her creations. Really feel the love. Then, feel the love you have in your heart for the Father of Creation, of all that exists beyond the Earth. Then, consciously feel your connection to both aspects of God, Mother/Father, and feel the love they have for you, their Child. This invokes the Trinity in a special way, through your love and their love for you. Next, feel just one love—for all of life itself. Stay in this feeling of love for a few minutes before you proceed. This is the most important aspect of the work. The processes and the techniques are secondary to the love you feel in your heart, so take the time to really feel it.

2. Asking permission

Focus your attention on the Being that constitutes the Spirit of the Land, also known as the Deva of the property with which you are working (name it by name, if you know it). Ask permission of this Deva to do this work. This is a process of co-creation, not dominion over Nature, and so it must be something entered into mutually. You can ask with a pendulum, or kinesiology, or simply listen quietly for an inner voice giving you the answer. Be sure that your own will is held in abeyance.

3. The Buddhic Column of transmutation

If the Deva is willing to be involved in the clearing session, then begin by invoking the Buddhic Column for the Deva of the property. Start with a five-pointed star on the top, form a column, and anchor the column to the Earth with the six-pointed star at the bottom. Then visualize a swirling energy that starts at the top and moves down the column. (Note: Do not try to determine the direction of the spin. Allow the Devas or the Masters of Light to determine this.) Ask that all geopathic stress, negative thought forms, lower vibrational energies, or lower energy states be taken into this swirling energy and that those energies be transmuted into a higher form.

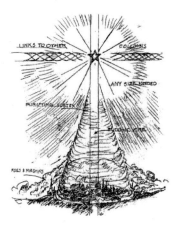

Once the Buddhic Column is constructed, offer it to the Deva via your thoughts and allow it to replicate this thought form of transmutation and place as many of them through the property as needed. Also, allow the Deva to make the columns any size it feels is appropriate. This gives the Devic being of the property the most latitude for making minor adjustments or attunements to the energies of the property.

I believe that if you work with these rituals you, too, will feel the power and changes that occur as a result, inside and out. They have had a powerful and positive effect in my life… I pray for the same for you!

Preparing for Sacred Time: Rituals for Greeting the Divine

Baiyina Abadey

Baiyina Abadey, an activist, nurturer, sister-friend, daughter, lover, and mother great and grand, always there to uplift and support. The sixth of seven children, she grew up in New York State but has made the Washington, DC, metropolitan area her home for the past 40 years. Abadey recently retired as the Deputy Director of the Howard University Center for Urban Progress, where she managed the research and urban development initiatives. During her 25-year tenure at Howard she held a few administrative positions and earned a master's degree in organization communications. Baiyina has a passion for progressive music, fine art, and vegetarian gourmet cuisine, as well as a keen interest to attain higher levels of spiritual consciousness and optimum health. www.artsdpc.net.

In the name of God, the Beneficent, the Merciful...

In my quest for peace and optimum health, I naturally progress to seeking a closer connection with the highest spirit, known by many names—Allah, Buddha, Jesus, Krishna, God, and the like. Performing some sort of ritual provides me with one way in which I can connect through my higher self to the Divine Source of all life. I see and experience ritual—be it simple or complex—as a custom, habit, ceremony, or practice of sacrament. I believe an intended daily or consistent spiritual practice can consist of an activity performed by a group of like-minded people or an individual activity performed alone, in private. In either case, the ritual can be as plain, creative, peaceful, stimulating, or beneficial as is felt necessary for the intended purpose.

In my personal and family practice, I often use ritual for calming or invigorating at the start or end of the day. Additionally, I use rituals to raise my inner power, to assist with healing, or to help myself and the participants to feel more positive about ourselves and about others. No matter the type or intent of the ritual, however, the most important aspects of this spiritual practice involve feeling that the ritual is your own and, through its use, creating a sense of enhanced connection between yourself and the Divine Spirit.

Purification

In my personal spiritual practice, when preparing for any type of ritual, I first cleanse my body. I use traditional Islamic cleansing practices called wudhu (partial ablution) or ghusl (full ablution), meaning to wash or cleanse the body before presenting yourself to Allah, God, the Divine, or the Infinite Spirit. Both wudhu and ghusl give me a sense of cleanliness, both spiritually and physically, and are intended to show respect to God. I am most familiar with this type of cleansing, as I have practiced this faith for a number of years, and have found this simple process easily adaptable to others who do not choose to follow this way of life but may choose to follow another spiritual path.

To begin the wudhu, in preparation of your intention to pray in a clean state for God, you make an intention to perform a cleansing of those parts of the body that have been exposed to possible impurities. Various oral teachings indicate the following steps are to be done in sequence three times (unless otherwise stated) to insure that the areas are clean and to practice the habit of the prophet Muhammad, Peace Be Upon Him, who set the best examples for his followers. Wash the right hand up to the wrist (and between the fingers) three times, then wash the left hand in the same way. Rinse the mouth and spit out the water three times. Gently put water into the nostrils with the right hand and pinch the top of the nose with the left hand to expel the water. This, also, is performed three times. Wash the face from the hairline on the forehead to where facial hair begins and from ear to ear three times. Wash the entire right arm, including the hand, up to the elbow three times; then wash the left arm three times. Wet the hands and, starting with your hands flat on the top of your head near the hairline, wipe them to the back of the neck and back again to the front. This is done only once. With wet fingers, place your thumbs at backs of the ears; use the index finger on the curves of the ear and the middle finger to wash the ears (front and back). This is done only once. Starting with the right foot, wash both feet from the toes up to the ankles three times.

Traditionally, a special prayer is recited with this cleansing. However, I suggest you use the "Water Cleansing Prayer Poem" I have written (see below) or another prayer of your choice. Several years ago I was invited by a dear friend to join a communion of light workers representing various spiritual paths for a Native American prayer vigil. We met on the grounds of the Washington Monument in Washington, DC, to offer a prayer for Mother Earth. As I began to ponder my prayer offering, I was inspired by the abundance of water on the planet Earth. I wanted to give thanks and praise for it, and I began to write my thoughts down in the form of a prayer.

Water Cleansing Prayer Poem

I offer... I adore... I give thanks and praises

My prayer is but one note in the great chorus of
prayers being offered each day
As we evoke the blessing of the
Spirit Water

As pure water from the Divine, is a sacred symbol of
purification of our faith...

We are humbly grateful for rain, the rivers, and the
fountains that provide us with Water—the primary
element for all living things—which existed before
Heaven and Earth

Most High Spirit we ask that you continue to provide
us with this pure essential element, and teach us how
to preserve it better...

Accept this offering of our gratitude for this blessed
life-giving, sustaining and purifying resource

As we evoke the quickening of the Blessed Water

We ask that you accept this use of water cleansing as
a symbol of our hope for world peace, and the end to
starvation among the people of the world.

I share this poem/prayer and the cleansing ritual because they have proved profoundly settling for me. When I cleanse myself prior to performing another ritual, I am easily transported to a place of calm and receptivity that aids in strengthening my connection with my spiritual essence. Though this is a traditional Islamic practice, it is a ritual that can be beneficial for anyone. Choose what works best for you.

Creating Sacred Space

Once I have cleansed myself and made my intention, I usually create a private sacred space that serves as a point of focus for me. I often use a prayer rug, a small cloth, or a small table or shelf, which I can either store away or set aside, for private and sacred purposes. To further intensify my focus, in the sacred space that I create I may include the use of a holy book, candles, incense, a symbol of my faith, a plant, and/or flowers.

Silence… Stillness… Sound… Movement

I know that sound also helps the centering process prior to participating in a ritual. You may find that the sounds of nature, chimes, bells, instrumental music, and soft vocalizing aid in your relaxation. Or you may feel much more relaxed in silence or using movement, dance, and song as tools of relaxation. I am most often called to silence and stillness.

Chakra Meditation

I personally find that the Chakra Meditation is a powerful tool to begin hearing your inner voice with more clarity. It took me a while to build up to the Chakra Meditation, which focuses on clearing and cleaning the major energy centers, called chakras, in the body. (I would not necessarily recommend it for beginners.) To establish comfort during this exercise, it is best done lying down or in a lotus position. I begin to focus on each chakra and its corresponding principle.

There are many energy fields in and around the body, and for this exercise I will focus on seven major chakras. The first one, the root chakra, is located in the sexual gland area and corresponds with the color red. The second one, the sacral chakra, is located in the navel area and relates to the color orange. The third chakra is located in the solar plexus area and reflects the color yellow. The heart area houses the fourth chakra, which is associated with the color green. The fifth chakra is found in the throat area and corresponds with the color blue. The sixth chakra is located on the forehead, or in the third eye area, and relates to the color purple or amethyst, and the seventh chakra, the crown chakra, is located at the top of the head and reflects the colors of gold, violet, or white.

Once I am totally relaxed, I begin to visualize the energy flow in my body going from one chakra to another and the corresponding color of the energy field in the order I have listed. I picture myself brightening each area and clearing it of any debris. This ancient Hindu custom is believed to help clear blockages in the body that can cause stress or illness. Clearing these energy fields has been known to transform aspects of human life for the better.

Breathing Meditation

Once you have prepared yourself with cleansing and creating sacred space, another simple meditation I find particularly relaxing involves a simple breathing meditation. To enhance this relaxing meditation, I often create a calm atmosphere with the use of candles and pleasant fragrances. I assume a comfortable position on the floor, sitting or lying down. As I begin to relax my body, I inhale through my nostrils, counting slowly to three as I inhale. I retain the air for a moment and then exhale it, counting slowly to three as I do so. I repeat this a few times with my eyes closed. (I am careful never to hold my breath to a point where it is uncomfortable.) This releases the tension in my body.

As I breathe in air, I think positive thoughts of happiness, love, peace, and good health, and I begin to visualize these things. While I exhale, I visualize releasing negative energies of anger, sickness, fear, and the like. During this deep breathing exercise your body should be straight; use a pillow to support your lower back if necessary. If you are sitting, your hands should rest on your knees and your palms should be open and facing upward, with your fingers relaxed.

I do this for several minutes as I forget time and place and just relax. I often imagine the tensions and worries of my life and body exiting while I breathe. The more relaxed my body becomes, the more open and alert my consciousness becomes as well. I begin to talk with the Divine Spirit of God and to just listen for a response or to my own inner voice.

You may stay in this position for 15 minutes or more, or for as long as you can keep your concentration and focus on the meditation. I gradually come back to my familiar surroundings and open my eyes gently as I return to my "normal" space. The more I have practiced this over the years, the more it has become a way of centering myself to listen to my inner voice and to release some of the chatter of the busy world in which I live.

These rituals in no way are intended to take the place of any present or future religious practices or beliefs that you enjoy or to replace the peace and serenity of your religious worship. I hope you will see these rituals as positive enhancements to your life and as a way to continue a warm, loving, spiritual connection with the Source of all living things.

References

Mohamed, Mamdouh N. Salaat: The Islamic Prayer from A to Z (self-published, 2003).

Ozaniec, Naomi. Essential Tips, Basic Meditation (DK Publishing, Inc., 1997).

Simpson, Liz. The Book of Chakra Healing (Sterling Publishing Company, Inc., 1999).

Simplified Water Practice
The Venerable Dhyani Ywahoo

Venerable Dhyani Ywahoo is Founder and Spiritual Director of Sunray Meditation Society, holder of the Ywahoo Lineage and Chief of the Green Mountain Ani Yunwiwa. Her training to carry the ancestral traditions began in early childhood, under the direction of her grandparents and elders. As repositories of the sacred knowledge of their people, they passed to Ven. Dhyani Ywahoo the spiritual duty and blessing to carry the traditions on which the work and teachings of Sunray are based. The elders foresaw Ven. Dhyani's duty to be involved in the manifestation of world peace, and that this work would bring many people and nations again to see the clear light of right relationship. For more information visit, www.sunray.org.

Water Offering Prayer

As I sip this water, may this water become medicine.

*As it rises as a vapor from my body and perspiration,
may it become medicine for the atmosphere.*

*As the water flows may it become medicine
for all the hearts and emotions for all the people.*

*As this water flows into the ground in all the streams
and rivers may it become medicine to purify the
water again*

*May this water stabilize the emotions of the people
so we can see behind the appearances; that the
hypnotic effects may be washed away and we may
see things as they are.*

*May the element of earth within us and our bones,
remember the pulse beat of the Earth.*

*May our well being resonate with the pulse beat of
the Earth.*

*May the element of Earth, as it is expressed through
our stomachs, our spleens and bones, may the
element of Earth come again to balance.*

*As we give thanks for the precious gift of life,
may the element of Earth come again to balance
within us.*

*May the Elohi Mono, may the Earth Mother
know our appreciation, our thankfulness
for the gift of life.*

Water Practice Teaching

Whatever is the emotion, we have the antidote inherent in the emotion; especially if we see the elements as the elixir that we can offer as a means of transforming the suffering, attachment and aggression. Each time we drink water, for example, we make a prayer while drinking the water:

Prayer for each time we drink water

May this water become a medicine that washes away sorrow

May it nurture the wisdom potential in all the people.

May this water as it passes through my body,

May it arise as a vapor to clarify the emotions,

May this water be medicine for all beings.

May it know my appreciation and

*May it carry the message of my appreciation
to all its forms and into all the realms.*

Just to practice appreciation with our food and our water is healing the circle of good relationship and actually creates a network through which we may connect and re-weave the circle of life.

So what is it to re-weave? It means the thought forms of yesterday of scarcity, of colonialism are recognized as not supporting wisdom and that they cause harm. We see they are like a drowning man, the thought form tries to expand the form again and it is for us to create around the threads of good relationship by weaving a tapestry of light.

The vision of Tecumseh I understand more and more these days. It is that something old is collapsing and something wondrous is being built by our hearts and our prayers and it is built through the circle of appreciation. By recognizing that each element has a relationship to our emotions and supports our physical body, and that through the transformation of these emotions into their inherent awakened state, we are putting the weapons that cause suffering at the roots of the tree of peace.

The connection of the liver and its ability to synthesize and transform the wood element is saying, let us put at the roots those old habitual patterns of fighting against so we may give life to one another. There are practical ways we do it internally through breathing and stretching and most importantly through appreciation. When we eat something green give thanks, "Oh, green, you are nurturing the power of synthesis, you are nurturing the power of life, you transform the ignorance of jealousy. You, the special tree of life, thank you. As you flow through me, may all beings benefit."

In this way we are contributing to weaving this world of beauty and from the laundry tube we understand forms arising and dissolving in a great display. The meditation on the torus ring actually becomes a meditation on your own luminous rainbow body and you begin to notice the rainbow circles everywhere and in this way we are nurturing the dream as it is arising.

THE THREE LEVEL PRACTICE

The following prayers and practice are based on teachings from Ven. Dhyani Ywahoo's grandparents and Chief Thunder Cloud. There are three levels to the practice as well as a dream practice. We have had success in reawakening dry springs through the following prayers and practice.

LEVEL ONE

Realize water is medicine. Prayer when drinking water:

As I receive this water and it flows through me,
May it become medicine dispelling all ills.
May it become medicine revealing the wisdom within and throughout.
I offer apology for any harm done through wrong speech & action.

As this water flows through me and becomes vapor,
May it purify the atmosphere.
May it nourish the wisdom potential in the people.
I offer apology for any harm done through wrong speech & action.

As this water flows through me, and returns to the water table,
May it remove the impurities of chemicals placed within the water.
May the water be made new again.
May this water become medicine for all beings in this and all worlds.

LEVEL TWO

When people are without enough water, go outside, preferably to a place where there has been a spring. If the spring has dried up, go to that spring and stand near it and look to the east and hold either a gourd, a cup, or a glass full of water up to the sky and say the following prayer.

Prayer to bring forth water:

Thank you for this gift of life,
Thank you for the gift of water.
We appreciate this water that you have given.
Now the earth is dry and the trees are crying,
Please accept our offering of this water.
Please accept our apology for any harm done through wrong speech and
action.

Then:

> *Pour some water on the ground.*
> *Then turn around and, in each direction,*
> *Take four steps forward and repeat this prayer.*
> *Step four steps back and turn to the next direction.*
> *Repeat the prayer, praying to all four directions.*

LEVEL THREE

This level is done at night to see and hear the sounds of those who are crying. Pour fresh water in a special glass that you use just for the purpose of this practice. Before going to sleep go to each corner of your bedroom and offer a bit of smudge, incense, or smokeless incense. In each corner of the room make this prayer offering.

Prayer to see & hear the sounds of those who are crying:

> *May what is outgrown become compost for the wisdom seed to flourish and grow.*
> *May what is outgrown become compost for the wisdom seed to flourish and grow.*
> *May what is outgrown become compost for the wisdom seed to flourish and grow.*

Then:

Take the special glass of fresh water to the window holding it up so you can see the moon (if it is not visible, simply hold the glass up) saying the following prayer:

> *This water, may it become medicine to benefit all beings,*
> *May this water be a mirror that reveals all.*

Then:

> *Sip the water.*
> *Put it beside your bed and as you are lying in bed review the day.*
> *Look at, how did I listen to others? Did I respect the people I met today?*
> *See above you the light and bring it into your heart and central pathway.*

DREAMTIME PRACTICE

It is significant in the dreamtime/dream body to be able to raise your hands to the sky. This may take some time. When you have accomplished this, then you have awakened the awareness of the illusory body and the body of light. Through doing so you may benefit others through the dedication of your actions and the manifestation of ever more skillful methods.

This awakening is also able to bring rain. Once you get your hands up in the air in the dream body, then invite the rain to fall in gentle ways to nourish the seeds of wisdom in the people. Pray for the sweet waters to flow to give the people all they need.

When you wake up give thanks that another day has come, that the sun rises again, and hold your glass of water up to the sun, giving thanks for this medicine and pray:

> *May this water flow through me as medicine.*
> *May it return to the atmosphere as medicine.*
> *May it return to the earth as medicine.*

How we receive water is very precious because water is the gift of life. Close each of the Three Levels of practice with the following prayer of dedication:

> *May this practice benefit all beings in this and all worlds.*

Commentary

As you inhale you heal the air, and as we exhale we can give thanks. Our mind, by observance of the circle of air, becomes stable and our innate wisdom state is revealed. As we receive the gift of water, we sense the water flowing through us, and we give thanks. Conflictual emotions are pacified and their inherent wisdom state is revealed. As we eat we give thanks to that which is grown and those who have handled it. As we receive the gift of water and we sense the water flowing through us and we give thanks, conflictual emotions are pacified, and their inherent wisdom state is revealed. As we eat we give thanks to that which is grown and those who have handled the food. And the element of wood and sound within us also remembers its inherent pristine state.

The Earth through our appreciation... a-ha... our stomach becomes well; the digestion is clear. The fires that break down reveal their innate intrinsic awareness. And the blue-black waters of the kidneys and the bones, through our songs of appreciation, through the recognition of water as consciousness. The blue-black water of the kidneys and bones they too are stabilized and reveal their innate intrinsic awareness and thus dissolving into space and revealing the pathways through which all forms arise.

I invite you to make a torus ring for yourself as a tool of exploration and to remember that this is hollow space. From the emptiness all forms arise and we ourselves are inseparable from that great potential. The empty space and through the dance of the elements and the interaction of our thought, word and deed, appearances arise and we are born. Let us give thanks for the gift of life and let us step back from the habitual patterns; let us recognize the power of our minds to conceptualize a world of peace and people in good relationship and visualize and energize the skillful methods arising so you may transmute those patterns of confusion and bring forth skillful awareness of co-operative action.

May we energize that wisdom seed within ourselves and others, and may we each day do what needs doing and listen to the sounds of those beyond the horizon.

May all beings benefit,

Wadogh.

I Give Thanks

Barbara Daniel Cox

Barbara Daniel Cox possessed vast experience in planning, development, and special events production. A native of Louisa, Virginia, she lived in Philadelphia, Pennsylvania, most of her life. She served as executive director of the Mayor's Commission for Women in Philadelphia for four years and as adjunct faculty at Temple University, Antioch University, and Bryn Mawr Graduate School of Social Work and Social Administration. Cox served as director of consultation and education at a mental health center, where she designed and conducted self-help workshops, including "Blues and the Black Woman," which she conducted in several cities and at national conferences. She enjoyed facilitating and participating in "Sister Circles".

I try to practice offering gratitude to God for all that I am, all that I receive, and all that I see and experience in the world around me every day and in every way I can imagine. This constitutes my daily ritual, my spiritual practice. For me, the practice of gratitude seems like a constant prayer, a flow of poetic words from my mind and heart to God all day long.

I give thanks to
The One Most High
When I open my eyes
When I rise
When I move

I give thanks to
The One Most High
Quietly
Consistently
Reverently

I give thanks to
The One Most High
When I'm alone
When I'm in congregation
When I'm in transition and in between

I give thanks to
The One Most High
When I'm sitting
When I'm standing
When I'm moving

I give thanks to
The One Most High
For my family
For my friends
For my associates

I give thanks to
The One Most High
Silently
Quietly
Joyfully

I give thanks to
The One Most High
All day
In every day
In every way

I give thanks to
The One Most High
I give thanks!

SECTION TWO

THE VOICE OF GOD/GODDESS

THE VOICE OF GOD/GODDESS

**The first sound vibration and utterance was birthed
from the silence in the stillness.**

**The creating/manifesting Voice of God speaks
in, through, as, and to us… Listen!**

I have learned that the voice of God is not always gentle and calming…
sometimes it can be downright alarming! I once attended a spiritual event
in Washington, DC where many of the city's leaders of traditional-African
spiritual cosmology and the members of their temples, shrines, and "spiritual houses" were in attendance. Much pomp and circumstance, powerful
prayer, ritualized chanting, and calling-in-the-Divine-singing had taken
place during this auspicious gala event. As the ceremony was nearing its
end, I decided to move my car closer to the door so that the spiritual elders
who I was transporting would not have far to walk.

When I returned with the car, I pulled into a space right in front of the door. Just as I was exiting my car, I "heard" an alarming voice say, "Hurry! Get out of the street, there's about to be an accident!" Before I could completely formulate and express my first thought and say, "No, I don't think so; I don't see any other car . . ." my second non-verbalized thought manifested: "Who *is that* talking?" Before any of that was fully processed, I heard a car screeching down the street... I quickly closed my car door. I had already exited when the alarming voice spoke, so I ran as fast as I could in front of my car toward the curb. I heard the screeching car collide into another car... "Hurry!" the voice now screamed. I was almost at the curb when the car crashed into my parked car which then hit me and propelled me down the street a few yards to where my body was stopped by the fender of another parked car. I lay on the ground watching *my* car traveling toward me, in what looked like slow motion along the same path that I had just been slung. People were leaving the event now and several saw the accident happen. I heard someone scream, "Oh God, it's Amshatar!" as my car was coming toward my head! I saw no way to move to avoid being crushed. I remember saying (to the Voice), ". . . but who is going to take care of my daughter?" The answer came in the form of nothing less than a *miracle*!

My body was somehow, in a *split* second, miraculously repositioned. Instead of my car colliding into my head, it pinned my *knees* between it and the parked car! My body had been magically turned just as a master midwife would skillfully reposition a fetus to prevent a breech birth. My head, back, and feet were safely planted on the ground, and my knees were where my head had been. The first people to arrive at the scene were amazed when they looked between the two cars and saw me—living, breathing, and able to speak. The look in their eyes showed clearly that they expected something FAR worse... I could see their undeniable shock and relief.

No doubt the preponderance of ritual and ceremony and powerful uplifting prayers of the evening had summoned the Voice on my behalf! I Give Thanks!

Listen, as you read through the personal stories in this section as the Voice of God is heard in the dance of the wind and sage, through our hearts and hands, angels, our truest self, psychic phenomenon, intuition, and Spirit Itself!

Morning Light: Assessing Intuition at Dawn

Sharon Franquemont

Sharon Franquemont, an author, coach, and consultant, focuses her work on the wisdom of intuition and its application in integrative healthcare, sustainable development, and world citizenship. Franquemont works primarily with the Life Science Foundation in Excelsior, Minnesota, and also serves the Shumei International Institute in Crestone, Colorado, and in Japan. Her books include *You Already Know What To Do* (Penguin Putnam), *Intuition: Your Electric Self* (Sounds True), and *World Citizenship: The Philosophy of Mokichi Okada* (Shinji Shumeikai Press), released in 2011.

It is promised. The light will dawn. We will remember who we are; we will remember what to do. The climate crisis, armed conflict, poverty, hunger, and disease will abate as a more peaceable kingdom arises. It is our inheritance.

Our intuition provides one key to the kingdom. What is intuition? The word intuition comes from Latin, *intueri*, meaning unmediated, direct perception. Pure intuition—intuition not clouded by interpretation, wishful thinking, or projection—is often associated with light. People say, "I've seen the light," or, "We felt illuminated," or "May we be enlightened." Intuition dawns upon us as a morning sun. It illuminates the path to present wisdom and future enlightenment.

In the past, intuition primarily has been experienced or seen by people as an individual's gift, challenge, or oddity. Intuition is labeled as a gift if the recipient can integrate its illumination into useful knowledge for self and others. If someone can't integrate and apply intuitive knowledge successfully, society—and often the recipients themselves—categorizes the experience as not real, reliable, or relevant. Instead of understanding that many cultures lack societal training in processing, integrating, and applying intuitive knowledge, we have a tendency to ignore or condemn intuition itself.

Times are changing. We are awakening to a new dawn. Now and in the foreseeable future, intuition's gifts will not come from the "star" individual that can integrate intuitive wisdom. Intuition's greatest gifts will arise as collaborative intuition—the collective knowledge needed for teams, organizations, communities, nations, and the world to make wise decisions for present and future generations. Intuition calls forth the cohesion of soul that leads to group insight. The Earth and our evolving planetary community ask this of us. As author Peter Russell said in *The Global Brain*, "Things are soul sized now."

Intuition, which can be thought of as knowledge that arises without the use of known rational processes, is a full-spectrum experience. You already use words to describe non-rational knowledge along the intuitive continuum. For example, you call the capacity to know without logical input at the body level "instinct." At the emotional level, communication occurs across space and time with "psychic experiences"; at the creative level, we experience the great "Aha breakthrough." While these three levels of the spectrum (instinctive, psychic, and creative) are well known and documented (although not always believed in), four other intuitive levels have attained less public identity.

Systems intuition, the fourth level, reflects the innate capacity of some people to see, know, and respond to complex systems—for example, successful market analysts, stockbrokers, or advertising executives. Throughout history, visionary intuition, the fifth level, reveals the yet-unlived future with amazing accuracy. To pre-cognize is to know beforehand; therefore, we refer to this fifth level as precognition or prophecy. Sports teams can exemplify a sixth level of intuition—collaborative intuition. When this level of intuition is operating, people step into a field of being where they directly perceive their own role, the roles of others, and the role of the whole. In these moments, we are amazed at a team's capacity to flow "in the zone" and act as one. The experience feels electric. We watch it unfold on our TV sets and enjoy our team as it turns the tide and executes a mind-boggling, last-minute victory where every action is perfectly timed to match every other action. Collaborative intuition is magical and exhilarating for everyone involved. Mystics, athletes, artists, and innovative people in all walks of life speak of a seventh level of intuition: Unitive Intuition—the transcendent, omniscient, Oneness level.

For the sake of clarity and distinction, each of these levels is described in a linear way, but they are profoundly interconnected and interactive. This afternoon you may be reminded of a friend you haven't seen in years and, within a few days, hear from him or her. While this might interest and pique your curiosity, it will probably not impact your life as greatly as a transcendent communion in nature or a profound sense of inner calling. Yet, each level is equally important. An awakened person or group can tap into the intuitive continuum and apply whatever level of intuition is best suited to the situation.

It is this full-spectrum intuition that we need. In addition to instinct, psychic experience, and creativity, the world needs your system insights, visionary boldness, collective wisdom, and the sustainable peace of your Oneness. The Earth is calling. The stars are watching and waiting.

We are more than we realize, claim, or master. We have a greater potential that includes the instinctual and intellectual *and* the intuitive, where we can actualize greater knowledge and wisdom. But where does life-affirming intuition reside, and how do we tap its illumination? What do I need to do to identify my particular role in the creation of a successful planetary community? How can I manifest what the Hopi tell us: "We are the ones we've been waiting for"?

Developing Intuition through Relationship with the Earth

There are two approaches to answering this question. The first is found in establishing a personal intuitive relationship with the Earth through conversation, ceremony, or ritual. Some may ask, "Is it possible to have a personal relationship with the Earth? She is so big and impersonal." If you find yourself doubting the possibility, consider your efforts to do so as an experiment. If it works, you have much to gain.

Remember that the Earth, the Divine Feminine, birthed us into life. We are bones of her bones and flesh of her flesh. Our chemistry is her chemistry. When you converse with the Earth, in essence, you have a conversation with the roots of your chemistry and the rhythmic beat of your heart. When you overcome any barriers to the ancient tradition of consulting the Earth your logic creates and, instead, trust, you find that you are not alone; millions of people before you have sought an Earth relationship. Know that the Earth has cast you onto the sea of her existence for a reason. You can talk to her about your reason for being as you might talk with a deep friend or a wise mentor. Assume that the code of your path and place, your spiritual DNA, is written within you and available for claiming.

What has this to do with intuition? Intuition is not a tool to pick up and put down; intuition constitutes a path of life, a field of wisdom within which we dwell. Thousands of years ago an Indian philosopher, Patanjali, recognized that meaning serves as one of the four ways we can know anything. While intuition is like a surprise supper guest when you live at the surface of life, after you begin guiding your life by purpose or meaning, intuition pervades the field of your being. No longer a surprise guest, it becomes integral to the fabric of your everyday life. Therefore, find a time and a place to converse with the Earth, whether your purpose lies in discovering new directions or renewing and rejuvenating your vows to all life.

If you decide to take on this ritual, sunrise provides a good time to speak to the Earth. Bring offering gifts to the morning light, such as your favorite prayers; living flowers to plant; fruit that returns its seeds to the Mother; sacred substances, such as sage, tobacco, and copal; stones you cherish; or precious objects. Let abundant joy provide an expression of your gratitude for life. Invite living things all around you—the insects, birds, grasses, mountains, waters, city park creatures—to partake with you and be your witnesses.

In this company of friends, talk over your situation with the Earth as you would with a beloved mentor, friend, or family member. Ask the Divine Feminine for guidance. State your intentions to the best of your ability. Ask the Earth to plug you into her intuitive world-wide, innernet community where a wealth of companions await. Consider telling the Earth that you are willing to be wherever she needs you.

When you finish your morning conversation with the Earth and the sun has fully risen, look around. Before you go, write these moments upon your heart so your imagination can return you to them whenever you feel the need. In the coming days, weeks, and months, remember: You no longer need to search for answers or make guesses as to how the Earth and your intuition are responding. In fact, doing so may prematurely funnel intuitive energy in directions mentally created by you. These tend to cloud, fog over, or delay the intuitive sunrise of knowledge. Ease and patience provide your keys. Now, whenever you are reminded of your challenges or lack of connection, say to yourself, "I can let go. The 'work' belongs to the Divine Feminine, the Earth, her intuitive field, and the prayer. I know answers, like the morning sun, will arise of their own accord." When opportunities begin to enter your world, say "yes" to all those that activate your heart; hold back on those that have little heart connection.

The More You Love, the More Intuition You Awaken

Henceforth, intuition awaits you at dawn. As you awaken each day—even before you are fully awake—greet the Beloved. Flood yourself with love. Saturate your bones with love; gift your thoughts with love. If worries, plans, or emotional unrest arise, gently invite them into this field of love. Know that you are loved; know that you love. Rest within this love. You do not have to work at intuition. Intuition travels on love.

Once upon a time, I thought intuitive genius was a matter of birthright— Einstein, Mozart, and Watson were all born with a lot of it. After many years of pondering intuition, I realized that they didn't have more intuition; they had more love. They loved the subjects of their profound questions intensely. Love itself had opened the gates of intuitive wisdom to these individuals. Therefore, to enhance your day-to-day experience with the intuitive field, begin each day soaking in a bath of love. Let this love extend to the global family of souls to which you belong even if you do not yet know who they are.

While performing this ritual at dawn, the morning light may bring you another awareness: emptiness. Oddly, love empties us. In a state of love, our worries, preoccupations, and plans fade into the background. Urgency disappears. Old habits of thought and perception that tend to clog intuitive space fade into the background. When they do appear, you are more likely to see them for what they are. You truly experience a new dawn.

Contentment hangs its hat in the corner of your being. Your mind is made clear. The light of intuitive understanding assumes its rightful place within your intelligence matrix.

You may recognize a common form of this emptiness. Sometimes we say, "I'll put the problem on the back burner," meaning that we'll turn our attention elsewhere and cease looking for solutions. Creative breakthroughs often happen when they are least expected—in the shower, out for a walk, listening to music, or daydreaming. Yet, do you… do we, as a human family, know that we can find solutions to the global challenges of our times?

The Value of Emptiness

This brings us to the second approach to the question, "What is my role in the creation of a successful planetary community?" Poet Ralph Waldo Emerson believed "Knowledge is light." As you greet the dawn, in addition to talking to the Earth, empty yourself of old notions about knowledge. Surrounded by a sea of computer and media information, you no longer need to be a "vessel" into which information and knowledge are poured. Retention skills give way to your ability to (1) discern relevant information from irrelevant, (2) generate, organize, and communicate knowledge, (3) create multiple scenarios for the application of knowledge, (4) build in feedback loops that generate flexible responses, and (5) learn to release the old, no matter how effective it has been.

The latter—releasing the old—serves as an emptiness skill. Preconceived ideas, past assumptions, looking for familiar answers, or spending a lot of time admiring your past successes delay or thwart the creativity and adaptability necessary in a rapidly changing world.

Emptiness allows flow; retention clogs the system. The flow from others and to others catalyzes our collective abilities and enhances collaborative intuition. Emptiness is a profound skill that requires new forms of trust.

For example, trust that the knowledge and wisdom field surrounding you will be available in the moment of your need. You don't need it sooner than that. The knowledge needed may arise in conversations, come across the television, visit during deep reverie, or come in nighttime dreams. This level of trust embodies the full package of your intelligence, of collaborative intuition. Guided by your intuitive relationship with the living Earth you represent, the path opens before you and your contribution is assured. As you leave the dawn and walk into the morning light, you bring with you a life-long relationship with the Earth, an enlarged planetary family, and your intuitive inheritance. Days of discovery lie ahead; no rush exists. Love warms your heart and peaceful emptiness graces your mind. You receive the sacred gift. The new day is yours to share.

Dream World: A Prose Poem

Margaret Wheatley

Margaret J. (Meg) Wheatley is a writer and management consultant who studies organizational behavior. Her approach includes systems thinking, theories of change, chaos theory, leadership, and the learning organization, particularly as it relates to its capacity to self-organize. She writes, teaches, and speaks about how we might organize and accomplish our work in chaotic times. Meg received her doctorate from Harvard University and holds an M.A. in systems thinking from New York University. She has worked on every inhabited continent in "virtually every type of organization" and considers herself a global citizen. Her practice as an organizational consultant and researcher began in 1973. Since then, she has served as a professor of management in two graduate programs. She is co-founder and president emerita of the Berkana Institute, a global charitable leadership foundation. To learn more, visit www.margaretwheatley.com.

I am dreaming the world. This world is an illusion. It is not as it appears. A wise one tells me this, so I dutifully recite the mantras.

"It will help you awaken," I am told.

In a moment of inattention, I scrape my index finger. It's a small cut, really nothing, but it throbs painfully. It hurts enough to keep me awake that night. How strange that this tiny break in flesh exposes the full pulse of my body. No statistic (only .003 percent of my body surface) describes its impact.

Small cuts.

I'm standing at a newsstand. *Time* magazine has a special issue, "Can the Earth be Saved?" We humans have changed the climate and now the planet is responding to our arrogance with violent weather. Another weekly magazine features "Botox," the new government-approved drug that can change the face of America. It deadens facial muscles and eliminates wrinkles. To look younger, all we have to do is numb ourselves.

The world is an illusion. It is not as it appears.

Can a planet be saved by the numb at heart?

I'm driving behind a big black truck. It's been "lifted"—raised high on its chassis by big tires and super suspension. The chrome bumper and wheels glitter with exuberance. Inside are three teenage boys, riding high, torsos dancing together to music I can't hear. I love watching them as we cruise down the road. They remind me of how it feels to own the world, those moments when it's all working just for you. A minute later, I am weeping. The world is not as it appears.

I'm sitting on the caked and dusty surface of a reservoir that has lost much of its water to drought. The wind raises only dust and I feel gritty from the inside out. I notice green growth on the dried surface, but when I stoop to see it, I realize it's not leaves, but a type of algae, the first plants to appear when Earth emerged from fire.

The sun sinks low and rose-colored hills appear in the east. Warmed by their radiance, I glance at those fishing along the shore. Are they, too, soothed by this light? They seem focused on casting artificial flies onto the water a few feet in front of them. I turn and face west. The world is on fire! Cirrus clouds flame passionately, burning at the sun's departure. I am watching the world dying. I am told this (who is telling me?): In the great turnings of life, this is the age of destruction. There is nothing to do but surrender. Gracefully. Even in death, life will be beautiful. I am stunned by this message. I hope it is an illusion.

It is night and I am sitting on the edge of my gentle bed. I open a jar of African honey butter and begin my evening ritual. Slowly I massage cream into my pedicured feet—first the soles, then the toes, then the cuticles. From the jar's label, I learn that this cream has been gathered for me by the labor of women in Zambia and Ghana. I read that my purchase creates work for them and income for their families. I do not know how they harvest honey in Zambia or make the cream in Ghana. But I do know African women, many of them. Often I have stared at their feet noting the muscular calluses from never wearing shoes, the flaking skin from never using cream.

In the peace of my bedroom, I imagine them in theirs. I know there is no comparison, not in comfort, not in security, not in fatigue. As the cream soaks into my soles, I picture them in fields, gathering the means for my life to remain soft. They cannot imagine my life. I know them well enough to know I cannot imagine theirs.

At a conference center in the U.S. where I sometimes work, I am told of the African women leaders who come there to attend meetings. Always, they are given their own bedrooms and not paired up with a roommate. This is offered to them as a gift. It's the first time they've ever had a room of their own.

I am dreaming the world. It is not as it appears. Yet I know that I spend more on a morning cup of coffee than half the world has available to live on for that entire day. Three billion people living on nothing as I walk dreamily into Starbucks.

I am dreaming the world. It is not as it appears. Yet I know that 35,000 children die each day from starvation as I watch the cooking channel. I learn to make small cuts in the peel of a cucumber to shape it as a rose. To cut open a mango so the fruit is revealed. To slice an onion so it doesn't make me cry.

But I want to cry. For the world I am dreaming.

I turn off the television and burrow into my pillows. In Zambia just now, the women are rising from their crowded beds. Soon they will walk on hard feet into the bush, carrying basket crowns through the high grass. They will find where bees have hidden the honey this day.

I awake and clean my favorite coffee pot. The metal filter slices the skin under my thumbnail, but this cut doesn't throb the way my last one did.

It is late afternoon in my world. The sun is still shining. The wind picks up the dust of drought and it becomes difficult to see. There are still a few hours left before the sun illuminates this dust and sets the world on fire. In Africa, my sisters are sleeping now. They, too, are dreaming the world. It is not as it appears.

I leave them sleeping to go draw my bath. I have been camping and my feet are a mess. I will scrub them clean and rub away the young calluses. Then I will massage them with African honey butter. In my dream, I do not know where my softened soles will lead me.

Women of Craft: Art as Ritual

Carole Schwinn

Carole Schwinn is co-founder of InGenius, a Michigan-based consulting practice that works with organizations committed to bringing people together for the purpose of improving the quality of life in their communities. Her work with InGenius and the Berkana Institute, a Utah-based global change organization founded by Margaret Wheatley, has taken her to Japan, India, Thailand, Canada, New Zealand, and South Africa. Schwinn feels most passionate about her family, fiber arts, and gathering together with women of craft.

The inspiration for this piece comes from anthropologist and Buddhist teacher Joan Halifax, who commented in a 1996 interview:

> *Traditionally, there are three female archetypes: the maiden/virgin, the mother, and the crone. I think there is also a fourth, and that is the woman of craft. She is the woman who takes her creativity and turns it toward the healing of the world. She can be a weaver of textile or a weaver of text. I think that's where the women of the 21st century will find themselves.*

Many women approach their work as a ritual, a meditation, and a spiritual practice. Each time they engage in their craft, their intention, focus, and reverence connect them to their own Spirit and to the greater Spirit, thus healing themselves and all those that their creations touch.

In her hands, pen poised over paper, mind focused, nothing comes. Anxiety rises until, after washing the dishes, making the beds, sweeping the floors, and bundling children out the door, she pauses for a cup of tea. The words come full blown, poetry, a gift of the Great Memory. Thankful, she breathes through another day, knowing why she came, remembering that her craft resides deep inside, available when she steps out of its way, free of fear.

In her hands, the wool of Corriedale and Cotswold sheep is shorn, cleaned, carded, and spun on the Michigan farm, then tinted with wode, walnut, Queen Anne's lace, goldenrod, madder root, day lily, or onion skins and prepared for lesson plans teaching Lakota children in South Dakota their own forgotten traditional craft. The wool, woven into a shawl and worn to the Sun Dance ceremony at the invitation of the leaders, becomes her gift of gratitude for being allowed to observe her hosts' ancient ritual of growth, renewal, and replenishment.

In her hands, in honor of her friend's gracious beauty, scraps and remnants collected from the sisters—tea-dyed lace, a bit of flowering vine from Auntie Joanne, Grandma Aiuto's placemats crochet-trimmed for Aunt Phyllis's trousseau, Nonna's infant dress—are stitched around the diamond-shaped pearl pattern center from about-to-be Grandma V's wedding dress. All wrapped in stories of the women whose pieces they were and little bits of advice for baby Kadence: Be proud of your Italian heritage; keep the traditions and pass them on; know that you are a member of a sacred circle, a woman of this world; be sure to claim your unique contributions boldly.

In their hands, hundreds made plates, mythic and historic memories, honored guests—Sacajewea, Elizabeth Blackwell, Margaret Sanger, Sappho, Hildegard of Bingen, Virginia Woolf, Ishtar, Sojourner Truth—setting the ceremonial banquet table for the Dinner Party, Judy Chicago's installation art piece celebrating the artistic contributions of women. The tiled floor is a tribute to 999 others, the whole a centerpiece of ritual gatherings, traveling across time and space, elevating both women and women's craft, re-entering their achievements in the records of our common truth.

In their hands, the weaving war widows of Chimaltenango—husbands, fathers, brothers, and uncles dead or disappeared in the Guatemalan Violence—flee to safety in the hills. Now 500 strong from 15 villages, they send tablecloths, placemats, towels, and napkins woven on backstrap looms for sale to travelers and tourists so they can buy sugar, salt, soap, corn, notebooks, pens, schoolbooks, clothes. This generation of women is blessed by Ixchel, Lady Rainbow, Mayan Goddess of weaving, fertility, and childbearing, birthing the cloth on the loom, transforming the skills of the grandmothers into a future for their children's children.

In their hands, the shantytown women of Pamloma, Peru, sew *arpilleras*—scenes of their lost villages—on garments for markets abroad. Their skills and designs are a gift from Rosbita, refugee from Chilean political prisons of Pinochet, where in their cells the women sewed messages to helpers outside into pockets of their handiwork, blithely passed on by guards who never suspected the subversion of craft in the hands of these women imprisoned by terror.

In their hands, the grandmothers carry ancient memories of linear designs infused in droplets of piri piri plant seeds, placing them in the eyes of infant girls as their birthright. Now 96 mothers' clubs, 400 members in seven Shipibo communities in Peru's Amazon Basin, mold pots from Lake Yarinacocha mud mixed with wood ash from open fires. They glaze the pots in the air and set them out to dry, they paint the remembered geometry on the pots with brushes of their own brittle hair.

In her hands, Margarita of the Bolivian Cochabamba secures the brightly dyed, balled yarn under her arm, knit into pieces for markets, thrown over her shoulder while she walks to join the women's meeting. The women repay Freedom from Hunger loans, ponder new ventures, vote on distribution of the money, share their successes, laugh at stories of the men in their lives, thrive on their independence, care for their children as only they know how.

In all of our hands, what is at hand—earth, wood, wool, clay, glass—is taken up, shaped, shorn, woven, worn, whittled, sewn, transformed, becoming warmth, wisdom, treasure, artifact of beauty and utility. We create each piece with the intention, focus, and reverence of a spiritual act, a meditation, a ritual. We lose ourselves to our craft, connecting with the creation and the creator at the same time. We are women of craft, women of care, women reweaving the world. Alice Walker said it best: "Helped are those who create anything at all, for they shall relive the thrill of their own conception and realize a partnership in the creation of the Universe that keeps them responsible and cheerful."

Beginning with the End in Mind
...The Evolving Self...

Queen Mother Osunnike Anke

Queen Mother Osunnike Anke is a natural Healer's healer, Spiritual midwife, Priestess of Osun and spiritual teacher and guide. She is the co-founder and president of the Institute of Whole Life Healing, an organization designed to assist individuals and groups in rebirthing their divinity. She is also the founder of One Million Wombs United (OMWU) and the chief priestess of the Sacred Feminine Mysteries Initiation–Passage into the Great Mother (SFM). The mission of OMWU is intended to ignite the luminous light within the wombs of women across the world. The SFM initiation is a sacred journey for women designed to re-awaken the ancient wisdom and knowledge of Self that lays dormant within their sacred wombs and ultimately contributes to the continued healing and transformation of humanity. Queen Mother Osunnike believes and demonstrates that the healing of Mother Earth and humanity rest on the healing of the Sacred Feminine and that healing must happen NOW. www.manypaths1truth.org

During my earlier years as an actor, poet, short story writer and playwright, I would spend countless hours rehearsing lines, identifying and perfecting my characters' traits, developing intricate plots and story lines, making sure that they were believable, realistic and of star quality. However, more importantly I learned that a great story always begins with the End in Mind.

Even if the ending changed once you got there, you at least needed to have some clue up front about how you wanted your story and your main character to end up.

Little did I know at the time that all of my countless character preparations and Academy Award-winning "wannabe" performances, were just a mere reflection of how we as humans are really acting out our lives on the cosmic stage, screen, and bestselling book called **LIFE**. You see this spiritual knowledge and awareness only began to unfold for me when I had consciously made a serious commitment to assume responsibility for my own life, to stop being a victim on all levels, and to listen to and know my evolving **Higher Self**.

> *As I began to ask deeper, more penetrating questions about my personal role here on Earth, the Truth about our collective human purpose and, of course, who and what role does this universal creator play, sure enough I began hearing faint whispers echoing from somewhere deep within me and around me. Soon the whispering became piercingly thunderous.*
>
> *"STOP!!!!! Please," I begged. "Stop screaming… please. I can't hear you when you scream…" The raspy bodacious roar of this voice was deafening. It bellowed throughout my inner sanctum like a whispered echo riding on a frequency familiar–yet way, way too far away to comprehend. This was a primordial tone; rich, pulsating, vibrating, alive, however older than old… it was ancient… it was God, and it was feminine.*

The words, "listen within" were whispered through a veil of dissonance to me. "Be STILL my sister," I heard spoken from a distance that was coming closer. "Now, listen from within." The echo is on the inside, somewhere. Where? Deep… no deeper. "You must delve deeper to reach the higher frequency of absolute truth. The higher frequency of your deeper know-ing… your deeper truth. Go deeper… go deeper inside the inside of the inside pocket. Listen… in… ”

The deeper I listened, the whispered echoes of the **Ancient Mothers** rever-berated throughout my entire BEING, and their vibratory beams of sound waves began to weave the fragmented tapestry of my soul into a melodic mosaic of authentic wholeness… listen…

> *"What if this role you are playing is just that? Imagine,*
> *my sister, that you are really a part of a much bigger*
> *story, a cosmic story with a much greater role. Perhaps*
> *the bigger cosmic story that you are starring in, audi-*
> *tioned and rehearsed for is a part of humanity's story…*
> *and what if you are actually playing the role of God…*
> *manifested in the form of YOU?"*

Wow!! Well, these whispered echoes added more fuel toward my commit-ment and deep yearning to KNOW and understand the highest meaning and truth about my life as an African Native American woman, mother and healer. And, so with tremendous fervor, I began a serious sincere intellec-tual search to understand the meaning of my life story. Thirsty for truth, I gobbled up every morsel of sacred knowledge that I could get my hands on.

Often, when I was showering, praying, crying, writing or just waking up, I would vividly witness and re-experience my soul in its physically man-ifested form time and time again, and the myriad of lives I chose merely to enact my karmic drama. And slowly but surely I began to realize that in this lifetime I was also responding and reacting to the numerous other lifetime dramas and unresolved karma that was stored within my soul's cellular memory, deep within my womb.

During this time I also had begun to have an intense longing to go "home." To return to a place that clearly was not my Earthly residence. Sometimes I would awaken in the middle of the night sobbing and longing to return to this home that seemed so far away and yet, somewhere inside of me I knew was as close as my fingertips. Yet, I didn't have a clue as to how to get there. It was a deep, deep longing–much like the ET character who was so home-sick and longed to return to his home in the stars. You see, this longing for home began to mimic a pulsating sensation that I was feeling in my heart for a closeness that I just couldn't put my finger on. I was looking for something deeper, higher, much more organic and authentic than what I had been experiencing. I had no clue as to where this longing was coming from or taking me to—until two incredible, life-changing experiences.

The first happened as a result of a rebirthing breath session. Rebirthing is a powerful healing tool that involves continuous circular breathing patterns that can transport you into the bowels of your emotional body. I had experienced several cathartic individual breath sessions with a trained rebirthing facilitator. After running out of money and thinking I had to end my private sessions, she suggested I attend weekly group sessions. So I did and what I experienced was life transforming and affirming. Once I was able to get over the awkwardness, fear and vulnerability of doing this very personal work within a group of strangers, I began to feel a cocoon of safety woven all around me. Soon I sensed myself slipping inside the inside of the inside of my body and becoming one with the vibratory sounds of the **Ancient Mothers**.

Inside this awareness I soon began to sense these incredible pulsating waves that seemed to have their origin somewhere in the core of my body. This motion was subtle initially, and then intensified with my deeper levels of breathing and body awareness. My brain could not fathom these waves of sensation, but my body knew them well. You see, up to that point in my life I had never experienced sexual orgasms. I had been faking them all the time and now when the real deal was happening in a room full of people (all in their own worlds, of course), I was awestruck. How did my body know how to do this all by herself? What was the impetus for this? Where is this coming from and how do I do it again? These were the questions my brain was begging my body to explain. And as those thoughts began to in-trude on my level of body awareness, a slither of pain so deep and so sharp began to penetrate and almost obliterate my ecstasy. Within a matter of seconds, some way and somehow I began to comprehend that my ability to have sexual orgasm had been circumvented by some kind of unconscious sexually painful experiences embedded within my womb. But the gateway to ecstasy was now open and despite the pain I did not want that door to close. I needed to know more. I was ready to experience the truth about my divine essence–to remember who I really am. With a flash of light, my body began to tremble and I heard the echoed whispers of The Ancient Mothers…

> *"My sister, do you know who you really are? Do you*
> *really know? Are you willing to look beyond the veil of*
> *illusion into the portal of your own ancient wisdom and*
> *reenact your divine herstory? Do you remember from*
> *whence you originated? Do you remember what your*
> *authentic cellular essence is made from? Do you remem-*
> *ber how far back or forward the umbilical cord of your*
> *magnetic feminine soul reaches and stretches? Can you*
> *remember resting deep within the primordial fluid inside*
> *the cosmic womb of* **The Great Mother?"**

As I surrendered my mind and body, they ushered me into the Akashic re-cords, the inner dimensions of Self, the etheric living library, which houses THE ALL KNOWING–The Absolute. There I began to slowly remember and gather the fragmented pieces of my soul, not only from this lifetime, but from infinity.

There, within the realm of the infinite, the eternal, I started to uncover the puzzle pieces from many of my lifetimes. Accessing and reconnecting to many of the pertinent roles that I have engaged in have illuminated my journey home to the Absolute. I realized that many of my major lifetimes carried a consistent theme that was being played out in this lifetime, and that these lifetimes were just the multicolored clothing of the Great Mother that adorned my soul.

We are not our stories. The entire play that our soul is engaging in is a series of chapters, acts and scenes in the book of life. All of our karmic lessons are personally selected, specifically to aid us in the various areas of self-mastery. As we individually and collectively remember our multidimensional beingness, we are able to transcend our 3D reality with all of its emotional baggage and consciously assist, like the Ancient Mother's Mothers as Spiritual Midwives, at this time, in the grand ascension of Mother Earth and humanity into the fifth dimension and higher.

So as I began to gain a clearer understanding of why and how I had co-created my personal myth, the Ancient Mothers continued guiding me deeper into the abyss of my evolving self.

With a ferocious hunger for absolute truth I opened myself wider and deeper to their whispered echoes… listen.

> *"Oh my dear sister, do you really, really know who you are? Do you remember who and what you were and where you were 10 billion, trillion lifetimes ago? Do you remember your second dimensional self 45 million years ago as one of the aboriginal vibratory beams of molecular and atomic sound rays and bands of light that formed the energetic grids spanning across the continents linking the North and South poles to the Earth's axis, anchored deep down within the womb of the earth mother whose breath still sustains life for all living beings today? Or, do you really believe you just showed up 20, 30, 40, 50 or 60 years ago?*
>
> *"Do you have any conscious knowing of how many dimensions you have existed within prior to being a third dimensional being, what other universes you've traversed, and why you chose to incarnate within this universe and on*

this planet as a womb-an this time? Sister, my dear sister, do you really want to remember who you are and why you are here this time? Are you willing to reawaken the dormant serpent of ancient wisdom embedded within the recesses of your womb? To reawaken the memories of your Sirian stellar and Venetian planetary and galactic origins connecting you to the Sacred Serpent Wisdom encoded within your cellular consciousness stored within the multi-dimensional genetic library of the collective Mind of Self?

"Memories of your ancient ancestral mothers and daughters descending from the stars to co-create the civilizations of Lemuria, Sumeria, Mesopotamia, Ethiopia, Egypt, India, Tibet, and so many other highly spiritually advanced ancient civilizations entrusted with the knowledge of the sacred mysteries of the universe. Sister, do you remember who you truly are and your secret covenant with the Great Mother sustained with the DNA that flows through your sacred menstrual blood. Sister, sister are you willing to remember who you really are?"

Gently tumbling like a silken feather from the abode of The Absolute through the Interdimensional Crystalline Water Portals that exist before time and beyond space, I began to remember. My soul graciously experiencing its self as a beam of light... Re-eese ; Keeper of the Sacred Feminine Mysteries, beaming in from the Star of the White Sand (Selenium). Delicately encased in a silent symphony, I...ree; Keeper of Sacred Sound from the star system Sirius permeated my entire being. As more divine knowing flooded my conscious awareness, I observed myself taking on the feminine form of Vonnia; a Priestess and Keeper of Sacred InSight during the time of Lemuria. And continuing to view my soul's evolution, I witnessed myself through the kaleidoscope of time as a High Priestess Seeress in Peru and the Maori tribes of New Zealand. In the Polynesian Islands, I was Huna: Keeper and Weaver of the Sacred Cloth and member of the Koubehenii. And in still another lifetime, I knew myself, as a Cherokee visionary and medicine woman, Keeper of the Earth Plane.

And then, I remembered, Ma fa ra el, Egyptian High Priestess and Keeper of the Serpent Wisdom and Sacred Sexual Rites. Living and breathing in the energy of Ma fa ra el, Vonnia and Re-ees holds me in the remembrance that I have returned at this time to uphold my covenant to the Great Mother. To reawaken and ignite the seeds of The Sacred Feminine Mysteries sheathed within my womb and the wombs and hearts of humanity. And as I live and breathe in this moment retracing the footprints of my soul's journey by way of my personal mythology, I remember *Beginning With Our Ending In Mind*.

Tapping Into the Oneness:
Co-creating Your Life with Intentional Rituals

Rhonda Anderson

Rhonda Anderson, a recognizable television personality, produced A Different Perspective, a successful Atlanta area television program (www.rhondatv.com). Anderson hosted the program, interviewing celebrities, scientists, and best-selling authors in the fields of global consciousness and spirituality. She has also been interviewed by national television network programs for her mystic abilities and perspectives. She was invited to guest on "The Oprah Winfrey Show" to talk about her prophetic dreams. Anderson also produced and hosted a short film, "Making a Difference with Sustainable Communities." Her current work and passions are a continuation of her counseling, and individual and community soul development. It's through the alchemy of design and renovation of stale dwellings, she transforms homes into sanctuaries which heal body, mind and spirit. Rhonda is currently revising and editing her novel *No Matter What.*

Rituals have played a significant role in the creation of who I am today. Over the years, my work as a counselor, teacher, healer, TV host and producer, speaker, and guest on several national televised programs derived from the rituals, prayers, and meditation tools I developed to enhance my life. I attribute my business success and personal fulfillment to intentional rituals, by which I mean rituals I consciously have added into my life and participated in on a daily or regular basis as a way to "intend" my life's experience. If I sometimes get caught up in the day-to-day business and go without these rituals, I find myself missing their presence. I feel disconnected from Universal Consciousness and God.

However, it took me many years—several decades—to formalize my rituals, despite the fact that I had a proclivity for rituals from an early age. In fact, I had a spiritual nature and a tendency towards ritual behavior.

Angels' Blessings and Other Spirit Gifts

I was born with several gifts. At age five, I remember distinctly sensing and feeling the presence of angels on Christmas Eve. I sat in front of the nativity scene my mother displayed with a candle lit on each side and cupped my hands in prayer, offering reverence and simply listening. I could see the angels directly in front of me, large and luminous in stature. They were not in third-dimensional form; yet, my much younger self sensed and knew them in a way I assumed all could. With their hands in upright prayer, or Namasté position (a Hindu hand position with hands together at chest height), the angels nodded, acknowledging me. I now realize that I engaged in the age-old ritual not only of prayer but also of giving and receiving blessings between myself and the angels. That night, in the middle of my experience, I suddenly heard whispers. Looking up, I saw my parents and brothers watching in the doorway. When I turned back to the angels, they were gone.

I will never forget the love that filled me in the angels' presence. I later asked my family if they saw the angels—they were certain they had not. Looking back, I wonder if I learned this ritual in Sunday school, or did my old soul in a young body simply know what rituals were destined for me? Either way, making my way into a spiritual and ritual life proved a pivotal time for me, and I realized at a very young age that I was different.

In addition to seeing angels, I could often hear what people were going to say before they spoke. Frequently, I would *literally feel* what others were feeling. I must admit this could be a little disconcerting, though it was quite instrumental in helping others. Looking back, I was giving counsel—even as an adolescent and young woman—in my own unique way.

I could sometimes "feel" deep restrictions within my mother. She, too, had gifts of spirit—always speaking of spiritual concerns—but this kind, beautiful, and talented woman felt bound to society and family constrictions. She and I grew up in the south—she in the '40s, I in the '60s. The social, political, and religious climates were not nurturing for either of us. Psychic gifts were often referred to as "of the devil." In retrospect, I often wonder if this suppression contributed to her alcoholism and divorce.

Daddy gained custody of my three brothers and me. Their divorce was finalized on my 12th birthday. My mother moved three states north to live near her sister. Many phone calls and visits ensured that she and I always remained close. For many years, I felt saddened and angry; however, I saw her as a victim of her circumstances.

Now, my awareness clearly understands that we create our own reality. We do so through our core beliefs, the thoughts we think, our intentions, and our actions. There's no one to blame for our station in life or our current experience. My mother served as one of my greatest teachers. Being a witness to her difficult life placed me on my path to creating a better reality for myself.

At an early age, I assumed I was equal to any boy. It was a matter of fact to me. As I grew older, I began to realize that the rest of the world didn't always see through my lenses. I was stunned and dismayed at this revelation. A year prior to the divorce, as well as after it, I had more than my share of domestic duties for an 11-year-old. I would come straight home from school to clean house and prepare a full dinner for my father and three brothers. Innately, I understood how to help my father and brothers, and I sincerely chose to do it since it was a difficult time for the family.

Simple Daily Rituals and Prophetic Dreams

However, it was at this point in my life that I created more rituals, which saved me from feeling isolated and insignificant. I wrote lots of poetry—it was a wonderful release and a fun way to communicate my thoughts and feelings. Also, every night after my chores I would escape to my room, close my door, and sit in my closet… simply being still and listening to the quietness surrounding me. In my young mind, perhaps I was waiting for the angels to return; looking back now, I know I was meditating at a young age—I just didn't know it at the time. I believe these simple, natural, unplanned daily rituals helped me evolve from a little girl caught up in the midst of a controlled, patriarchal world into a young woman whose soul yearned for meaning and connection.

By my late teens and early twenties, I began having prophetic dreams. I would dream of local or world events, only to see them the following morning on the TV news. Even though this was amazing, I still would dismiss my dreams and the reality before me. At this point in my life, there were few people with whom I felt comfortable sharing these revelations. Frankly, by this age, my "gifts of spirit" didn't have the full respect they deserved. I was caught up in family, college, and dating, so I didn't bother with them.

By my late twenties, though, the dreams became intense, and typically involved a loved one's health or well-being. These dreams got my attention! One night, around 11:00 p.m., I dreamt a female family member was being chased by an angry man. It frightened me, so I immediately woke up and woke my husband up, too. The woman lived nearby, and we called her. She picked up the phone, screaming that an old boyfriend was at that moment bursting through the front door and she was running out the back door. My husband dressed quickly to go help her and I called the police. The old boyfriend had left before the police arrived. She was shaken, but safe.

By my thirties, I had an insatiable yearning to know God and myself, to understand the tapestry of life. I began familiarizing myself with various religions, philosophies, and rituals. I read over 100 books in one year. I took a meditation class, and I participated in an energetic healing group. I came to see myself as a "spiritualist," someone who embraces aspects of many religions, philosophies, and indigenous cultures. I also viewed myself as a mystic, although at times a reluctant one; I wasn't sure I wanted the responsibility or visibility. A mystic interprets the world through a different lens than those of ordinary experience. Oftentimes the words of mystics are difficult to convey—we see beyond the linear, often seeing the bigger picture and a broader perspective, which can seem vague or surreal to many. A famous line from the *Tao Te Ching* describes this well. It reads:

> *My words are very easy to know, and very easy to*
> *practice; but there is no one in the world who is able*
> *to know and able to practice them.*

When I first began formal meditation, I created a sacred space with a white candle lit for purity, soothing melodic music, and burning incense, reminding me of far-off, exotic, spiritual places. I was taught in the developmental stage of learning meditation to lie on my back. After only weeks, I could feel myself rising from the bed. The first time, this startled me and caused me to descend quickly. The next time, I simply enjoyed the levitation experience. I had not intended to levitate. For me, the little I knew of levitation seemed fanciful and only experienced by master yogis—way beyond my experience.

As time and experience progressed, other numerous and interesting "gifts of spirit" came into my life quite unexpectedly. Simple yet life-altering abilities from my youth were finely tuned through the practice of my daily rituals of meditation, prayer, self-healing, and setting of intentions: *Clairaudience*—the ability to hear audibly and directly from otherworldly beings such as angels, masters, saints, etc.; *Healing*—I could lend myself as a conduit to Universal Consciousness and God for the healing of others; *Clairvoyance*—the ability to see for others and to see world events through the third eye became stronger for me; *Prophetic Dreams*—these were frequent and quite accurate; and *Discernment*—the ability to glean messages from Spirit (in representations of different symbols, numbers, animals, and synchronicities) through intuition, practice, knowledge, and skill.

The Reluctant Mystic Creates Intentional Rituals

I was incredibly thankful for these gifts, but I knew in the recesses of my heart and soul that I had much more to learn. In some ways I was still the Reluctant Mystic who steered myself away from visibility for fear of being looked upon as oddly different. Yet, a stronger part of me was determined to understand my space and place in this magnificent universe and to make a difference.

Ultimately, I chose to listen to that stronger part of me. It was time to place what I had learned into a more formalized set of intentional rituals. I call them this because they are my intentions for life's experience. I created these daily rituals, which healed many wounds, and through healing I gained wisdom to share with other seekers. These rituals open doors of joy through manifestation and create a more meaningful life!

Meditation constitutes the first intentional ritual. Meditation is like air: When I practice it, everything flows; when I don't, life becomes congested. My main form of meditation involves sitting upright with legs crossed in the lotus position. I breathe in long, deep breaths, bringing in renewed energy, holding it a few seconds, and then releasing the stagnant energy slowly. Through practice, I've also learned to breathe in through the right nostril, up and across the bridge of the nose, releasing the breath out the left nostril; then I reverse the process. My count is always 12 breaths in and 12 breaths out, for either breathing style. Both breaths are yogi breaths, which balance the yin and yang, or masculine or feminine energy, at the same time purifying the breath and bringing in more oxygen. This breathing style also creates vitality, providing a younger appearance to the practitioner.

After the breathing process, I say my invocation. It's my way of formally announcing my purest intentions for meditation. I usually say something like, "I come to you, God, to sit and be with you, to love and cherish you, to trust in you and to be in you. I serve in the highest of regards for all concerned." I find the experience so beautiful that often tears stream down my cheeks. I usually see, with closed eyes, the color indigo pulsating with edges of gold and/or silver.

After the invocation, I say my Christ and Goddess Intentions. This only takes a few moments once practiced, but when spoken with purest heart and intention it is very powerful. The attributes and qualities of the Christ Consciousness and the Goddess Consciousness are balanced in the masculine and feminine; therefore, the qualities overlap. I choose, and am always changing, the attributes I want to integrate—to create my highest self possible here on Earth: "I am my Christed Self. I am love. I am compassion. I trust fully. I am forgiving. I am faith. I am abundance. I am grateful." I say these three times each. The Goddess Intentions work in the exact same manner, only saying those you choose to integrate: "I receive beautifully. I nurture myself and others in a balanced way. I am passionate about my heart's desire, which creates my life's purpose. I set boundaries clearly. I am creative. I am unconditional love. I am charity. I am wisdom." With continued practice, these intentional rituals can be spoken quickly and with profound results.

If you say these intentions with sincerity and humility, you will become these attributes. They may show up through grace, or they may come through an opportunity for growth. Both ways, it's an honor. It's important to be grateful for the gifts of attributes, regardless of the manner.

It's also important to discern whether you're ready to integrate these attributes. For example, if you intend, "I am creative," then creative opportunities will come your way. As Jesus said, "Ask and you shall receive." They may not come in the manner you self-perceived, but they will arrive in a manner that serves your highest good. It's that simple. Sometimes it takes a lot of strength and courage to move forward with these opportunities from God/Higher Self, but you'll never regret following where you're being led.

After saying the attributes, I sit quietly while releasing all needs, emptying my mind of mental clutter and controls, which are of the ego. I may be in this space of pure freedom for 30 minutes to an hour. At times I go very deep, feeling a little numb and removed from the mundane world, while at other times I'm aware of my surroundings. Both states of stillness are of equal importance for spiritual growth. As I feel myself coming out from meditation, I send healing energy and prayers for those in need and for the planet as a whole.

Another intentional ritual of mine involves working with glands in my body that enhance my higher consciousness. Twice weekly, I perform exercises for my pituitary, pineal, and hypothalamus glands. These represent our master glands and can ignite Higher Consciousness. They also serve as the control center for the endocrine system, which keeps us in optimum health. Twenty years ago at a meditation group, a friend shared with me the pituitary, pineal, and hypothalamus exercises in cassette form. I've used it, off and on, with wonderful results. You can find out more about this or purchase a CD at www.Lazaris.com.

I also do chakra work twice a week as part of my intentional rituals. Chakras are vortexes of energy—unseen by most but seen by some and documented through scientific instruments. There are seven main chakras in the physical body (and many smaller ones scattered throughout the body in strategic divine places), but there are many others extending outward toward our ethereal bodies. Many people have seen these auras—in photos of saints and angels or around someone's head or body. These auras are energy fields, or the ethereal body. They encompass our emotional, mental, and spiritual bodies. If we are indeed one with God, we must be multi-dimensional beings. I find it exhilarating journeying myself, and others, into other dimensions during extensive chakra work. It's an incredible tool for expansion of consciousness.

I have many more rituals and use them daily, weekly, seasonally, or by the placement of the moon. Please use any or all of mine as suggestions or guidelines to fashion your own. Be creative! Get personal! Invent your own ways of connecting with your Higher Self. There is no right or wrong way. Intentional rituals provide a wonderful opportunity to act as a master of kindness to oneself. Decide where it is you want to be, what it is you want through life, and watch while you participate magnificently, co-creating the best you.

An Example of How Intentional Rituals Allow Co-Creation of Life

As an example of how these rituals pay off, I'd like to offer you an example from my life. An exciting moment came for me when I received a phone call from a producer of "The Oprah Winfrey Show" asking me to be a guest on her program. David Rybeck, Ph.D., who authored the book *Dreams That Come True*, was scheduled to be a guest, and I was asked to share my prophetic dreams. This Reluctant Mystic was scared to death, so I politely replied, "No, but thank you for asking." The whole world would've ended up knowing who I was. I wasn't ready, and maybe I would never be ready for such exposure. Yet, God knew better, and within a couple months I was invited by TimeLife Series to be interviewed for a program they were filming for HBO, called *Unexplained Phenomena*.

A friend of mine commented, "You know you'll keep getting these opportunities… It's here for you to do, Rhonda!" What she said truly resonated with me. Relinquishing control, I agreed to do the show. I was a nervous wreck at the taping. I was there for hours, watching others being interviewed and becoming intrigued by the entire filming process—the cables, cameras, and crew, all with their independent tasks. An unexplained excitement came over me, along with a shivering from head to toe. I heard a voice not of this world say, "You can do this." I knew that instant I was being guided to a new chapter in my life.

It thrilled, yet frightened me! I had never in my life considered television or film as an occupation, yet the feelings, the synchronicities, and *the voice* were too strong to deny. Later, at home, I continued with my rituals of intentional prayers and meditations. Two days later, a friend called about an acquaintance that needed an assistant at a cable station in Atlanta. Without hesitation, I said, "I feel that's mine." The next day I took the 45-minute drive from my home north to downtown Atlanta. I met with the director. I then became the new assistant. I took the appropriate classes in producing, editing, directing, and screenwriting. I learned from these studies the importance of the full integration of the right and left sides of the brain for synergistic success. A year later, I advanced to co-producing a program.

My first project was an off-location shoot at the World Congress Center in Atlanta. If I still had the least bit of doubt, it certainly was cleared that day. I was doing exactly what was intended for me at this stage of my life. In one day, in just over a few hours, I (along with my co-producer) interviewed and gathered footage to produce shows on Deepak Chopra, Wayne Dyer, and Shakti Gawain! These bestselling authors had been on the leading national talk shows, and now they were on my program!

From Reluctant Mystic to Nurtured Mystic

I obviously overcame the Reluctant Mystic stage, becoming the Nurtured Mystic instead as Spirit and I nurtured me. These rituals continue to keep me in alignment with my purpose. They are a part of who I am. Sometimes I get busy and caught up in the monotony of my days, inadvertently going though life without them—only to understand once again that I need them as much as I need water.

Rituals go beyond enlightening ourselves. We are *all* a part of God and Universal Consciousness. Mother Earth is a living, breathing entity. Love is the energy that binds the collective whole. We're mirrors to one another, to Mother Earth and her inhabitants. An outside reflection reflects an inner condition. The beauty and wonder of healing ourselves, one by one, constitutes the process by which we heal Mother Earth. Universal truth says, "We are all one." We're in a reality where we continually create. And I've chosen to utilize intentional rituals for a healthy, abundant, and love-infused reality.

Listening for God Within: Achieving Balance and Guidance with a Variety of Practices

Patricia Moore Harbour

Patricia Moore Harbour, founder of BreakThrough Coaching and Healing the Heart of Diversity resides in Suffolk, Virginia, and is an internationally recognized transformational coach, trainer and social change leader. She is, also, a public speaker and former educator who inspires individual, community and organizational change. Her work encourages those who make a difference in the lives of others to "do their own work," taking the next step to achieve their highest capacity. Dr. Harbour coaches one-on-one and in small groups with individuals, self-employed practitioners, and entrepreneurs to help them achieve breakthrough performance and personal and professional excellence. Visit her website, www.mybreakthroughcoach.com.

When there is no satisfaction with where I am with my life,
I feel I do not have a home,
There is a fear of being separate, being on the outside.
Yet, I notice a yearning… to write, to find and call forth my voice.
I feel a profound calling to bring forth something so deep,
More than I can ever imagine
And beyond where I feel ready.
Stuck at the edge, not risking nor stepping out,
Rather, stepping back from being "the one."
In a word, settling to place second,
Wanting to fit, belong, and be accepted outside myself

How can I live the full value of who I am? Find my true self?
Oh, just to be, to be whole, gifted, and accepted by me
Can that be the value of truth to embrace?

What would I have to give up?
From here, it seems too great a loss.

What would I lose?
I want to feel at home in my spirit.
Let goodness, integrity, dignity, and respect… Lead me,
These I value.

I fear I've judged, not wanting to find myself identified with that which is
judged by me;
Now, at my doorstep I face the mirror of my own judgments
Is this a mean trick life is playing or is it the content for my life's journey?
Is this why I am here… to learn what I must?
Hidden is the voice of my truest self...

How do I find that voice and speak from it?
And, what if people would not believe me, would doubt me?

How then shall I listen?
Embracing the voice of God within, who is
Moving me toward fulfilling my life's purpose?
Perhaps, I am the one, after all!

©2002 Patricia Moore Harbour

When I truly operate on my "A game," on center, connected to the Spirit within, I realize with deep humility what an awesome privilege and responsibility life itself represents. It is our "job" to represent Spirit here on Earth, learning on God's behalf what it means to be in the world. At these times, I am engaged in living life knowing the work I do is God's work, and I honor my relationships as Spirit's gifts for enjoying the essence of my life on Earth.

I'm not always on my "A game," though, and often I fall off the "hobby horse," so to speak. I remember when I was a child and received a bicycle for Christmas. During my first ride, I fell off and lay there crying. My grandmother told me, "When you fall off, you get up, and get right back on again." Of course, I thought she was telling me to get back on my bicycle. I didn't realize that, in her usual wise way, she was teaching me a life lesson. I make mistakes, forget my purpose, suffer, whine, and remember again as I walk through life. The question is, what does it take for me to "get back on" that "hobby horse," my life again, and again, and again—and again?

All my life, I've been inspired by special experiences and powerful places, learned from others, been enlightened through spiritual awareness and study, and used ancient rituals and practices. I discovered these are tools I use to lift, to support, and to give me the strength to get back on my "hobby horse" again and again. Specific rituals, such as spending time in nature, journaling, photography, chanting, meditating, writing poetry, and praying, when used as a practice, have at various times brought me deep within to listen and to hear the voice of Spirit. In these experiences, I have been inspired, directed, reinforced, and redirected, and learned life-changing lessons. I have come to great clarity about issues and problems with which I was struggling and thought there was no answer, no consolation.

Reading Poetry and the Giving of Yourself as Ritual

One of my favorite poets is Khalil Gibran, and in many of the personal and professional development trainings I lead, I often share Gibran's poetry. One of my favorites is "On Giving," from *The Prophet*. I love his words, "… you give but little when you give of your possessions; it is when you give of yourself that you truly give, for what are your possessions but things you keep and guard for fear that you may need them tomorrow." I find this is important for me to remember, particularly when I want to change something or make a difference. Too often in our culture we throw money at our favorite charity and at that which we say we are committed. Both the giver and the receiver benefit when I give of myself—my time, my energy, my talent. My true generosity of spirit lives with giving of myself. Authentic generosity of spirit is the genuine gift of self. When it feels difficult some-times, I say out loud, "Give yourself away, unselfishly, and you will always have you." When I do, I experience the height of joy.

I remember the last days with my father. These were days mixed with sadness, joy, hope, and hopelessness. Looking back, the deep gift of giving unconditionally—from my heart, without concern about what I must safe-guard—seemed so "normal," so easy. A wise friend said to me, "Oh, you can get another job, but you can't get another father." That was so true. Giving sustains my being. Perhaps this is who I am at my core.

When my Dad was transitioning, I had the privilege of being there with him throughout the last two months of his life. The gift of life and death in this particular relationship was so full of love and moments of grace. This experience was beyond anything in my wildest imagination. Together, we learned to live in every moment, which often constituted a challenge. Death was an "in-my-face" reality in our daily living. During this time, one of our most nurturing shared experiences came from the readings of Khalil Gibran before my Dad went to sleep. We faced our fear that death would separate us and read aloud the sections of *The Prophet* that offer ageless wisdom about these issues.

We read Gibran's writings at bedtime: *"On Life," "On Death," "On Joy," "On Sorrow."* We found comfort, peace, and an unspoken closeness. I discovered, to my amazement, a deeper understanding of one of my biggest life lessons, in real time. I began to see that life is *one coin* with two sides. I recognized that I could not know one side of the coin nor experience the beauty of either without knowing both. My experience with my Dad taught me that to know life fully I must see life and death as they are—they are one and from the same source. I believe one cannot know the experience of joy without having the experience of sorrow. This became evident at his passing. In my deepest sorrow, when his voice fell silent for the last time, my soul felt incredible joy—just as I had during the special, brief last moments we shared. We focused on living, not dying.

I have other favorite poems and poets, but I still read and reread sections of *The Prophet* that may be relevant for particular times in my life. I find great value in this practice.

Journaling to Access Guidance

Along with poetry, I find journaling another source of enlightenment that lifts and empowers me to sustain living from the inside out. For as long as I can remember I have written in a journal. As both a little girl and a teenager I recorded my thoughts. An only child, I remember thinking of my diary as a special confidant. I could tell my diary my deepest thoughts and dreams. In fact, I could say to my diary things I dared not say aloud. I would figure things out by writing about them in detail. I also wrote about times my heart was broken or when someone special noticed I was there or walked me home from school. I recorded dreams and wrote about what I thought they meant. I continue, less often, to write about these things— what I see, hear, and think—and I follow my meditations and prayers with a period of journaling.

When I am on my A game, I rely on journaling to gain guidance, wisdom, and the truth necessary for me to make the "right" or best decision about the major challenges in day-to-day living. When I do so, I remain centered and grounded. However, when I am scared, not on my A game, or want to avoid the truth, I notice I don't "go there." I let my journal fall by the wayside and don't seek that guidance. I allow myself to fall into things or to let my circumstances decide for me.

I had one of my most powerful journaling experiences in Tucson, Arizona. I was attending a staff and board retreat with The Fetzer Institute. We were at the beautiful ranch home of John Fetzer. It is located in a valley surrounded by a series of mountains with diverse terrains. I was standing by the pool in the garden, noticing that all of nature seemed to encircle this home. It was one of the most beautiful desert locations I had ever seen. I could see all of the different mountain ranges, some barren and rocky, some lush and green.

I sat down quietly in the stillness of the day, pulled my journal from my bag, and began writing. The sun was hot and bathed me while I looked at the beautiful, lush, green mountain before me, so unlike the picture in my mind of the desert. It reminded me of my home in the far western corner of Virginia, where the mountains are rich, green, and lined with trees and wildflowers. This mountain before me felt familiar. I was soothed and comforted as the words describing this incredible natural beauty poured from my heart's core onto paper. I wrote and wrote.

Glancing back over the pages, however, I noticed there were words and sentences I did not realize I had written. I thought I was writing about the beauty of the mountains—the lush green that stood so distinctly in the middle of the desert, yet something else had come through me.

Instead I had written, "Act now. Act with deep connection—close to the nature of things… Truth lies in the nature of things." Amazed and shaken, I wondered what the words meant. Once I recovered from the shock, I knew I had been given a gift, a message to guide my way. Over time, I have learned that being in relationship represents "being in the nature of things."

I believe Spirit has divined us to love, give, receive, and learn in relationship with each other. In relationship we both teach and learn from one another. All my life I have been surrounded by love—the love of God, family, daughters, and my own unlimited capacity to love. Because of my relationships, love has been present in every dimension of my life. It has lifted and supported me when I needed it most and has been there when I was totally unaware or thought "no one loves me." Every relationship, especially those with my daughters and grandsons, and including those with people I thought I had "quit on," brought the richness of God's love into my life. Thus, as I contemplated the words in my journal, I came to believe I had been given this message to ground the new work emerging from the center of my being: the founding of Healing the Heart of Diversity (HHD). Through love and support, The Fetzer Institute supported me to bring this work into reality.

Peace settled over me, and then, I heard it. I looked around, but as far as I could see I was alone—no one, no houses, no cars. My colleagues had disappeared, but I heard clearly the sound of music. It was a simple melody played on a flute or clarinet; I don't remember the instrument or the tune now, just that it sounded so beautiful and both haunting and internally exhilarating. I did not know what to think. I didn't normally have such experiences. I thought I would not say anything, or the group would think I had flipped.

Later, though, as we were sharing our "in nature experience," I transcended my fear and told the story about my journaling and the message that came as a result. Then, before I knew it, I had asked if anyone had heard the music outside. There was silence. I described the music, and hesitantly, from the other side of the room, someone said, "Yes, I heard music." Just the two of us heard it. I can't explain it. No one could.

I am grateful I was chosen to experience these moments of grace and I value the blessing. In that instance, I hoped the work I was called to do would create a space for participants to work with diversity and diverse relationships from the inside out. I imagined we would be available and conscious to moments of grace and that each of us would learn to act from that place "... close to the nature of things," with or without the music.

After this experience, my work escalated to bring diverse groups together. These groups created community and relationships beyond the social, cultural, economic, and historical boundaries that separate us. In these diverse communities we gained a deeper understanding of each other and learned what it means to work and live together. We discovered that treating each other with respect, love, and dignity is a powerful way to sustain diverse relationships. In Healing the Heart of Diversity Retreat sessions, this message continues to inspire the authenticity and truth-telling that support core healing and reveal valuable, substantive learning. Over and over again, through this work, people have discovered how to access that space beyond difference and connect. In this manner, not only do we gain an understanding of others but we gain a deeper understanding of ourselves as well. This understanding includes knowing who we are, individually, collectively, and in relationship to each other. It means we understand the profundity of our purpose and our relationship to the issues and circumstances that challenge us.

The Ritual of Spending Time in Nature

I would say that my moment journaling in the desert garden by the pool was one of grace. Nature provides a key source of strength and inspiration to feed my spirit, and for this reason, I incorporate time in nature in all HHD retreats and leadership programs.

I love to go to one special place in nature—Point Reyes, near San Francisco. I call this my special doorway to the edge of the Earth. I love being there.

For me, traveling through the mountains and hills to the ocean, standing at the lighthouse and listening to the crash of waves while hoping to see a whale pass, offers a combination in nature hard to surpass. I enjoy looking at the ocean from a particular place along one wall, where a huge rock stands rooted to the floor of the ocean and towers above the water, pointing to the sky. Reflecting on this image one day, I noticed the relationship between the rock and the ocean waves. The water banged against the rock, and the rock remained, strong and centered. The water redistributed itself and flowed back into the ocean. Waves and ripples flowed outward, from the inside out, bringing calm, re-inventing the quality and capacity of the water to reach out and touch edges far beyond where it began. I became conscious that for me, this scene represented an important metaphor for living. The image of the water rushing high against the rock, falling away, spiraling out, yet constantly increasing the ripples many, many times over made me realize that when I take a stand—not a position—the power of its authenticity and integrity touches others and empowers them to be in the world in new ways. Taking a stand serves as the cause of effective change and personal transformation. We want the good we do to multiply and have a ripple effect that encourages others to act, speak, and live differently.

Finding Your Center in Silence and Prayer

At Point Reyes, as in Arizona, I am still and silent in nature. I am grounded by this stillness. When I can be still in nature, clarity, focus, increased concentration, confidence, and peace of mind abound. This also is true when I meditate, pray, or chant.

I am nourished by such contemplative practices as journaling, meditation, chanting, poetry, and prayer, which come from ancient religious and spiritual traditions. Silence is a powerful tool in each tradition and provides me with a primary source for sustaining and grounding myself. Silence, as well as other contemplative practices, helps me connect and listen to my God within. During and after contemplative practice of any type, I always feel uplifted and healed. My mind is clear and my energy shifts. I am energized. It feels as though my burdens have been lifted, and I am free. Obstacles become opportunities. This new attitude, if you will, then shows up in my work and decision-making, and new ways of being also manifest in my personal and professional relationships.

When I lived and worked in an urban school district in Ohio, my life and work were embroiled in political challenges that shattered the purpose and vision I believed brought me to Ohio in the first place. I was the super-intendent's chief of staff, working with her and the leadership team; we faced pressures that targeted schools, the district, and us, individually and collectively. This constituted business as usual, and the struggle was never ending. At the height of this struggle, life threw me a curve.

My father died. I was just returning to Ohio from Virginia when the superintendent left the district. I found myself lost and in deep grief. I felt disappointed and frustrated. My ability to help create the change I had envisioned was derailed. Suddenly, the actual change I saw involved a changing of the guard. A new superintendent was hired, and I was given a different leadership position—one I neither asked for nor wanted. I also found myself relocated to a city in which I never wanted to live, and the person I had come to work with was let go immediately.

The loss of my Dad left me without parents or grandparents. I struggled to regain my perspective, find myself and a way to move forward. Every day I felt like Sisyphus, the king who, in Greek mythology, was cursed to roll a huge boulder up a hill, only to watch it roll back down, and to repeat this throughout eternity. Each night I returned home extremely tired, gravely distracted, and totally disconnected.

During this period, I had a flier posted on my refrigerator to which I had not responded. One evening after a very trying day at work, I noticed it. The flier announced the schedule for *Satsong* (chanting) and lectures from ancient wisdom teachings by the current leader of the Siddha Yoga Lineage. This caught my attention when I needed centering and healing most. I contacted the people on the flyer and began attending Satsong every Wednesday. We chanted ancient chants. Each session always included a reading and a period for meditation and chanting.

This sustained me through what I thought was one of the most difficult times in my life. It led me to quiet, peace of mind, and prayer. Chanting touched my soul, and I listened to my God within. This centered me. I grew stronger each day and every week until facing my challenges no longer had the capacity to weigh me down. I reconnected the loose ends and loose parts of myself that had been shaken by the loss of my father. I deepened my relationship with God at a profound level. My spirit was rejuvenated and renewed. I moved through the trying time and emerged intact, whole, and complete. I reconstituted myself and became stronger. I possessed a clear view of my direction and how to get to my destination. Plus, I felt empowered to conquer this and I also prepared myself to let my father go. Most of all I felt rested. The remaining months of my tenure were manageable and focused. Prayer provided a vital source of strength and a pathway for me to gain access to my higher self, the God within.

The Prayer of Jabez is a short passage in the Bible. The story that surrounds this passage involves a man named Jabez. Jabez means "pain." Upon his birth, his mother said she named him Jabez "… because I bare him in sorrow." Jabez prayed. His request from God was immediately granted.

Oh that thou wouldest bless me indeed,
and enlarge my territory,
that thine hand might be with me,
and that thou wouldest keep me from evil...

1 Chronicles 4: 9–10

This prayer has become my prayer of gratitude. I consider it a prayer of unconditional giving and of selflessness. The request to "expand my territory" means to increase my opportunity to serve God and to serve others. To "keep me from evil" corresponds to how I behave with others. Jabez asked to be healed and "protected from evil." For a long time, I thought that literally meant what it said: "protect me from evil." Actually, these words request that God keep me from imposing evil or acting in an evil way toward others. I love the simplicity and depth of these few words.

I have witnessed the magnitude of this prayer's power in my life. I often travel with a copy of this prayer. I repeat it silently several times during a day. A source of prosperity, this prayer has enriched my life with a multitude of caring people, work, resources, and physical comforts. Most importantly, the prayer offers me opportunities to give unconditionally and be in service. I feel so blessed, even during moments of "personal drought." Indeed, this prayer taught me that at such times I must give the most—I give of myself rather than of my possessions.

When I think I have lost my footing, my rhythm, my center—when I fall off the "hobby horse," or find it difficult to get back my "A game"—I regain my balance by giving of myself, reading poetry, sitting in nature, journaling, or engaging in a specific contemplative practice. When I do these things, I notice I am more consistently on center and enjoying my life's rhythm. My inner experiences have awakened me to my Source for guidance to live in the world, which has given me access to my Higher Self, helped me discover my hidden wholeness, and unveiled gems of Divine wisdom that continue to transform my life… beyond the edge.

The Smoke Always Tells the Truth

Adelia Sandoval

Adelia Sandoval serves as the cultural director and liaison for the Juaneno Band of Mission Indians/ Acjachemen Nation and resides in San Juan Capistrano, California, the hub of her tribal homeland. A ceremonial leader, bear dancer, re-burial rites ceremonialist, and keeper of songs, Sandoval has been taught native ways by tribal spiritual leader Ka'chi. Additionally, she holds the role of director of the tribal women's singing group Tushmalum Heleqatum (Hummingbirds That Sing). She was ordained through Life Blessings Ministries in Descanso, California, where she centered her studies on the indigenous teachings of her own tribe as well as interfaith and metaphysical teachings. Her interfaith work in Orange County, California, and worldwide has led her to the Global Council of the United Religions Initiative, which creates cultures of peace through interfaith dialogue. She serves as the group's North American trustee. She is currently on the board of the Interfaith Council for South Orange County and is an active member of the Spiritual and Religious Alliance for Hope (S.A.R.A.H), a women's interfaith group.

The Old One held the shell carefully and watched the smoke dance heavenward, smiled, and then began to tell the stories. I remember the story of the Great Wind and the Ocean as if it were yesterday, for it was a personal story.

"The Great Wind began its sacred dance in the canyon. This Holy Ritual began with the stirring and swirling of the sand between the mountains not far from the coast. It seemed as though a longing was groaning in the Wind's belly, a hunger that nothing could satisfy but her. It had been waiting for months, and now the time was right. This Great Wind knew she would be waiting, longing for the rush of its powerful ways.

"Suddenly, bursting forth, the Great Wind made its way desperately to the shore. Everything in its way tossed and twirled and moved to make way for this turbulent passion. There she was, waiting at high tide. She arched her waves in complete submission as the Great Wind met her in mid-air. She threw herself against the cliffs, the sound echoing the pounding of an enormous heart."

It was during this ritual of the Great Wind and the Ocean that I was born. My spirit was waiting for a moment so spectacular. From the north I came, ready to take on another journey. I settled softly in Yolie's womb. Perhaps this is why I have been drawn to ritual ever since that November day when the sycamore leaves tumbled down Washington Street.

Now that I have stepped into my wisdom years with my childlike heart, I still sit and watch the sycamore leaves tumble down the street as I have done for over 50 years. In fact, everything repetitive, everything chanted over and over again, fills me with joy. Repetition, ritual, exists in my blood.

When I settled in Yolie's womb that autumn day I became *Acjachemen*. I became part of the Earth that day, part of the ocean, part of the sky. My attention is drawn to the daily rituals of creation around me because of what I am made of.

Ritual becomes a way to overcome the everyday world, to discover what is real. I find the dance of the swallows on a summer afternoon real, their twittering chant softening me and making me smile. The determined ritual of the honeybees bobbing from bloom to bloom gives me respect for a hard day's work—another reality of life.

I go to the Mission, to the Old Stone Church, to pray as I have done many times before and to feel the presence of my ancestors. I see their copper-skinned hands as they carefully placed the shells and crystals between the stones and the yellow-colored mud. I hear their chants, and I smell the smoke of long-ago days. I see the Old Ones holding the sacred shell and watch as the column of smoke rises from its center—the same ritual I witnessed. I see their eyes sparkle as the smoke once again tells stories and the truth.

As I walk home, I keep thinking of the smoke swirling its way heavenward as it merges with all that is. I recall the morning and its familiar repetitive actions and experiences that feel sacred, ritualistic. It began with the cry of the hawk.

The hawk wakes me almost every morning. The crows and the hawk do their dance above my house, up on the hill in the large trees. I listen to the soulful cry of my sister hawk for a few moments before I open my eyes.

Once I do open my eyes, I belong to my dear four-legged companions, who wiggle and stretch on my bed. Together we pad out to the front yard to greet the morning. When my feet touch the grass I am physically connected to my beloved Mother. I let That Which Is Weaved Through All Of Life fill me up as if I were an empty shell waiting to be filled. I feel sweet life touch every cell of my body as if it were an elixir, defying time. I feel young for a brief moment and wise, as my heart fills with the stuff of the cosmos.

Turning to the west, the direction of my homeland, I honor my ancestors and Grandmother Ocean. I turn to the north and honor the direction that I came in from as I entered this life. Turning to the east, I honor *Aswut* the golden Eagle and *Temet* the sun. I turn to the south and pray for my family and community. Stretching my arms above me, I give thanks for the heavenly bodies and honor the sacred resting grounds of the People. I sit and open myself to the Earth, my Mother.

Reaching then for my abalone shell with its few dried leaves of white sage, I breathe deeply and relax. After I light the sage leaves, they slowly transform into the sacred smoke. No need exists to burn more than a few leaves. I have been taught only a little smoke is needed for this solitary time. The smoke knows when I am ready for my day. The smoke always tells the truth. Always.

A song of gratitude comes forth from my mouth: "Oh Great Weaver, thank you for weaving me into this life. The grasses you have used are those of my ancestors, and the bear, the pelican, and the dolphin." I wipe away the ashes of the abalone shell and see my reflection....my copper skin, my great paws, my white wings, and my smooth, wet skin. I am ready. I am alive!

Just as I was born during the dance of the Great Wind and the Ocean, each day I am born again during my morning rituals. And each day, as I retain awareness of creation occurring around me and the reality of the constancy of creation, life begins anew.

Journeying Into the World of Spirit: The Mourning Process

Iya N'Ifa Farinola Efunyale

(Mother Pamela Taylor)

*Iya N'Ifa Efunyale (Mother Taylor) was born on the island of Grenada and raised in Trinidad, where she was educated in the Shango Orisha tradition. Her spiritual training began at the age of four under the tutelage of her parents, Thomas Cox and Lillian Mitchell Cox, who were both priests in the Congo and Yoruba traditions, respectively. She was baptized in the Spiritual Baptist tradition of Trinidad at age 17. In 1982, she founded the Yoruba Temple of Spiritual Elevation and Enlightenment in Washington, DC. Mother Taylor was a gifted spiritualist who, for years, humbly offered herself as a channel through which Spirits spoke and worked.

I was born in Trinidad in the late 1920s into a family and culture firmly grounded in a spiritual tradition rich with ritual practices. Since my father was a descendant of the Congolese (Congo) and my mother was a descendant of the Yoruba (Nigeria), our family practiced traditional African spirituality and culture. While I was still a teenager, traditional divination practices revealed that I was one day to cross the "big water" and, in preparation, I was to be trained in both the traditional African (primarily Yoruba) spiritual practices and the synchronized (Christian/Yoruba) Sango Baptist spiritual teachings. Though my father initially strongly opposed my

This contributor is deceased.

exposure to spiritual teachings outside of the traditional African practices, he finally agreed with my mother and allowed me to go for training in the Spiritual Baptist faith.

One of the Spiritual Baptists' foundational beliefs and teachings says, "Spirit is the best teacher." Additionally, this tradition believes one of the best ways to contact Spirit is to journey into the Spirit World via a process called "Mourning." My first mourning experience was an amazing journey into the Spirit World that made my life complete and affirmed my desire to never turn away from my culture.

Mourning constitutes a deeply personal spiritual adventure that usually lasts for seven days but can last for 14, 21, or even 40 days. The Mourning ritual can be likened to Daniel's experience in the Bible, in which he speaks of his vision and communication with Spirit. He, too, "mourned" for 21 days, and when his journey ended, he sat by the river and offered his account of being in the presence of Spirit (Daniel 10:1-20).

Everything in the mourning process is done "ritualistically." My father told me that the mourning work, which uses the seals of Moses (believed to have magnificent or magical powers), is based on ancient Egyptian practices. Much of what is done in the mourning process is not spoken of outside of the experience; the ritual itself is kept sacred and secret, so much of the ritual I cannot share here. However, I can say that the greatest ritual element of the process involves faith. During the mourning process, you are asked to perform the ritual of repeated prayer, and you are given a sacred word to use continually throughout your journey. You are told to talk to and ask questions of anything and everything you encounter. The repeated—never-ending—use of the sacred word you are given, and your prayer, opens the door to dreams and visions. Your faith in the spiritual power of your word and your prayers allows you to continue using them until the doors of Heaven open for you and reveal visions, just as was done for Daniel of old. That is the powerful gift of this ritual of faith and perseverance.

Mother Awai, one of my primary Spiritual Baptist teachers, "pointed" me for my first mourning journey (the person overseeing the ritual of mourning is often referred to as the "pointer"). For the first three days of my seven-day mourning ritual, I was "pointed" to the bowels of the Earth. On the third day I arose (spiritually) and looked down into the belly of the Earth where I had lain for three days. Suddenly, I remembered how Spirit took the writings of the scripture and opened the crown of my head and placed the Bible in my head and closed it again. To this day, I am not a reader of the Bible or knowledgeable of the Bible in the usual "chapter and verse" sense that many are who actually read and study the scriptures. I just "know" most of the stories; they come to me "spiritually" when needed.

From my first mourning experience, I also remember seeing the biblical valley of the dry bones as discussed in Ezekiel 37:1-14. Just as Ezekiel asked, "Can these dry bones live?" I wondered, "Can these people 'spiritually' live again?" I also remember saying that I was like John Bunyan's *The Pilgrim's Progress*, though at the time I didn't know of this book that spoke of someone's spiritual journey quite similar to mine. It had been revealed to me by Spirit!

At another point on my journey, I found myself waiting to be received into the presence of the most high—God. I saw the clouds, and I saw the throne with cherubim and seraphim over the throne. Off to the right, as if in a deeper valley, there appeared to be tribes of ancestral spirits. I wanted to know from which tribe in Africa I originated. The ancestral spirits stood in the light wearing white. I was told (by Spirit) that these were my ancestors, who had risen to that high plane of consciousness. I was told which tribe I was from, and I was shown my destiny. Later, I realized that, even though we may be from different tribes, we all are on a journey to the seventh stage of consciousness, ascending as if into the seventh heaven (the heaven of heavens, the Creator's heaven) to be at the feet of the same one God.

Then, I saw a cloud of smoke and felt the presence and energy of a higher power. I was told I stood in the presence of pure being; thus, I had the ability to ask for whatever I desired. In the power of that awesome moment, however, I could not think; I was filled with wonder and deep humility. The only words that came to mind were those of *The Lord's Prayer*.

Upon rising from this deep meditative dream, I told my spiritual mother, Mother Awai, about my experience. I said I felt so humble that I did not know what to do or say, so I just sang *The Lord's Prayer*. She said to me, "Daughter, you have asked for everything with that song."

Over the years I have participated in the mourning process more times than I can count. As I walked into the footsteps of my destiny, I became a Spiritual Mother to many, as Mother Awai was to me. I have been blessed to include the teachings of the Spiritual Baptists with my work as a traditional Yoruba Priest and, as such, have "pointed" over a hundred or more journeyers into the world of Spirit. As they returned, I have been privileged to hear first-hand of the visions and messages they received during the mourning process and to watch them grow spiritually as a result.

I could tell you about many other experiences from my mourning journeys and my work, but most of all I would like to impress upon you that the experience is real, it is rewarding, and, most of all, it leaves you with the knowledge that the Spirit of the Lord still dwells with man. You only have to begin to enter into the realm of consciousness of light and peace to find God. The simple ancient rituals of ceaseless prayer, faith, and spiritual perseverance serve as formidable guides even today.

SECTION THREE

SANKOFA

SANKOFA

The Wisdom-message from the Voice of God often gives us pause... calls us to reflect... to remember... to reconsider past thoughts, deeds, and actions!

The West African ageless wisdom, as expressed in the Adinkra symbol, Sankofa, reminds us of the efficacy of retrospection. Sankofa suggests that we look back in order to go forward. Learn from the past to build for the future!

I love music. I am a connoisseur of female vocalists. I do not know any song by Rickie Byars that I do not greatly appreciate and enjoy. One that I particularly love, however, is one of the Congregational Hymns at Agape International, called "Use Me." *All* of the lyrics of the song speak to me, and I am especially moved by and *love* the lyrics of the chorus—my personal prayer:

Use me, O God
I stand for You
And here I'll abide
As you show me
All that I must do

Rickie's song, "I Release," was to my dear friend Zainab as "Use Me" is to me.

I release and I let go
I let the Spirit run my life
I am free in the Spirit
Yes, I'm only here for God

I met and got to know Zainab during an extended stay at a holistic healing center in San Diego, California. We "connected" upon first meeting, our bond quickly solidified when we discovered that we had several Atlanta, Georgia, friends and experiences in common. Years after we met and several months after Zainab passed, I was in my prayer room offering my morning prayers. On this particular day I really wanted to receive more clarity on my mission in life, my work of service in the world. I wanted more direct Guidance on how I could be a greater channel for God to work through… to use. After an extended period of "begging" prayers to the Creator, I began to sing "Use Me." Something stopped me mid-way and I received a clear message from Zainab. She told me that I had to come *through* her song ("I Release") in order to get to mine ("Use Me")! Wow, I was stunned, both at the clarity and the profundity of the message. I knew she was right. I knew that before I could be ready to be used to the degree that I was willing and desirous, I had to first do the work of releasing! I had to take a deep Sankofa-look back and identify those things (mostly aspects of ego and self-doubt) that I needed to completely let go of. I had to totally let Spirit run my life so that I could truthfully say that "I'm only here for God." *Then*, I would be ready for Spirit to Use Me.

The spirit of Sankofa serves both as spiritual anchor and springboard. In this section these wise women writers share stories about the multi-dimensional eternal continuum of life. Retrospectively, they are able to see how the puzzles of their lives have been constructed; how the lives and tried-and-true rituals of their ancestors inform their rituals and traditions of today; how the life and "story" of the dearly departed is now intricately woven into the story that we continue to weave... even as we explore the wisdom and power of emptying into retreat, seclusion, and quiet in order to emerge full and charged.

Ritual: Food for the Soul

Sobonfu Somé

*Sobonfu Somé, one of the foremost voices in African spirituality, was destined from birth to teach the ancient wisdom, ritual, and practices of her Dagara ancestors to those in the West. Sobonfu, whose name means "keeper of the rituals," traveled the world on a healing mission, sharing the rich spiritual life and culture of her native land, Burkina Faso, which ranks as one of the world's poorest countries, yet one of the richest in spiritual life and custom. Since the beginning of her journey, Sobonfu traveled extensively throughout North America and Europe, conducting workshops on spirituality, ritual, the sacred, and intimacy. Her work has moved African spiritual practices out of the realm of anthropology and into a place alongside the world's great spiritual traditions, and offers a message of profound significance and practical application for the lives of westerners. Sobonfu authored several books and articles, including *The Spirit of Intimacy, Welcoming Spirit Home,* and *Falling Out of Grace,* addresses ways to respond to disappointment in oneself and in others with strength, creativity, and faith. For more information on Sobonfu, visit her websites: www.sobonfu.com and www.wisdomspringinc.org.

This contributor is deceased.

For me, ritual constitutes a way of living life wholly. It is a way of connecting with Spirit and with other people's spirits. It also is a way of celebrating, praising, healing, blessing our lives. Many people feel ritual is something they do not know what to do with, or they think it's something so far away that they do not connect to it. For me, however, ritual seems as essential to the soul as food to the physical body.

My ritual practice is determined by what's going on in my life. Living in the West, I have found it important to do ritual that connects me to the Earth. All the political, missionary, and other misplaced attachments to religion and spirituality in a western context make it easy to become disconnected from self, Spirit, and life altogether, so I have found it helpful to go outside in nature barefooted or to lie down on the ground and call out to Spirit. Gardening, which I see as a form of prayer, has served as a way for me to stay in touch with the Earth and its vibrations around me, and that has helped me to not go crazy.

A meaningful ritual for me could be something as simple as calling out to Spirit, saying, "Spirit, today I feel fragmented. With all the things happening in my life, I feel overwhelmed. I'm reaching out to You to help me be grounded, to help me connect to You, so I don't lose what is in my essence." I then touch the Earth to feel it and to take its healing and grounded energy.

I have earth from home and sometimes I even eat it, because that's what I need to do just to stay grounded. Sometimes I take a little bit of it outside, I lie down on the Earth, and I put a little bit in my mouth and say, "As I take this in, remind me that I am a part of this realm, of this Earth. Help me be rooted and keep me focused with my purpose and form."

I learned these tools and practices growing up. This particular ritual is easy and simple, and was incorporated in everyday life. When children are running around wild, especially teenagers, parents create a mound of earth, put water in it, and ask the children to go and play in it. In this way, the children meet the Earth and take some of the energy from the Earth into themselves. All of a sudden, they find themselves so grounded, and all the wildness and craziness basically stops.

That has been an inspiration for me—just remembering. When I first came to America, I realized, "Oh, my God, I don't even live on the ground floor. I am even further away from the Earth, and I now know why I'm going crazy." Remembering this ritual to keep me grounded and keep me aligned with the Earth has inspired me and provided ways for me to be at peace with myself and with my environment.

I also learned early in life that building a shrine to Spirit helps me connect. If you would like to build a shrine—also called an altar—ask yourself, "What kind of shrine should I create to begin to communicate with Spirit? What kind of materials, colors, and elements would support such a shrine?" Ask permission from the land and start out with a prayer to focus your intention. Then let Spirit guide you in creating your shrine. You cannot start to do spiritual work without having a shrine. This provides your anchor, your compass, to help you navigate throughout your spiritual experience.

We need a purpose for doing a ritual, because without any purpose a ritual cannot be done effectively. Without purpose, the ritual may not have as much impact. The prayers that arise from a ritual are dictated directly by its purpose.

We also need community. The community is the human support system that bears witness and helps the individual through the various stages of the ritual. Yes, it's true that when doing an individual ritual we do not necessarily need our community. However, there are many rituals that require the involvement of the community—for instance, the grief ritual. We may grieve on our own, but part of the reason we cannot shake off the grief lies in the fact that it becomes too isolating and we get stuck. We really are not able to share the pain of the grief, so we need witness-bearing, blessing, welcoming. We need the community to be there to hold us and say, "Yes, you are doing the work. Yes, we support you." When you do the work by yourself, no one is there to cheer you up and support you. Somewhere in your psyche, it feels as if you have done something wrong and that's why you are being punished with grief. Your psyche is unable to release everything, because it is like one person trying to empty a lake with a bucket.

The last part of a ritual is the closure, during which we say "thank you" to Spirit. If the shrine was created in a space that requires that it be dismantled, we ask permission to take the shrine apart. Otherwise, we simply thank Spirit to close the ritual.

The Grief Ritual: Making Peace with Yourself and Others

The grief ritual constitutes a huge part of our Dagara culture, and I use it in many ways. The grief ritual is actually one of my favorite rituals—not because I'm a crybaby but because it has many different purposes. The grief ritual offers us a way of making peace with ourselves, with our ancestors, with our Spirit, and with family and friends. It has the ability to purify us, to bring back peace, to bring back balance, so we can be realigned with our vision and our Spirit.

For the Dagara people, the grief ritual has great importance because it provides a way to say goodbye to a person, to a dream, or to something that causes pain in our lives. It gives us a way to bring different experiences to closure. We can use the grief ritual to release everyday frustration. There are many, many different uses for the grief ritual. It provides a powerful way of letting the soul shine and of not getting depressed.

Of course, this ritual also offers a means for us to say to a person who has passed, "We care for you. We love you, and we are going to miss you." It is a way of cutting the umbilical cord as well; a lot of people, or a lot of spirits, get caught between realms because they're still so attached to their families. This makes it difficult for them to leave the physical realm. When a family member is not willing to accept a person's death, or is not willing to let that person go, a bond is created that connects that person to the deceased, thus preventing the deceased from moving forward into the realm of ancestors. At the same time, the person who lives here on this side, on the physical plane, is unable to live life fully because he or she is tapping into energies that do not sustain life or the soul's purpose.

The grief ritual generally is done as a collective, in a group, and certain elements traditionally are part of the ritual. For example, we use water, which, in our tradition, represents emotion. Water is used as a way to draw out our grief and also serves as the container for our grief, so that our emotion does not spill out and attach itself to others or run everywhere.

Rituals Provide a Spirit Connection

Ritual connects you to Spirit. For me, it's like feeling at home. You can be in your home and not really feel at home. When I am connected to Spirit, I have a sense of security, a sense of being at home, a sense that I am living the life I want to live. I can feel Spirit, sense It, smell It. This connection feels like being a part of a huge picture in which I hold a piece of the light that radiates throughout the whole scene.

In our tradition, we serve as the eyes of the ancestors on this ground, this plane of existence. They benefit from this connection, because in many ways we help them achieve their overall purpose. For instance, maybe someone in our family has used her purpose incorrectly during her life-time, has been mean to other people or has destroyed the family life. Upon her death she realizes, "Oh, my goodness, how could I have lived my entire life being this way? I really need someone to help me make amends in the realm of the living so I can go on to the world of Spirit." So, she might pick someone in the family and ask that person to do a specific job. This is why you will find yourself thinking about this deceased person. You won't know why you're thinking about her, but something definitely drives you to connect with the spirit of this ancestor, and this process then reveals the nature of the relationship that will exist between the two of you. Thus, you benefit by being the one who could stop a pattern of behavior or dysfunction in your family. This not only enhances your purpose, but provides a healthier way to live your life as well. Additionally, it allows you to correct the behavior of your ancestor so he or she can move on to the world of Spirit.

How Ritual Quenches a Spiritual Thirst

So many people are searching spiritually right now, and people who may have been very religious all their lives are realizing they want something more than religiosity. They have a spiritual thirst. I would tell these people, first, to stop running around so much and to look closer to home. If you are searching it means something in your life has made you do so. You need to stop and ask yourself, "What was the trigger?" You have to know the source of your search, your need to search, so you can begin looking into it and see what it really means to you. Often people run so far on their search that they lose track of the starting point of their spiritual quest.

Second, I would suggest that any spiritual searcher connect to the spirit of the place where he lives. Connecting to the spirit of your immediate environment will help you connect to the greater Spirit.

Third, I suggest taking your search to the community. We all want to have an isolated experience, but when we find pieces we have been searching for and discover that we need community to help us complete the last bit of our spiritual journey, the community may not be there for us. This, then, becomes another crisis we have to address beyond the original spiritual thirst or quest.

Ritual: Life's Guiding Force

If ritual weren't an important part of how I live my life, my life would be like being in a boat at sea without any kind of direction, without knowing where I was going. I could be anywhere. Ritual provides me with direction. It also provides me with a way to bring clarity into my life and to free myself of things that keep me trapped. It is a way of defragmenting my spirit and my soul. It serves as a way for me to celebrate. It gives me a way to unite body, mind, soul, and Spirit. Ritual offers me a way to find a sense of purpose. For me, it's important to use ritual every day, whether it be personal ritual or collective ritual. It all creates the map I need to live my life in a whole manner. I don't know what my life would be without ritual—and I don't think I want to find out.

Spirit is not some alien thing we think about that doesn't really exist. It is as real as you and I. Spirit serves as a guiding force in our lives, and we need to recognize that fact and stop running away from Spirit. We have nothing to gain by being divorced from Spirit. By including ritual in our lives, we can not only connect with Spirit, but enjoy all the benefits of that connection.

Honoring the Past, Embracing the Future:
Healing and Prospering with the Ancestors' Blessings
Michelle Coghill Chatman

Dr. Michelle Coghill Chatman (Iya Omo Olofina) is an anthropologist, educator, vocalist, and devotee in the West African based Ifa/Orisha religious system. For many years, she performed with Blacknotes, a Washington DC-based spoken word and jazz ensemble. Dr. Chatman is a professor at the University of the District of Columbia and she enjoys teaching and inspiring others through her music, writing, and public service. Dr. Chatman especially enjoys lecturing on the use of culturally responsive mindfulness and contemplative approaches in education as a means of supporting student learning, fostering community, and promoting justice and equity. She wrote this essay while expecting her daughter, Zora. Learn more about her work at www.wisdomfromthemat.com.

As I recall the moments of great joy in my life, I find that they have often involved children. Within the Yoruba religion it is believed that children are ancestral souls who have returned into the family. As I write this, pregnant with my first and long-awaited child, I am also literally waiting for my sister to deliver her second son—all ancestors returning.

As with numerous belief systems around the world, the reverence for ancestors is part of the cultural ethos. Thus, it is reflected in the daily lived experience of the family and community through the erection of altars, maintenance of burial sites, and cultural festivals that commemorate the deceased. The ancestors often are entreated for favor and blessings, for they are not considered to be sleeping in some far-off place awaiting resurrection. Instead, they are believed to be alive in the ancestral realm, watching over us, protecting us, and, when invited, intervening on our behalf—gently nudging us in the direction of our highest good. For African Americans, reclamation of our ancestry is a central component in our healing and uplifting. For generations, our native land, people, and customs have been denigrated and devalued, and we have been psychologically con- ditioned to shun anything pertaining to Africa. The tradition of honoring those who came before us allows us to move beyond this consciousness and to connect with and become proud of our traditions and our history.

The relationship with the ancestors is one of reciprocity, a core element in many indigenous African belief systems. Not only do they help us, we do the same for them. We pray for them, asking that they be surrounded with light and elevated when they return to this plane once again in the body of a newborn child. Of course, not all our ancestors departed this life in a state of peace. In fact, many of them lived lives filled with hardship and died tragically. For them, we also pray for their peaceful existence in the next life and for their purposeful return to this one.

Honoring Ancestors with an Altar

In my particular spiritual community, The Yoruba Temple of Spiritual Elevation and Enlightenment, the establishment of an ancestral altar serves as the first step in reclaiming one's spiritual heritage and beginning the journey toward oneness with Spirit. When I learned of this practice shortly after joining the Temple, it made perfect sense to me, though at the time I could not articulate the reason why. In fact, my grandmother, a very religious and spiritual woman, was, and continues to be, one of the major influences in my life. She had a "direct connect" with God and, without hesitation, would share divinely received visions, dreams, and messages with our family. She anointed my siblings' and cousins' heads, as well as my own, with holy oil she blessed herself. Although we would laugh at our oil-stained foreheads bearing the sign of the cross, I now realize what a powerful ritual she performed. Indeed, I have been led to a place where my spiritual leader, Mother Taylor, performed the very same ritual anointing during the third eye opening ceremony, which activates one's spiritual site. My grandmother foretold family tragedies and blessings alike, and I truly believe she has directly influenced the ways I've grown and the woman I have become, although she died when I was 23 years old. Perhaps that explains why I welcomed the opportunity to make such a visible and honorable connection with her and my other ancestors through the creation of an ancestral altar.

I remember performing the task, placing the pictures of my ancestors and relics that reminded me of them in a dedicated place in my small, two-room apartment. Upon a white cloth I placed handwritten letters from my grandmother, an intimate act that inspired my love for words and learning; a photo of my grandfather, a handsome, cocoa-brown man who was a painter, fisherman, and hunter; pictures and mementos of a host of other relatives and friends; and a sand painting of the "Door of No Return" in Senegal, where captured Africans were held before being shipped off to endure enslavement throughout the diaspora. The painting represented the many ancestors I never knew and would never know. I then lit a white candle, symbolizing peace and purity, and gave an offering of flowers, drink, and prayers.

That was the beginning of a healing for me, and I believe it represented a long-awaited moment for my ancestors as well. When I acknowledged them, I could feel their gratitude. So many things about this ritual just felt right to me.

Using an Altar for Connection to Ancestors

As I sat in front of my altar one evening, I poured out my heart to my ancestors. I gave thanks for all they had endured and sacrificed. Somewhere in the midst of praying and talking, I began to cry and say to them repeatedly, "You have not been forgotten. You have not been forgotten." It was a cathartic experience for me, and I deeply believe it can be the same for all people and for the ancestors. We all need peace and reconciliation, and this ritual helps us find these things.

An impenetrable connection was made that day between my ancestors and myself, and it has inspired and guided me ever since. It gave deeper meaning to the song lyrics written by one of my favorite groups, Earth, Wind, and Fire: "Sound never dissipates, it only recreates in another place." The ancestors are that sound, that immortal energy that cannot be destroyed but persists in our dreams, resonates in our songs, and returns in the form of our young ones.

One morning, as I shared my breakfast of Cream of Wheat and toast with the ancestors, I began to sing the ancestral songs we sing at my temple. An aunt had recently passed, and, as I reflected upon all those that had crossed over, I considered the fact that I had never visited a cemetery after the burial of a loved one. Suddenly, I heard them speaking to me as if they stood in the flesh before me, saying, "There is where we die, but here is where we live."

And indeed they do. The ancestors live in our songs. They live in our physical features and personality traits, in our habits, in our stories, and in our words of wisdom and sayings passed down through the generations. Just as we inherit their phenotypical and expressive characteristics, we also inherit their energy and spirit. We are their energy and spirit. At our personal sacred sites we can remember that they live in us and are still with us in that eternal place, the "now" place—this very moment, never too far from the place we call home.

The ancestors guide us. They share information with us in our sleeping state and in silent, intuitive ways. I recall my first visit to the house of a young man I had recently started dating. In his office he kept a beautiful, wall-sized color photo of his deceased mother. I found it a touching and honorable sentiment to have her photo so present, so near. Immediately recognizing it as his ancestral altar of sorts, I silently prayed that she would confer her blessing upon our newly established relationship. I also prayed that her son was the mate for whom I had been searching.

On my next visit to his house, I placed a small arrangement of yellow roses under her photo, which just felt like the "right" thing to do. I would later thank her for raising such a fine son, the man who grew up to become my husband and gleefully expectant first-time father.

Honoring the Ancestors Returned as Children

Children are the ancestors returned. With great expectation I look forward to the birth of this little one I am carrying. I can't wait for him or her to join the brilliant offspring of my siblings, my niece and nephews. I anticipate sharing with all of them the stories and history of our family and creating memories they will cherish long after I am gone—when I become an ancestor. As we mold these returned ancestors with the love and sternness our predecessors offered to us as well, they will grow in the spirit of those who have gone before.

So we honor them, the best of who they were—and the not so best. We recognize that they were only human and did the best they could with what they had. We acknowledge them, the ones we knew and those countless and nameless ones that we never knew but from whom we descended. We claim them, the ones that made us proud as well as those that didn't shine so brightly, with the hope that when their energy returns, when their souls reincarnate, they will occupy a higher level of consciousness and master the lessons they came to this lifetime to learn. We also claim them, because, either directly or indirectly, they helped us become who we are. Thus, it is our responsibility to express our appreciation for life, a blessed journey.

I invite and encourage you to honor those who walked before you in the manner that speaks to your heart. You may not be called to set up an elaborate altar, but you can share with other family members the history and stories of your transitioned loved ones. Every so often, you can cook a meal consisting of the favorite foods of a loved one and perhaps even set a little to the side "for the ones who ain't here." Consider inviting the youth in your family to create poems and stories dedicated to ancestors, maybe even identifying particular ones in whose shoes they would like to walk— or think they do walk. Glance through your many photo albums and walk down memory lane with your departed loved ones. Look at the children in your family and acknowledge the fact that they carry forth the spirits of the ancestors, the energies and traditions of all that came before. For when we acknowledge and honor the ancestors, we connect with the strong and soulful roots from which we emerge and now stand strong. Indeed, doing so helps us stand stronger.

From Seeker to Finder:
Co-creating Your Life with Spirit
"Gabriella"

German-born Gabriella has lived for much of her life in the United Kingdom, where she feels her spiritual connectedness and receives most of her inspiration. She has a background in farming, psychotherapy, and social work, as well as in music. In the last decade, Gabriella has developed her own style of intuitive, improvised meditative healing and transformational music as well as her own method of sound-healing through what she calls "sound weaving." Inspired by the Celtic lands and her deep connection with nature, her music opens hearts, lifts veils, and allows souls to remember their connection to Source. Gabriella's sound-weaving work takes her all over Europe and the Americas, where she accepts invitations to give workshops and to share her healing and inspirational music. www.peace-trails.com.

Many of us start our young adult lives searching for something we seem to miss during our early religious or spiritual education. Much of what we are taught in our society about these subjects doesn't seem to make sense to us. In particular, principles taught by religious organizations get contradicted by the lives of those who represent the organization and don't seem to correspond with what we see working or holding true in the world. Those of us who feel this discrepancy strongly enough, therefore, start to search.

We go on a quest to look behind and beyond the commonly agreed-upon normality and so-called "reality" to find something that makes more sense and meets our souls' thirst for meaning and connection. This search—sometimes deeply buried in the subconscious rather than being part of our awareness—then shapes our life's journey.

Yet, a major turning point occurs in that journey when something in us wakes up, or becomes aware, and we stop being "seekers" and become "finders." At that moment, which actually represents the culmination of a gradual process, we realize that we are the creators of our destiny and of our own journey. We know that the answers are within rather than outside.

From that moment on we stop going after things, and they begin coming toward us. We also begin living a life of connection to Spirit, a life filled with a different spirituality and spiritual practice than we learned in our youth. This mysterious, mystical, magical moment is experienced differently by every single person, and, while it can be invited, it cannot be planned or forced. Like a moment of grace, it is received and recognized—sometimes only much later!

If you haven't experienced this process yet, I want to encourage you to invite it into your life—and I will do this by sharing my story.

The story I am telling is not about rituals and practices in themselves, but the journey towards an inner alignment where practices and rituals emerge daily—by themselves, effortlessly. The raking of leaves becomes a practice of meditation and of the clearing of space on the inside as well as the outside; the weeding of a flowerbed becomes a communion with nature or a moment of rewriting old scripts and stories.

The activities of cleaning and decorating become acts of raising vibration and frequency in a particular environment. Today, all my music-making has become a deeply aligned practice of weaving strands of consciousness in communion with Spirit whenever I pick up an instrument or use my voice. The following is my journey toward a connectedness to Self and Source, Nature and Life. My daily practice includes ongoing work with intention, alignment, and awareness.

Asking for Guidance

As my 33rd birthday approached, I found myself enjoying my life but not really satisfied with it. I couldn't see the "thread"—my soul's purpose—running through all aspects of my life, or the destination towards which I was heading. I had started my working life farming, then went on to play music, explore the field of mental health, train in psychotherapy, and finally work in children's homes and other institutions. No matter what job I tried, I didn't see how I was contributing, where I was making a difference, or how I was fulfilling my purpose. Everything I did seemed random and unrelated. Here and there in my work, I could see I had made a positive contribution to people's lives, but I wasn't happy with the institutions and organizations I worked for and represented. More importantly, my jobs offered me no fulfillment. I was really fed up. Plus, I was still searching, but wanted to stop.

On the day of my birthday, I decided I'd had enough. I banged my fist on the table and said to Spirit: "I've had enough of not knowing why I'm here. I want to know now! I want to see the 'thread' and live my purpose."

This obviously provided a firm and clear enough request, since the beginning of an answer came to me just three days later in a meditation. As I meditated, I saw a clear vision of my future self walking along wooded paths. The vision caused me to know certain things about myself in the future, but without specific details. For instance, I knew I was working with sound. I knew I was facilitating people's deeper connectedness with Nature. I knew I was traveling the world and teaching, and I knew I was living in a conscious ecological community. In all cases, I didn't know where, with whom, or how I would come to be doing these things.

This vision left me feeling so uplifted that I began to look at my life to date differently. I was able to see that everything I had done so far had prepared me for everything I might be doing in the future. My farming experience could form the basis for my connection with nature. My music training could serve as the perfect preparation for my work with sound, and my training and experience in therapeutic work offered the perfect preparation for teaching and living in a community as well as for healing and teaching.

I tried to get a sense of when this vision might become a reality, and the feeling response I received said "a little over 10 years." When I tried to see how I'd get there, how I'd create this vision, I drew a blank. (As I write this, however, 11 years have passed and most of what I saw that day has become a reality. At the time I first envisioned this future, though, I couldn't have imagined the path I actually took to create it.)

Receiving Spirit's Response

A week after my meditation experience, I reconnected with an acquaintance and felt compelled to tell him about my vision. He responded to my story by telling me that he and a few friends had recently moved to the Scottish Highlands. They were hoping to buy a piece of land upon which to start a conscious community living in harmony with the land.

I realized Spirit was responding quickly to my birthday request. However, I couldn't integrate the gifts so fast! Not wanting to turn away an opportunity obviously sent by Spirit, I agreed to visit Scotland when I could to "feel out" the situation.

While I waited for that time to come, I consciously noticed all my attachments to my current life and what seemed to be a notable resistance on my part to big change. For this reason, it took me several months to gain enough momentum and reasons to visit Scotland.

When I did get there, I was clear that it was not yet time for me to move. However, I felt the energy of the land so strongly that I verbally committed to doing anything necessary to fulfill my soul's purpose. If that plan included moving to Scotland, I would take the necessary steps to make it possible.

Spirit heard my commitment! The day after I got home to Devon, in southern England, my partner decided to end our relationship, I was given notice to move out of my apartment, and changes began happening at work. For the first time in my life I didn't feel upset by any of these events. Typically, any one of these events could have easily sent me—or anyone, for that matter—into all sorts of emotional states and reactions, if I felt a victim of them. This time, though, I knew I had created them.

Indeed, I understood these events as a direct response from the Universe, or Spirit, to my commitment to taking the steps necessary to live my life's purpose. Anything that wasn't serving that process at that moment was falling away with ease and grace. I didn't need to do anything to make it happen.

Yet, instead of feeling disempowered, I felt empowered by the turn of events. In fact, I have learned to recognize that this feeling of empowerment signals the shift from seeker to finder. At that point, we recognize our own creatorship and stop feeling like victims of circumstances and events.

Sensing Energy in Your Life

Someone offered to let me apartment-sit for a few months over the winter, and I accepted. Those winter months in that apartment represented the first opportunity I had ever had to live on my own. During that time, I became much more aware of the energy of my activities. I noticed which ones, as well as which people in my life, increased my energy and which depleted my energy. Also, I started to drastically reduce my busy social life, which had served like a drug, keeping me entertained and distracted but not really fed. I made conscious choices as to what I did and with whom I spent time, according to what I was learning about energy. By the time spring arrived and I had decided to move out onto the moors, I was ready to experience being a hermit, to let go of my town job and life and to connect with Nature. I knew this experience would expand my energy tremendously.

When spring came, I found a caravan to live in up on the moors and, after years of town life, prepared for the total wilderness of the Scottish Highlands. Within a short time after my arrival, I found gardening work, which kept me going financially and, at the same time, strengthened my connection with Nature. Every morning upon waking, I started by clarifying my intention to deepen my connectedness with Nature and my own inner Knowing, and to attract those events and situations that would lead me to the next step in living my soul's purpose. This practice was so strong that many magical meetings happened and things seemed to become manifest really easily and fast. Often I would go out to particular trees, sit, make contact, and enter into deep communion with them. The world of Nature and nature spirits became very alive to me and those trees became my entrusted friends that would advise me. Late in that same fall, I suddenly felt that by spring of the next year I would be ready to move to Scotland.

And I was: By then I knew clearly what I wanted to contribute in that community. Having worked in gardens all summer, I felt a longing to work in a garden created by listening to Nature. This garden would not be designed from a human, mental perspective of tidiness and organization, but instead would be co-created in harmony with the nature spirits. So, I moved to Scotland in the spring, ready to create a garden with flowers, vegetables, and anything that wanted to grow there for the little retreat and healing center the small group had established there. The first feeling I had in the space of the potential garden was a sense of excitement and joy and an inner Knowing that Nature was rejoicing at the prospect of co-creative partnership.

Working with Inner Fences

As soon as I began establishing this garden, I received a great teaching. In the strath, the Scottish name for a long and wide river-valley, herds of deer, cows, and sheep roamed freely and rabbits proliferated. If I didn't want to share all that grew in the garden with these animals, I would need to build a fence. As my first step in creating the garden, therefore, I sat down with my new friends to tune in and commune with the nature spirits and guardians of the area about the garden plan and fence. We sat in the garden in meditation with the desire to connect and commune with the intelligence of the garden, holding a question in mind and allowing the answer to arise. The answers we received would sometimes come as feelings, images, words, or an inner Knowing. The answer we received at this time was that we would benefit from spending a week working with our own inner fences before attempting to build an outer one.

As part of this beautiful process, we took deep journeys on the inside through meditation, and on the outside by going for walks in search of fences. When we saw a fence, we would stop to feel the effect it had on us and on the surrounding area. We also would look inside ourselves at the walls, fences, divisions, separations, and compartmentations that filled the landscape of our inner world. We discovered that these inner walls actually caused much pain: Our collective and personal beliefs, judgments, and experiences made us feel separate from Nature and from Spirit, and made us even doubt their existence or our ability to perceive them. We also discovered issues of needing to control and defend what we "own". We spent time with inner journeying to give love and healing to these insecurities, wounds, beliefs, and doubts, many of which came from early childhood experiences and also seemed ingrained in the collective psyche.

The process of looking at our inner walls provided a great gift. It offered us a chance to stop, to explore emotions and energy, and to heal before taking action. At the end of that week, I was ready to build the fence. I wanted it to be a creative and playful structure that clearly created sacred space within the larger sacred space of the valley and the mountains. I built it to create a caring, loving, nurturing, welcoming energy. Had I built a fence before looking at my inner fences, I would have built one with the intent of keeping something out, which would have only created more separation of energy. Now, I was building a fence that had the gesture of caring, loving, and nurturing the life and co-creative activity that would be able to happen within this inner sanctuary.

As the gardener for our little retreat center, I sometimes felt moved to bring my cello out of the closet and play for our guests. On those occasions, I wouldn't bring any music with me; I would just close my eyes and "tune in" to the energy field of those present and let the music flow intuitively for them. When I did this, people would say they felt deep transformational shifts, burdens lifting off their shoulders, buried memories resurfacing, and old wounds being healed. Some said they heard the soul call them to remember deep dreams or had other profound experiences. This led me to use my "intuitive music" as another healing tool in our little retreat center. I had asked Spirit to show me the thread, and it had appeared. Out of my garden, through my music, it was beginning to wind its way into and through my life.

Connecting with Nature

My intuitive music moved to a new level when I met a visitor who also worked closely with the nature spirits. During her extended stay at the healing center, we experienced a connection with the nature spirits in many of the beautiful places in the area. To help integrate these experiences, I played my cello in the evenings. On one of the evenings, as I played, it seemed as if the veil between the dimension we usually dwell in and that of the nature spirits parted and we moved with the sound of my instrument into the dimension of Nature. New sounds came from the cello, as if many more instruments and musicians had joined me. That night deepened my commitment to Nature and wove my "thread" more intricately through this part of my life.

The next day, as I drove through the familiar landscape of the valley, one of the mountains "looked" at me. The "stare" was so powerful that I stopped my car, stepped out, and was moved to ask aloud, "What can I do for you?" In response I heard/felt the words, "Play for us!" This request moved me deeply and informed the way my life evolved from there. My co-creative work with Nature expanded from the garden to music-making. My practice evolved: Every time I sat down to play my cello, I invited Nature to co-create with me, so that in partnership we would create the vibrations and sounds for the Highest Good of anyone present and for All Life Everywhere.

A couple of weeks later, the same visitor—now a friend—invited me to accompany her to the island of Orkney, which lies off the northern coast of Scotland. There, many ancient stone circles and sacred sites give testimony to a deeply connected culture of wisdom and advanced knowledge of the stars and the earth. I agreed, and on this island, sitting for hours amongst those ancient stones—portals between many dimensions—I began to receive songs, poems, and messages from Nature and the Earth.

After Orkney, the two of us visited the island of Iona off the west coast of Scotland. There I felt an overwhelming sense of "coming home." This tiny island, which houses an ancient spiritual center where the veils between worlds remain thin, is difficult to reach from any location. Yet, every single day during the summer months, its energy and power attract hundreds of visitors who make the long pilgrimage to set foot on its sacred ground. More songs and inspirations came to me there, and with them came a growing sense that they wanted to be shared. Time had passed, but Spirit was still responding to my request, and my commitment was still to co-creating my experiences. The thread was getting longer and more apparent in my life. I could see where it was leading me.

A year later, our little community at the healing retreat center came to the knowing that our time there was complete. Each of us needed to follow his or her own journey for a while. I returned to Iona for a second visit and was offered a job in one of the hotels for the following year. My body responded with a powerful "yes" to this opportunity, while my mind tried to catch up.

However, when I moved to the island the next spring I arrived prepared, with several powerful dreams and a little voice from inside suggesting I needed to share my music there. In fact, Spirit had told me that doing so constituted the primary reason for being there.

I felt nervous about sharing my songs and music, but the path had been paved for me, and the hotel received groups of pilgrims regularly who often were grateful to include an evening of music into their program. Plus, it seemed as if I was offering just the right music at just the right time in just the right place. The souls of those on pilgrimage—opening in the energy of Iona and undistracted by ordinary daily life— could hear the messages through the music, sounds, vibrations, and songs I co-creatively played and sang. Many of those souls had deep transformative experiences.

By the end of the summer, I had so many invitations to play my music all over the world that I began to travel as a peace-troubadour. I followed the invitations, singing the songs and messages of Nature and the Earth, co-creating with them the sounds and vibrations of peace, wholeness, and healing wherever I went. Ever since that time, I have traveled in the same manner, but with ever-expanding sounds and messages, weaving the vibrations of wholeness and connectedness into the fabric of the collective consciousness as I go.

Vision into Reality

For the first few of years of my travels, I didn't have a fixed home any-where—at least not for very long. I moved around, stayed wherever I was welcome, had a base with friends for periods of months, and enjoyed the troubadour life tremendously. There came a time when I felt the need of a home, of replenishment, of a firm base to return to after my travels. As with most things in my life since the day I had made my request to Spirit, as the need to search arose, what I was seeking found me. I was offered a long-term house-sit in a very magical place—an old mill cottage in southern

England. That home's owner and I have since become "family," and we continue to share the house in a way that makes life and our residence a beautiful place of flowing love.

So, a decade after my original vision, I found myself working with sound, facilitating connections with nature, and traveling the world singing and teaching. My vision of community has expanded to include many forms of intelligence and consciousness and spreads far across the globe.

Along the way, I found it helpful to have my vision as a light on the horizon guiding me, but often I needed to release my expectations. I had to let go of the thought that the vision might come to pass in the way I had seen it, and when I did so, things unfolded in unpredictable and surprising ways. It felt powerful to invite the opportunities, yet when they appeared it took courage to step through the doors, especially since often they led me outside the known and predictable comfort zones. My practice has evolved into an attitude and belief that everything that comes my way is to support me in some way, even if, at first, it might appear to be a disturbance and I might resist it. At those times I need to go back into a place of stillness and inner connectedness, from there give love and acceptance to the resistance or fear, and allow myself to come back into balance and alignment with what is.

I give thanks to the Universe for this amazing continuing journey and all the magical moments along the way, and for the opportunity to share it. I hope that by doing so, I can help you to experience the quality of living as a finder, rather than as a seeker, always open to Spirit's response to your requests and to your commitment to fulfill your soul's purpose. I believe that living in this way, we can begin to create our own destiny.

I wish you much joy in the discovery of your own wonderful and mysterious journey.

Cool Revolution

(From *Now Is the Time to Open Your Heart*)

Alice Walker

Alice Walker is an author, self-declared feminist and womanist—the latter a term she herself coined to make special distinction for the experiences of women of color. She has written at length on issues of race and gender. Alice Walker is most famous for the critically acclaimed novel *The Color Purple* for which she won the Pulitzer Prize for Fiction.

My father's mother was murdered when he was a boy. Before she married my grandfather, Henry Clay Walker, her name was Kate Nelson. This [story] and 3 [part of] a memorial to the psychic explorer she might have become. It also made clear to me in the writing how much I miss her. And have always missed her.

Kate Talkingtree sat meditating in a large hall that was surrounded by redwood trees. Although the deep shade of the trees usually kept the room quite cool, today was unseasonably warm and Kate, with everybody else, was beginning to perspire. They had been meditating, on and off their cushions, for most of the morning, beginning at five-thirty when they roused themselves, at the sound of the bell, from their beds. When they broke from meditating inside, they quietly made their way outside and into the courtyard. Up and down the path that led to the front door of the hall they did a walking meditation that had been taught them by a lot of different Buddhist teachers, some from America and some from Asia. It was a slow, graceful meditation that she liked; she enjoyed the feeling of a heel touching the earth long before a toe followed it. Meditating this way made her feel almost as slow as vegetation; it went well with her new name, a name she'd taken earlier, in the spring.

Ever since she was small she'd felt a wary futility about talking. At the same time she realized it was something that, in order for the world to under-stand itself at all, had to be done. Her old last name had been Nelson, and for a time she'd thought of calling herself Kate Nelson-Fir. She loved fir trees, especially the magnificent, towering ones that grew on the Northwest coast.

When it was time for the dharma talk to begin Kate made her way to a spot close enough to see and hear the teacher very easily. He was a middle-aged man of southern European descent, with an ecru complexion and a shin-ing bald head. His brown eyes twinkled as he talked. Every once in a while he reached up and stroked the silver earring in his left ear. Because of the earring and because he seemed spotless in his flowing robes, she mentally dubbed him Mr. Clean. She had been coming to his talks every day for more than a week, and had enjoyed them very much. Today he was talking about the misguided notion that a "hot" revolution, with guns and violence, such as the ones attempted in Africa, Cuba, and the Caribbean, could ever succeed. He seemed unaware that these revolutions had been undermined not only by their own shortcomings but also by military interference from the United States. The only revolution that could possibly succeed, he maintained, smiling, was the "cool" one introduced to the world by the Lord Buddha, twenty-five hundred years ago.

Something about this statement did not sit well with Kate. She looked at him carefully. He was certainly a well-fed-looking soul, she thought. Not many meals missed by that one, except by accident. Quietly glancing down at the program on the floor beside her, she saw he had grown up in an upper-middle-class home, had had educated and cultured people as parents and as grandparents, had studied and lived in Europe as well as in the East. Was now a prominent professor at one of the country's most famous universities. Easy enough for him to dismiss the brown and black and yellow and poor white people all over the globe who worried constantly where their next meal was coming from, she thought. How would they feed, clothe, and educate their children. Who, if they did sit down to meditate, would probably be driven up again by the lash. Or by military death squads, or by hunger, or by ... the list was long.

Looking around her she noticed most of the meditators shared the teacher's somewhat smug, well-fed look. They were overwhelmingly white and middle- to upper-middle-class and had the money and leisure time to be at a retreat. In fact, she noted, she seemed to be the only person of color there. What was wrong with this picture?

Her mind, which had been clear as a reflecting pool just minutes before, now became cloudy. This was exactly what meditation was meant to prevent. She took a deep breath, labeled her thoughts "thinking," as she'd been instructed to do if her mind wandered during meditation, and settled herself more firmly on her cushion. She would listen to this teacher, whom she indeed respected very much, and she would not be critical. Besides, she knew what he meant. There was a way in which all "hot" revolutions defeated themselves, because they spawned enemies. Look at those crazy ex-Cubans in Miami, for instance, who never recovered from having some of their power taken away, and the endless amount of confusion, pain, and suffering they caused.

After the talk she began to think in earnest. She felt she had reached an impasse on the Buddhist road.

That evening and the next day and the next she found herself unable to meditate. She kept looking out the window instead, just as she had looked out of the window of the Church of God and Christ, as a child, when she had been unable to believe human beings, simply by being born, had sinned. The redwood trees looked so restful, their long branches hanging down to the earth. Each tree created a little house, a shelter, around itself. Just right for a human or two to sit. She hadn't realized this before, how thoughtful this was. But on her very next walking meditation she slowly, slowly, made her way to the largest redwood tree and sat under it, becoming invisible to the dozens of people who continued their walking meditation and slowly walked all around her.

When everybody else returned to the meditation hall, she did not.

Becoming an Ideal Woman: Rituals for Developing Clarity and Spiritual Connection
Nana Yaa Densua

*Nana Okomfo Yaa Densua was a senior Akan priest, trained and graduated by the late Nana Yao Opare Dinizulu I. Nana Yaa was the Executive Director of the Sons & Daughters of Serwaa Family Institute. Through this institution, Nana Yaa served persons of all ages by offering spiritual and cultural guidance to foster health, power, and reconciliation. Nana Yaa was also a Certified Natural Health Professional.

"Becoming an Ideal Woman" is training based on traditional Akan ritual practices. The Akan people are an ethnic linguistic group of West Africa, primarily Ghana and the Ivory Coast. The training offers each participant a series of opportunities—encounters with Spirit, self, and community—to gain insight into her individual relationship with God, into living based on her true identity as an African woman, and into truly knowing and mastering herself. The training is not about expectations, but rather involves a journey of sitting and listening, learning, participating, and growing. It is about finding peace in the simplicity of our magnificent spirits, and drawing strength from that peace to build a magnificent life. The training honors the concept of an individual's divine and righteous growth and development, and the beauty of the moment as a testimony to God's greatness and the enduring beauty of the soul.

In the Twi language of the Akan, the name Serwaa represents the ideal woman—the pinnacle of beauty and royalty and the keeper of tradition. During our sacred time together in the program, we examine and reconcile our past, get in touch with the power and energy of God Almighty and our Ancestors, and use our own African traditional rituals to move towards clarity, healing, strength, peace, and transformation.

Libation and Spiritual Bath

We begin with libation to connect us to God Almighty, the Supreme Powers that rule the Universe, and our Ancestors. Libation is the ritual of pouring strong drink on the ground to pay homage to God, the Deities, and the Ancestors. We invite these Spiritual Forces to provide us with their power, protection, and guidance in our endeavors. All participants are then given a spiritual bath of organic herbs, roots, and barks to restore energy, cleanse, and provide emotional clarity, strength, and fortitude.

Bonding is an integral part of the program. The women are required to sleep at the retreat center, eat together, and share cooking, cleaning, and other responsibilities and duties collectively. Opening up and learning to lean on each other are greatly encouraged as well. The proverb that says "cross the river in a crowd and the crocodile will not bite you" sets the tone as the women engage in the principles of Umoja (unity) and Ujima (collective work and responsibility).

During that first night together after the Spiritual Bathing, songs are sung imploring God and our Ancestors to forgive us for anything done, said, thought, or felt that they might find displeasing. We ask for rescue and protection, direction and guidance on this journey and beyond.

The Cleansing Ritual of Full Expression

The next day begins with more cleansing rituals, training, and self-discovery exercises. The soul is that part of the Creator that is in every person. The soul is the bearer of destiny. These exercises help to awaken the soul so that it may be properly utilized in our daily living. The first of several circle exercises empowers each participant to reveal her individual voice and amplifies the power of the collective voice in the healing process. We gather in a circle and each individual takes a turn to express herself. We talk, and we listen; we listen, and we talk. We talk about the things each woman needs to release—past hurts, our families, our understanding of God, our connection with self, and the things we love and dislike about ourselves. Each participant is encouraged to speak until she has fully expressed her feelings. This is done to allow a release of buried feelings and negative points of view.

The healing power of full expression is rooted in the fact that often what we do not say or acknowledge causes the most pain and suffering. As the ritual continues, hard edges soften. Cleansing becomes evident as layers of mental and emotional suffering are discarded and released. As the participants begin to open themselves and relax, any reservations or fear present before joining the group dissipates. We are able to literally witness the discarding and releasing of some of the layers of emotional suffering and mental turmoil. We witness changed attitudes, positive body language, and newfound powerful voices.

Adorning the Body

The day continues with the preparation of semiprecious stones and beads that will be used for the "Adornment of the Body" ritual. After careful selection during travels to Ghana, West Africa, senior women purchase the beads and bring them back for use during this ritual. Beads symbolize beauty, desire, influence, and protective power and are worn to effect these characteristics in each woman. The beads are ritually cleansed and distributed to the participants. The women admire the beauty of the beads and there is great excitement and anticipation in the work that lies ahead to complete the beading. Because each participant must string her own beads, a mentor (someone who has completed the program) is assigned to each woman to teach her the ritual of bead stringing. The bead work is ongoing throughout the program. The completed bead work is again ritually cleansed and becomes a part of the participant's regalia on the day of the final ceremony.

Listening to the Voice of the Ancestors

Connection with the Creator, our Ancestors, our families, and our selves serves as the guiding principle of the program. The "Becoming an Ideal Woman" program offers a way for women to understand the primary importance of their individual relationships with God. During the program, women come to understand that knowledge and acceptance of our place in the Universe, our status as children of God, and that God is the only thing that does not change are the keys to a deep relationship with God.

The displacement and disconnection of African people from our traditions have allowed us to be brainwashed into believing that the adoration and commemoration of our Ancestors is "idol worship," or some other misnomer heaped on us by those who wish to keep us from self-determination and cultural reconnection. However, our Ancestors provide guidance, direction, and protection. In the Spirit World, they work very hard to protect and guide those of us still on Earth. We understand the African continuum of society… the yet-to-be-born, the living, and those who have returned back to the Creator, and the cycle continues. The souls of our Ancestors live on.

In fact, when we call on our Ancestors, they make themselves present. To honor them on a regular basis really translates into asking our Ancestors to keep their sleeves rolled up for us. Oftentimes one might say, "Something told me not to do that (or to do that)." In the "Becoming an Ideal Woman" program, we assure participants that this is the voice of our Ancestors guiding, directing, and protecting us… we need only to listen.

In keeping with connecting with our Ancestors, one of the Ideal Women we call on is Queen Mother Harriet Tubman. She led hundreds of our people to freedom as part of the anti-slavery resistance network known as the Underground Railroad. Through the years, our support of and participation with the Harriet Tubman Organization in Dorchester County, Maryland, has afforded the participants a first-hand connection in reliving the life of Harriet Tubman. The women spend a day in Harriet Tubman's birthplace, engaging in activities that recapture the movements of Mother Tubman. The participants learn about the life she was born into, the lives of her parents and family members, and the critically important work she performed. By reconnecting with the spirit of Mother Tubman, we are reminded, first, of her profound love for God. She spoke often of "consulting with God," and many of that era spoke of her "… confidence in the voice of God, as spoken direct to her soul." Mother Tubman's tenacity, determination, courage, fortitude, and undying love for our people serve as a strong reminder of our responsibility to perpetuate our heritage and culture.

Lifting Your Burdens

The "Lifting Your Burdens" doll workshop offers the participants further understanding of adornment and the release of emotional baggage. Under the original tutelage of Jean Lacey, a renowned artist, we developed this ritual to assist participants in releasing and transferring past mental pain and emotional distress. We perform this ritual at a place of moving water, such as a river. As we pour libation, we ask Nana Oyenni, the Akan deity of the water, to accept the dolls created by the participants. The dolls embody the personality of each woman. The participants are encouraged to let the dolls carry all the negative thoughts, painful experiences and emotions, mental suffering, and physical abuse from their souls. As each woman asks for the power and energy to release the negativity, she drops the doll into the water. This has proven to be an incredibly powerful release for each participant, as evidenced in the jubilation and joy exhibited after the ritual.

Rituals of Relationship and Sexuality

Looking at the male perspective on culture, family, and relationships are important parts of the program as well. The participants are taken on an amazing journey of self-discovery and regeneration led by highly respected and internationally known men of African descent who hold African women in the highest regard. The men offer the women a no-holds-barred dialogue and instruction on the male/female dynamic. The women come to understand the roles of balance and compassion in our relationships with men. They also build upon the concept of being a queen, which further enhances higher levels of self-esteem.

So transformative in nature, this ritual portion has been instrumental in the constructive reunion of couples and families. Women who come into the program with marital problems return home with new perspectives on their own relationships. Many have used this instruction to turn previously negative situations into positive and enduring relationships.

At this point in the program, participants are now deeply fortified with a real sense of overall clarity. They are ready to receive the rituals and training related to sexuality and healing. Unfortunately, many women carry the burden of sexual abuse on various levels. Guided by a medical professional, the participants are helped to release the tension, myths, pain, and trauma of past relationships while celebrating the beauty of love and fruitful relationships with our men. In the process, they come to recognize and honor the fertility of Asase Yaa (Mother Earth) and to accept their place in the Universe as sexual beings. Additionally, information on holistic health and healing is provided as a basis for establishing preventive care and a consistent program of well-being for participants and their families.

Ceremony of Higher Ground

We cannot help but lead joyful, fulfilling lives when we walk with humility, obedience, respect, self-respect, patience, self-control, nurturing, gratefulness, love of each other, honesty, cleanliness, and generosity in our dealings with one another. The eight-weekend program culminates with the "Ceremony of Higher Ground." To reach the place where the ceremony will be held, we travel through the forest singing songs to the Deities and our Ancestors, calling especially on the mmoatia (the little people) of the forest and asking permission to enter to perform the last of the rituals for the program. Gifts are presented at the banks of one of the mighty rivers as we call on Nana Oyenni, other Deities, and our Ancestors to thank them for opening the way and bringing us to the day of ceremony. We acknowledge the blessing of the presence of both the Deities and the Ancestors. They open the way for the preparation of the participants for the ceremony that both closes one phase of their training and leads them to higher ground and the next phase of living as an Ideal Woman. Adorned in West African attire and beading, the women are then presented to the community in a grand celebration of their achievement in completing the program.

Clarity is the catalyst for transformation. Once clarity is achieved, the exhilaration of walking the planet without baggage—with a clear aura, feeling a sense of cleansing and healing, peace, and self-worth—is a truly riveting and amazing experience. "Becoming an Ideal Woman" provides the necessary opportunities for women to be clear in their vision, hearts, minds, bodies, and souls. With this accomplishment, the women are truly on the path to becoming Serwaa in their own right.

The Ritual of Retreat: Restoring Balance

Pamela Ramadei

Pamela Ramadei, Master Certified Coach and Trainer, is on the faculty of Adler International Learning and collaborates with several coaching and consulting organizations. Her extensive background includes retreats and workshops on coaching, leadership development, and interpersonal communication skills, as well as group dynamics, conflict resolution, and synergistic collaborative learning teams. For over 25 years, Pamela has been recognized as an engaging, trustworthy, and innovative trainer and facilitator, and is currently engaged in leadership development programs in the U.S. federal environment. She has accomplished significant team coaching results with her "Group Synergy" team process and advocates life-long learning, mutual respect, and living with integrity and balance. For more information on Pamela's work, visit www.choicetochange.com.

I am blessed. I am calm and quiet as I surrender to the silence and the stillness. My serenity is reflected in my mind, and I am retreating into a space of not knowing, away from any judgments or analysis. I am relaxing into a cavern of mystery where my mind and heart can open with curiosity. I open to see what has been unseen and to know the previously unknown as truth. What once was unseen comes into view. I feel my connection with the Divine.

I wrote these words of reflection while journaling during the winter months of early 2008, from a space of silence and from a place of darkness when the moon is new. Light pollution was non-existent there, a place removed from the hectic pace and demands of life. I could easily be present with the images of my outer surroundings and my inner sensations and musings. With so few external stimuli, I found it easier to become aware of subtle changes arising both within and around me. Simply noticing, not judging, not expecting, not even wishing or hoping, I was practicing a long-honored ritual. I was on retreat from the usual, restoring balance to my life.

I had retreated into my cozy, little, newly constructed eco-nest—an alternative home built on sustainable development principles. The home is off the electric grid, and the Colorado sun supplies it with electricity and heat to keep it cozy even in sub-zero temperatures. Nestled in vast open space, the house offers a view of five towering 14,000-foot peaks in the glorious Sangre de Cristo (Blood of Christ) mountain range to the east. To the southeast, the view includes the northern edge of the Great Sand Dunes National Park, a 10-mile-long stretch of shifting, colored sands. To the south towers Mount Blanca, also called Tsisnaasjini' (Dawn or White Shell Mountain), the fourth-highest peak of the Rocky Mountain range. She is honored as the eastern peak of the four sacred mountains that mark the borders of the ancient sacred lands of the Hopi people. Mount Blanca, contained within the Navajo lands, elicits a prayerful feeling. To the west some aging trees dance in silhouette against the wind and setting sun, adorned with the Tibetan prayer flags commonly seen in this spiritual community.

All of this beauty and peace is a part of the tiny, yet influential town of Crestone, Colorado, a community that derives much of its economic viability from the many spiritual centers located there, established by world wisdom traditions that now offer retreats for visitors from around the globe. Here, too, the local coyotes sing and prance. The ravens circle. The eagles glide and play on air thermals, and the deer and elk commune while quietly watching the occasional "two-leggeds" (humans) go by.

What Are the Gifts of Retreat?

All religions and spiritual traditions have some form of the ancient and universal ritual called a "retreat." To "go on retreat" means to take time away from normal life to reflect or meditate. A retreat certainly can be taken with or without other people, momentarily or for as long as we choose to be "away." We can retreat on our own or guided by a spiritual or secular leader. These choices are best made after we reflect on what we might want from a retreat.

People go into retreat for many reasons. It may be to gain a new perspective on life or on an unresolved issue, to gain strength in preparation for an upcoming challenge, to restore after a period of stress or significant transition, or to make a major choice to change something in life, such as a career, living situation, or marital status. Planning or designing the actions related to a new path often happens in retreat space.

Into retreat we can bring our own version of reflection, prayer, and meditation, and we also can learn new ways to go inward, talk to Spirit, and listen to God. Using either the new or the old methods, we can more easily re-evaluate our core values and do the inner work necessary to resolve incongruent issues in our lives. Thus, if we go into the ritual of retreat looking for deeper meaning, our deeply held values will emerge. Various practices can lead to new awareness of deeper meaning and understanding. Reflection, prayer, intentional conversation, seated meditation, or even walking meditation can all lead to our core life values becoming more apparent. It was an intentional conversation with a peer coach during retreat that led me to synthesize my core values down into one phrase: Loving Connection.

When we give ourselves the gift of retreat on a regular basis, this ritual can become a source for restoration and relaxation, a chance to renew and recover from what needs our attention. We can't always do this while in the midst of stress, but we can while we are away from it. Moving away from what we have constitutes a useful process to see what we are now wanting. A pause from the fast pace and clutter of everyday life can provide deep renewal or release from what no longer serves us, and provide restoration of the soul.

Retreating also allows us to re-establish that delicate balance between our inner, more private personal life and our outer, more public shared life. This gives us a chance not only to see how we often restrict our minds to dualistic thinking, but also to transcend dualism into the context of wholeness where our interrelatedness becomes clear. To be beyond dualism is to be beyond the limitations of black and white thinking, not just thinking of the grey areas, but allowing for the full spectrum of the rainbow of possibilities. Holistic thinking goes beyond "either/or" thinking, beyond the judgments of simply right or wrong, good or bad, into the recognition that there is some right and some wrong, some good, some bad in everything and many choices in between. In the teeter-totter of dualistic thinking, balance is difficult. The ability to think holistically makes finding balance possible.

Retreat offers us a chance to go within so we can reach a deeper knowing of who we are as individuals with a higher self-awareness, with an awareness of who we are in relation to Spirit. This is a time to express self-love that, in turn, can blossom into deeper love for others. With this reaffirmation of our deeper selves, we feel better prepared to go back into the world, and we feel more willing and able to do so.

Choosing to take a momentary retreat means pausing from the routine of everyday life and becoming awake and alert to the present moment. By leaving the details and duties of life behind, each new moment brings the chance for renewal. Being present in the "now," we tune in and simply notice what "is" without attachment, without judgment. We notice our feelings and thoughts, sights and sounds, our sensations and subtle bodily changes happening right now. This allows for intuitive reflection that yields increased awareness and useful insights. A moment of quiet mind and peaceful heart gives us the chance to simply notice what is present. Noticing what is present brings our perspective to the moment of Now and attunes us to All That Is. For me, this attunement is a Spiritual Practice that connects me with the Divine. Eternity exists in every moment. As each moment comes to full consciousness, eternity comes into our consciousness.

What do these precious moments away from "life as usual" give us? What can be gained from stepping away and letting go of our attachments to so many commitments and responsibilities, even if just for a while? Retreating provides the chance to commune with our constant, pervading, yet sometimes ignored higher connection to God, the Spirit of life itself.

What is it like when we consciously move our attention and intention inward, with focus on that deep connection point with All That Is? When we give ourselves the gift of silence—and maybe even pure darkness in the middle of a moon-less night—to turn towards that connection, we gain a rare perspective on our lives. We can touch that place that has the ability to soften us so we can relax into the flow of restoration and renewal that rejuvenates and energizes. A practice such as this is life-affirming.

How Might Retreat Be Useful?

Going into deep reflection allows freshness, new insights, deeper awareness, and higher clarity to flourish. Sometimes we include silence as part of the ritual of retreat. Yet, from a silent place within us, a prayerful, peaceful mind can naturally shape a grateful blessing, invocation, or spontaneous prayer for the heart to circulate through life after retreat as well. In moments of deep joy, comfort, or relief, a sacred phrase of respectful appreciation can name the experience during retreat. A grateful blessing can be sent forth with intentionality, and this gratitude calls upon Divine Presence to wash over the space and replace negative emotions with love.

I use a simple invocation—God, Goddess, All That Is—and invoke Divine Presence into my retreat. From this I experience a reconnection to oneness, and any feelings of fear or separation I harbor fade. I learned this type of invocation early in life from my mother, who taught me one of Jesus's teachings. He said, "When two or more of you gather in my name, there is love." For this reason, I know the power of invoking Spirit together in group retreat and offering gratitude as a communal prayer.

Combining reflection, prayer, and meditation—all rituals in their own right—during retreat brings gifts beyond my expectations. For instance, the following prayer came to me during a Wisdom Circle retreat of women who gather twice a year in prayer and reflection as a response to the tragedies of September 11, 2001.

Daily Reflection and Request

May my awareness of the I AM presence be here now.
May love be shown to all people.
As sure as wind lifts a fallen leaf to fly again,
May wisdom be known in my soul.
As sure as water flows on the side of a mountain,
May truth be heard in my mind.
As sure as metal sings out as the bell is struck,
May trust be felt in my heart.
As sure as fire burns in our ever present sun,
May peace prevail on Earth, as sure as life itself.
With gratitude, compassion and awakened choice,
it is so.

How Might We Move Back into Balance with Retreat?

How does being on retreat impact our emotional well-being? Alfred Adler, the founder of Individual Psychology, tells us that our long-term goal as humans is to belong to a group in a valued and useful way. I find this quite true and feel so fulfilled when I contribute in some manner. At times, though, I can become overextended from overdoing or over-giving. When my level of activity becomes too much for me, I lose my balance—and doing begins to feel like too strong a need, sometimes nearly an addiction. At those times, I wonder, can I stop all the action and doing and still feel whole and complete?

This imbalance arises for me from the overuse of one of my strengths: productivity. I know well how to keep doing all the actions to produce results. Is the need to be productive and useful something that stops us from taking more opportunities to "do" nothing and to simply "be," to be not a "doer" but just a "being?" Can we remember our worth as people without all the accomplishments attached? In fact, to be connected to everything, to all of life, and to experience the deep peace of knowing we are not separate from each other, can be enough.

Simply remembering that we are not separate from the gorgeous snow-capped mountains and the trickle of water under the ice of winter or the little bird that provides the music shows us that we are enough without all the doing. As we pause, our awareness changes and we perceive the beauty around us, affirming life's fabulous interconnectedness. The cycles of life include us and surround us as we recognize that we are a part of this serenity and beauty. We belong in this place. We are a part of this delicate balance whether we are doing or being.

For some of us, even an attitude of retreat, rather than the actual ritual of retreat, can bring us back into balance and change our consciousness. The ritual of pausing to listen to the anger that may linger on the edge of our lives, hear the resentment that may surface and present itself to be viewed, or see the stress that affects our bodies and our relationships changes our awareness and how we may deal with them from a more relaxed, less attached perspective. A moment of reflection, prayer, or meditation can change our energy or perspective or give us a new insight.

A "retreat mindset" can be one of acceptance rather than judgment. When we judge our past, we are unable to heal it, unable to absorb the lessons of our experiences into useful material that may move us forward in our lives. Judgment leaves a condition stable rather than fluid, less able to transform and transport.

How Might Changing Our Questions Change Our Lives?

Once in retreat, how might we ignite deep reflection? Our brilliant minds function by processing information in response to a good inquiry. Just as software programs direct a computer to work to solve a series of instructions, our minds begin to seek the answers we pose in well-crafted inquiries with intention and purpose.

Notice how we may begin our day with questions: "What's the weather like? What do I have to do today?" These questions arise like well-run patterns, and, in much the same way, they invoke responses on many levels.

Some deep questions to ask are: "What might deep retreat ignite in me?" "What do I want?" "What might deep retreat space and time give me?" "What might it ask of me?" "How might I be different if I listened to the silence?" "What response might the silence elicit from me?" "How might the darkness contribute to me?"

Inquiries create movement in the mind. They invite the mind to move forward towards some thing or some place it has not been before—a new idea, a new level of awareness, or even a new aspect of consciousness.

Reflection in response to an inquiry yields new insight. When in retreat, we have the time and the setting to consider our response to any new insight or new awareness that arises from our questions. Considering new responses allows new possibilities to arise as new sets of choices. As new insights, responses, and choices are integrated during retreat, new changes may emerge and call forth new action upon return to our everyday lives. Indeed, the depth of a retreat experience can provide the motivation to sustain some behavioral choices that can actually change the course of our lives.

In my work as an executive coach, I work with leaders who are focused on helping their team members to accomplish results or to achieve their highest potential. The best of these leaders guide their teams toward innovation through the use of inquiry, helping them to access a place of increased awareness. They know when to be directive or instructional, and when to allow solutions to come from those who are most directly involved with the work. Asking questions at the edge of awareness and learning breaks trail to new avenues of wisdom.

In much the same manner, when in retreat we can more readily access our ability to resolve issues. Without the pressures of producing tangible results, we can free our imagination and creativity to arrive at new awareness or solutions. When faced with a dilemma—not just a "right versus a wrong" but two "rights" in conflict with one another—retreating into sacred space to sort out our conflicting values can serve us well. In our ever-challenging human relationships and communications, we are often faced with resolving incongruent issues that can cause tension. Deep reflection, along with leading-edge questions, leads to new awareness that makes a variety of previously unseen choices evident to us.

What Does It Take to Find Natural Balanced Energy?

In addition to the other retreat-related rituals mentioned—reflection, prayer, meditation, awareness in the moment, inquiry, silence—for me, a retreat must also include the ritual of journaling, which helps to deepen the new awareness achieved during retreat. Journaling offers time to capture my experience, my thoughts, feelings, wishes, dreams, visions, and musings in the written word, which, in turn, sets me free from judgment. When I journal, I just write what flows from the pen, and I turn my inner editor off and just capture what is in my mind and heart in the moment.

A poem emerged rather spontaneously at the close of my time spent in the dark and silent sacred space of my retreat time during those winter months of early 2008. It was one of the tangible outcomes for me of that retreat. Writing a poem, in and of itself, can serve as a ritual act when journaling.

In This Silent Darkness

In this silence, I feel myself alone and I see myself connected.
In this silence, I am not my feelings; I am not my thoughts.
In this silence, I hear beyond sound; I hear the chaos and the calm.
In this silence, I am my heartbeat; I am within, I am without.
I am the owl who knows the wisdom and feels the unknown.

In this dark, I see myself as separate and I feel myself as oneness.
In this dark, I am not my word; I am not my work.
In this dark, I touch the space between; I touch the earth and sky.
In this dark, I am my breath; I am within, I am without.
I am the coyote who freely lives both wisdom and folly.

In this silence and dark, I am one with all that is.

Practicing various forms of meditation and movement of energies during retreat can prove useful and enhance the experience. Practices such as Reiki, Yoga, and Chi Kong work for me to not only move energy into balance but also to help me notice the imbalance. Crestone is powerfully influenced by the energies of the towering 14,000-foot mountains of the Sangre de Cristo range, as well as the activities of the many retreat centers, such as the Buddhist Stupa and the Sumerian Ziggurat at the mountains' base. Knowing when to clear and release, and when to use these energies, represents an important aspect of my spiritual practice when I am on retreat. One of my goals is to live with more loving acceptance of what is, to notice the energy in my body, how I'm feeling, and to flow with it or address it as necessary. Some mornings I might have unused energy built up, causing an imbalance in me overnight. This might best be cleared by running with the wind on the dirt road toward the mountains and running into the wind on my return. Other times of the day I might take a meditative walk on a labyrinth, holding an issue in mind that I'd like to resolve or about which I'd like enlightenment. At another time I might simply walk to let all the energy gently release from my body. I take these conscious actions with a ritual awareness during retreat or any time.

What Is the Ebb and Flow of Balance?

I believe we naturally seek equilibrium like any system in nature. For me, the most meaningful retreat includes returning to nature, because doing so allow me to become more in touch with my Divine Source as reflected in the natural beauty of our precious Earth. For this reason, the ideal retreat setting allows me to immerse myself in nature, giving me a chance to feel a connection with the Earth so deeply that it elicits a sense of responsibility for the preservation of the harmony or the equilibrium of nature. This inspires the ebb and flow of balance in me. What is it to feel no separation from "other," and to be more conscious of your connection to Divinity? Accepting and acknowledging my relationship with nature's rhythm assists me in bringing peace to my surroundings. Nature seeks equilibrium at all times, and this inspires me to bring my self into attunement and balance as well.

And so this opportunity remains, to retreat from the things and the work of our lives to better see how and who we truly are—to discover our true selves without the ways and means by which we define our selves in the world.

What could it mean to step away for a moment or for a month to see more deeply the essence of who you are and what you stand for? What is it to feel no separation from "other" and to be more conscious of your connection to Divinity? What might be your rhythm for retreating? Once a month, at least for a short while? Once a quarter, to align with the seasons? Annually, for a longer time to truly rest and restore like the trees of winter? Increased awareness of self and of connection to the Divine might be the best gifts of the ritual of retreat. What might the gifts be that await you? I invite you to make the choice and be committed to retreat into this time-honored ritual—you deserve it!

Weaving in Ritual: A Weaver's Tale of Basket Making, Biodynamic Cranialsacral Therapy, and Conscious Dying

Janet Evergreen

Janet Evergreen was raised in Marblehead, on the north shore of Massachusetts. One of her lasting powerful memories is of her mother's Jewish Community Sisterhood. Janet is currently on a three-year sabbatical, reflecting, meditating, and writing poetry while living with her husband in Charlottesville, Virginia. She teaches Biodynamic Cranialsacral Therapy, Meditation, Peacebuilding (HIPP), and Zapchen internationally. She has a special place in her heart for children and is the Spiritual Director for a unique alternative high school called INEPE in the barrios of Quito, Ecuador. For more information, visit www.janetevergreen.org.

This is a story of how a caring community wove a sacred basket of light to hold and honor the last wishes of a friend named Prema at the end of her life. By the blessing of good karma, our lives were shared over many years, woven together and transformed in a way that now seems perfectly shaped by unseen hands.

I learned the art of basket making as an old-time tradition in West Virginia, amidst farm chores and a house full of children. Weaving locally available natural materials, I was drawn back to Source through my connection to the Earth by this ancient ritual. I wove myself whole again, weaving in my prayers with the mantra, "May we all be healed and whole again."

It seems these prayers, not I, are weaving this tale. I will tell you my story as a basket maker must, by spreading out the various pieces, the spokes which hold the form, and the weavers which bend in and out, gradually spiraling around and around.

In the beginning of creating anything—a story, a ritual, or a worthy basket, the yet-to-be-connected pieces are often wild and unruly. My mother would say I was a stubborn, headstrong, and wild girl. In the beginning of my life, I mostly figured things out on my own, the hard way.

Over the years I met others following their spiraling, spiritual path of deep inner work and training: Prema, who came from southern France near the Mediterranean Sea, and Connie, from western upstate New York's rural farm country, and others that arrived from as close as next door and as far away as Mexico, just as they were needed.

Native American healing rituals are done at all stages of life, and acknowledge one's continual relationship with the Circle of Life from birth to death. One can return to that original moment when Spirit first created man and woman in their sacred wholeness. In a Cherokee healing ceremony, I experienced prayers being sent for this purpose in a basket of light. Tibetan Buddhist meditation rituals, which are my core practice, contain both a Creation and Completion phase, mirroring the path to enlightenment. Training fully, one studies the Three Baskets (Tripitaka in Sanskrit). These include Morals and Ethics, the words of the Buddha as Sutra, and advanced practices "to see things as they are," such as The Great Perfection (Mahamudra).

A spiritual life is like a most precious basket. Like others weaving a conscious life, I carry a basket that is both light with happiness and joy and heavy with life's burdens. My basket is getting older, a bit worn around the edges. After carrying much, I am discovering, by facing end-of-life processes with beloved others, an eternal love. Even when I am at rest, empty.

Prema was diagnosed with ovarian cancer in the summer of 2007, at the age of 54. As the disease progressed, some close friends met to discuss and sign the hospice booklet Five Wishes. We spoke to Prema about rituals of death and dying. It was an open, honest talk about her options, choices, and last wishes through this transformation. Of primary concern to Prema was that there be no costly medical procedures, no heroic efforts to save her life. She did not want the hospital to have the power to put a financial judgment against her and a lien on the house. These discussions helped us prepare together for Prema's Completion phase of life.

Preparation: Gathering the Spokes and Weavers

In my twenties, after long hours of giving and doing, any number of things could have added up in such a way that I felt out of balance, overwhelmed, or restless. For me, the preparation, from gathering the materials to making and completing a basket, was steeped in meaning. It was a purification ritual and a body-mind training requiring the deep concentration, awareness, and communion that comes with the creation and completion of any task dedicated through prayer and intention to healing of self and others. I harvested wild vines and cut down white oak trees so I could weave. I looked for trees about my age. A tree, a beautiful being before me, grew out of a small acorn. I grew from an embryo. Mother Earth sustains us. I made offerings to the Earth of gratitude, praying that the Circle of Life continue for all beings.

To produce white oak strips for basket weaving, I divided a six- to eight-foot-long log into shorter and shorter lengths along the diameter of the log. That made it possible to slide a knife into the growth rings and pull a thick length of wood apart with my hands into equal halves many times. Just over five feet, I am not a large or strong person; only with absolute certainty that the wood, like me and all physical form, was not as solid and permanent as we sometimes think could I plunge in, meet the line of the growth ring, and then part the wood along its fluid space. This process was repeated until I produced a pile of wood splits. When I doubted myself, wavered, or became distracted, I would lose focus and ruin that strip. This, of course, happened a lot.

As the years went by, others came and asked to learn this ritual. I shared the art of basket weaving with people of all ages. It was a rewarding spiritual practice, an artist's way of being part of Creation and a conscious step toward contemplating one's own perfect Completion.

Creation: Shaping Our Basket for Spiritual Life

It is said in Jewish Kabbalistic mystical teachings that whatever happens anywhere reverberates throughout the totality of the Universe. Therefore, when we mend the soul (Tikkum ha-nefesh in Hebrew), it is inseparable from simultaneously mending the world (Tikkum ha-olam) and elevating both to Source.

For me, there is often a fork in the road between ordinary life and one's spiritual path, each one beckoning me to follow. Sometimes I follow one and sometimes the other. Occasionally they dance together. Ultimately, I believe we need to pendulate back and forth, alternating our reality, like weaving in and out between the spokes until they become an integrated whole. Intuitively, I was called to a new weaving, to weave a unity between duality and non-duality.

Living with children—my own three, one biological and two adopted, and sometimes others through emergency foster care—taught me to hold, moment by moment, each child's beauty and resiliency, as well as the depths of their suffering and terror from tragic circumstances. I sought gentle, natural healing for every child's injury, difficulty, and unspeakable trauma. Nearby, two osteopaths at the West Virginia School of Osteopathy responded to my love for children and generously offered to mentor me in what is now known as Biodynamic Cranialsacral Therapy.

I dove deeper into my process of mending my soul and mending the world, learning the ritual and healing art of listening to our bodies as living, pulsing tissues. Osteopaths offer this in a language of pristine nature and poetry, which describes the fluids in the body as liquid light that support and express balance. This ritual was described by Dr. William Sutherland, D.O., in the late 1800s as the "Breath of Life" which expresses the "Health that never is lost." Whether we know it or not, the Breath of Life, as it expands and contracts, is always informing our daily rituals. The Breath of Life can be observed in three significant rhythmic tides.

Healing others with the Breath of Life and the three Tides, like splitting white oak, involves being present moment by moment to shifting fulcrums. Just as a tree grows up from the Earth and branches into the sky, so our body tissues mirror vertical and horizontal growth. Growth rings in wood are waterways. They indicate the fulcrum in which to place my knife. So potent is a fulcrum that I could press without force, and a thick oak piece would divide into equally thin halves. What an awesome discovery! This ritual, practiced hundreds of thousands of times, helped me to experience fulcrums in our bodies. Membranes and tissue have similar cross-grain patterns, referred to as reciprocal tension. The body breathes in and out, up and down, circling around in naturally occurring reciprocal tension patterns. The fulcrum is held, usually between two hands, at these vital intersections. While holding fulcrums at the head, chest, diaphragm, pelvis, or joints with gentle touch, I learned to restore balance for my children and others.

In Biodynamic Cranialsacral Therapy, to connect with helpful fulcrums, the therapist rests in awareness of the tides that support and weave our experience through life, death, and rebirth. Each tide reflects meditative states which can be readily learned. The surface rhythm is the Cranial Rhythm Impulse (CRI). Beneath that exists a slower Mid-Tide, and beyond that the Long Tide. When we are aware of just what is in front of us, we are most likely experiencing a basic CRI, a physical movement that moves the bones in our bodies into external and internal rotation, flexion and extension. It feels like a waltz. In open attention, widening our peripheral vision, aware of nature, we find Mid-Tide; it is an energetic movement and feels like a slow, deep breath. With deep listening or using an intuitive vision, limitless light-filled space of love, compassion, joy, and peace is awakened. This is the Long Tide, our spiritual unfolding. Here we rest in non-dual awareness, free from illusions of self and other. It feels as if Universal Spirit is breathing for us.

My spiritual growth involved being with others while allowing my own growth and path to blossom. In 1988, just as I turned 31 years old, we left the farm and moved our family. I was unsure of my role as healer and spiritual teacher, but I was called to be with others and I had to leave my doubts behind. I discovered an old truth: That which we seek is seeking us.

For two decades, I enjoyed the good company of healers, teachers, and community peace and justice organizers in Charlottesville, Virginia. We held a common vision for meeting real needs to make a better world and did our own healing and hard personal growth work while mastering our craft. Our networking and connecting over various projects wove a strong basket based on our skills and compassion. Friendships grew, sometimes broke, and were mended—or not. Still we learned, grew, and came back to the question again, how could our lives benefit others?

Completion: Weaving a Final Life Basket

Prema and I moved to Charlottesville around the same time and graduated from the Virginia School of Massage together. As a young woman, Prema left her native France to come to the United States. She lived for many years in an Ashram, studying yoga and meditation, and had even taken monastic vows. She was well known for her ritual skills in flower arranging and French cooking. Prema encouraged Connie, her friend from the Ashram, to attend massage school as well. We became part of the Charlottesville spiritual body-workers' community. Prema and Connie both continued their spiritual paths as lay practitioners, learning to weave a deep spiritual life into ordinary activities. They married, had children, and studied Cranialsacral Therapy and many other healing arts. Through the ups and downs of life, they continued to be supportive friends. There was a time when they had difficulties and their friendship was strained by jealousy and competition. Their spiritual teacher had told them years before that in bumping into one another, there is rubbing and scrubbing of the ego, a necessary process to attain ultimate purification. For many years, they attended classes and rituals together and were part of the healing circle I supervised. In time, they skillfully and lovingly resolved their issues.

When Prema was very ill, a community of caring hearts gathered to support her in her time of need. Dozens showed up. Connie led our core group of about half a dozen people, plus Prema's family. We were given the honor of serving and living a spiritual rite of passage together until her death, which would come six months later.

Finishing an oak basket is the most difficult part. A strong and supple circular-shaped hoop is securely lashed to the rim. It is a different process than the earlier weaving described; it requires more attention to succeed smoothly. Through this finishing, we are brought into and reflect on the Circle of Life. In Completion phase, meditation light radiates out from the sacred form and penetrates the Universe. All becomes light and dissolves back into the sacred form. Finally, the essence of the most sacred dissolves into luminous light, returning to Source.

Prema's Completion phase wasn't always easy. For each of us, it was sometimes like an airplane going over turbulence. We used our spiritual training to notice whatever was causing the disturbance as sensation in our bodies. We did our best to be present to our emotions, touching the pain and the pleasure, the healed and the unhealed, the beauty and the terror.

Throughout her life, Prema believed in the perfection of life and she never gave up wanting to make a difference. She showed us how her body served as a container for her spiritual work up until the last moments, weaving her last wishes for herself and others until the container became unnecessary. Shortly before Prema's death, I was in her home and spoke with her 17-year-old son, Gabe. "The tumor is shrinking lately," he told me, "but it seems that even though the cancer itself is healing, it has done its job." I noticed that it was hard for him to take in his words, but he said he did understand. There was hope and the abandoning of hope all at the same time.

Sitting on the couch across from this beautiful young man who did not want his mother to die, the peace and love resulting from this six-month care giving intensive were palpable. When I went into Prema's room, our talk stayed with me and supported the weaving that came next.

In preparation for Prema's death, we had set up the shrine on a table near her bed. Prema understood this shrine, or altar, as the portal to her journey to the next realm. Having it there comforted her anxiety about breathing, which was becoming more and more difficult. With her permission, I climbed up on the bed and sat with my right hand on the back of her skull, and my left on her tailbone. I listened to her fluid-body movement and the three Cranialsacral tidal rhythms. I sensed our ability to be in alignment with these universal flows, how vital it was to create and hold that space, in this transitional moment.

Connie was Prema's spiritual friend for 25 years. She sat nearby offering love and encouragement. As a Cranialsacral therapist, she understood how to skillfully hold the space. Prema prayed out loud, her words setting a strong intention for peace and joy and healing. We tuned in and followed her prayer.

The previous weekend Connie and I had attended a Tibetan Buddhist teaching and empowerment on Phowa, a meditation practice and ritual, that helped us deepen our understanding of the dissolution of our elements and the transference of consciousness at the time of death. It is a subject we have studied for many years to learn to embody living and dying conscientiously. Now, the three of us talked as colleagues about how the Cranialsacral teachings and spiritual teachings lead us to the same place and prepare us for death and life beyond the body. We were no longer practicing. Leaning into the wisdom of our teachers, we held sacred space as Prema received gentle touch. We were weaving these teachings together and living their reality in the present, letting go of the past and healing into the moment.

In Buddhist cosmology, we are born from luminous space and these elements give birth to each other. The death process consists of the elements dissolving in the reverse order, one into the next, returning us to luminous space. It had become more and more difficult for Prema to move her body. That day it had taken three of us to support her while the bedding was changed. We talked about how that represented a natural part of the process. She felt her body get heavy, so heavy she no longer wanted to move. She was experiencing and letting go of the earth element. We encouraged her to let go. She did, and her breathing relaxed, which felt good.

We told Prema that Gabe and I had talked, and he knew she was dying. I spoke of what he had said to me and assured her he was ready for her death. She was amazed and accepting.

"He'll be okay," I told Prema. "He doesn't want you to suffer. It's okay to let go."

She relaxed from the relief of this knowing. I asked, "Do you feel the energy now?"

"Yes," she said. "It is calm and feels good."

"Good," we said, "go with that."

Earth becomes water as the body lets go. I could feel the Cranialsacral rhythm slow to Mid-Tide, a place of healing, as she talked about seeing and feeling the ocean. She grew up near the sea. Now she rested in her memories. We were quiet for a long time, then came another deepening. Our bodies became like the ocean at high tide on a full moon. Our eyes welled up and tears flowed from the depth of our love.

Water element becomes fire element. Prema was radiating light. My hands warmed, feeling the charge of the fire element emerging from her body where I touched her. The potency of the fire element is heat. The Long Tide, supporting her transformation, the fluids in her body like water into steam. Pure understanding and peace arising. We were permeated by a vast wisdom, realizing spacious emptiness. In Buddhist teachings it is called emptiness, because the truth is empty of illusions. The divine fire burns away all of our conceptualizations and ego identity. Then, the body and the space that holds us become light, luminous energy.

"I feel warm and comfortable. There is no pain now," Prema said.

"Good," we said, "go with that." We rested together in this new place. Then we talked about fire element becoming air element before quieting again, as Prema went deeper into the Cranialsacral Long Tide. In that place, we let go of everything and the Universe breathes us.

"Prema," we said, "let go of everything. Let the Universe breathe you." And she did. Again we rested together, healed, all of us, by the Long Tide. The healing session was an hour long. I said, "This is your abbreviated Phowa meditation. Practice it over and over. Now follow earth into water, water into fire, fire into air." She said, "Thank you, I can do this." And she did for a few more days.

Getting a Handle on Our Basket of Light

Prema had made her last wishes very clear to us and we were there to follow her wishes. After her death, friends washed her body in a ritual of love and prayer, led by her spiritual friend, Marcella, who arrived from Mexico for the last weeks. They dressed her body one last time in her favorite summer cotton colored dress. Elegant draped silk cloth represented her life as a spiritual yogini. Her body was allowed to be unmoved for three days before her cremation.

The week after her passing, during the Healing Group in which Prema previously participated, we circled without words, keeping the space open where Prema tended to sit.

Some of us in the Buddhist community kept a candle burning for Prema for the traditional Buddhist ritual honoring the 49 days of the Bardo (the intermediate state between death and rebirth). Our intention, held in our prayer, was that when the body was left behind, her spirit would move through the transitional stages towards a speedy and good rebirth.

For many of us who have loved each other over the years, the time has come to complete the basket with all its imperfections. Now, as wisdom keepers, we hold past and future in our sacred baskets. We tuck in the remaining pieces of our baskets, cut back and trim the ends. The handle, carved from rose-colored heartwood, is taken from the core of the oak tree. The Completion phase of life requires a return to the core self. Like the illusion of the solidness of the oak, our bodies and egos are illusory. We rest into our heart's true nature: inner happiness, love, and peace.

We know, like Prema, our time will come to trust, surrender, and let go into a sacred end-of-life ritual—the completion of a work of art, the final phase of a life, dissolving into luminous space until the next basket calls to take form again.

Ceremony for Maggie

Reverend Ione

Reverend Ione is an author, playwright/director author of the acclaimed memoir, *Pride of Family: Four Generations of American Women of Color; Listening in Dreams; This is a Dream!; the Night Train to Aswan; Nile Night: Remembered Texts from the Deep; Spell Breaking: Remembered Ways of Being and SB2: Listening to the Heart of Dream,* both Anthologies of Women's Mysteries.

Ione wrote and directed The Nubian Word for Flowers, A Phantom Opera, with Music and Sound Design by Pauline Oliveros. Premiere at Roulette Intermedium in 2017. She is the playwright and director of Njinga the Queen King (BAM's Next Wave Festival) and the dance Opera Io and Her and the Trouble with Him (Union Theatre, Madison, WI.)

Ione is the Founding Director of the Ministry of Maat (MoM) and a Dream Specialist, Center for Deep Listening, Rensselaer, Troy, NY.

(Websites: ionedreams.us and www.ministryofmaat.org)

I heard the news as I was returning home from the airport for a few days after a long trip. I heard a child's voice in tears, breaking up on my cell phone. Someone had died. She wanted me to know, but I could not hear the awful details. I sat stunned as my partner, Pauline, and I sped along the highway. I squinted at my phone, trying to understand the area code of the caller. My mind stubbornly refused to understand who had called and who had died.

Finally, Pauline said, quietly, tentatively, "Maggie?" I didn't have to answer.

"I'm sorry," she said, taking one hand off the wheel to touch my hand.

We stopped for dinner at a small restaurant near our house before driving all the way home, and, though it was summer, while at the table I developed a chill. Still dazed from the call, I headed back to the car for a shawl, tripping on a step as I did. The sharp pain of my scraped knee pierced through my consciousness, causing my mind to flit back and forth between the concept and the reality of the loss of Maggie.

As the reality began to become a larger part of my consciousness, memories began to arise, each one emerging with the beauty of a sacred ritual, reminding me of the preciousness of our times together.

For the almost 25 years I had known her, Maggie and I had had a therapeutic relationship that had developed into a deep friendship. I was with her through the perils and indignities of nursing school, as well as through so many of the other vicissitudes of life. We've all been there, attempting to solve the universal mysteries inherent in family, lovers, spiritual processes. She was my student; I was her confidante and her teacher of women's mysteries.

During those same years, many other women were part of Women's Mysteries, my ongoing training program in the intuitive and healing arts, founded in 1987—" for women who want to go deeper." We were then, and are now, women reclaiming our inherent wisdom while creating community with each other. Among these women, Maggie was a star, a wild card, a maverick who never ceased to startle unsuspecting listeners with her frankness, her sudden way of divulging her heart without filter.

Maggie hosted one of our most memorable Women's Mysteries retreats at her Colorado ranch. Her property has a direct view of the stunning twin peaks that the Native Americans call "The Wahatoyas," or "The Breasts of the Earth." The Utes, the Native Americans from that region, saw these mountains as important sources of power and sustenance for all life.

They said, "Wahatoya are two breasts as round as a woman's, and all living things on earth, mankind, beasts and plants, derive their sustenance from that source. The clouds are born there, and without clouds there is no rain, and when no rain falls, we have no food, and without food—we must perish all."

The events of this retreat on Maggie's land struck deep into the fabric of all our psyches. One such memory, a ritual in itself, saw two women of different ancestral heritage deciding to take a short climb up a nearby mountain. One of the women had been struggling with deep emotional and psychological processes, and while climbing upward, she experienced a moment of intense acrophobia and froze. The two women wondered how she ever would get back down. Inch by inch, her companion helped her back to level land.

There, the challenged woman experienced a major awakening. She came to me later in the small Tibetan shrine room on the property and described the spiritual mandate she felt she'd been given. She knew that no matter what difficulties she might encounter, she was meant to create an organization devoted to the sacred, an organization that would honor and be accessible to all races on the planet. Maggie, with her big heart and abundant land, were the crucibles for this powerful moment.

Indeed, with the peaks nurturing us, we each underwent our individual transformations and communed deeply with each other over four magical days and nights. Each morning, Maggie led us in our morning silence on a daily walking meditation across her land to a nearby stream. We passed the peaceful cows in one of her favorite places under small trees near a stream. After a few moments, I gave a signal and we broke our silence, telling each other our dreams from the night before. This is a daily ritual that is an integral part of the Women's Mysteries work.

In the evening, a half moon shone down upon us, and an enormous pale green luna moth rested upon the shrine room screen. As we do at all Women's Mysteries retreats, we created presentations for each other, bringing our creative reveries forth into potent performances—poetry, dance, visual art, and personal rituals that often involved the entire group. When it came to Maggie's turn one afternoon, we were pleasantly surprised when she appeared before us in her living room wearing a colorful dancer's costume from Egypt, replete with bangles and scarves. She gave an insinuating cue and taped music started up. Mouths agape, we soon began cheering her on as a small gyration of her hips developed into a wild and sensuous belly dance. We were delighted and impressed and truly inspired to love our bellies more.

In 1997, Maggie and her teen-aged daughter, Tiare, traveled with us on one of our Women's Mysteries Sacred Journeys to Egypt. There, we re-created rituals and ceremonies in the ancient temples we visited. We raised our voices in chants that resonated throughout the ages. As we toured Upper Egypt, Maggie, a deeply feeling animal lover, championed the cause of the skinny local horses, leaving our group to lecture their owners if she didn't feel the animals looked well cared for. She regaled us all one day with a hilarious description of an over-energetic massage by a long-finger-nailed masseuse at our hotel. Back in Ghiza, we sat together and smiled for the camera in the lounge of the luxurious Mena House Hotel, with the Great Pyramid visible through the window behind us. It was a peak moment, captured for the ages in a photo we enjoy looking at to this day.

Maggie was a traveler. She had a great fondness for the depths of Mexico and had begun to write about her experiences there. She was a devoted Tibetan Buddhist who had recently been to Nepal to visit an ailing teacher. She often traveled to what many might call wild and dangerous places. Indeed, she loved all that was deep and real and passionate.

I know that somehow she continues to explore the profound and timeless territories of the heart.

I left for New Zealand just a few days after I heard the news of Maggie's death. From there I traveled to Australia for performances I'd arranged many months previously. As I traveled in New Zealand, my memories continued to flow and a poem formed for Maggie. I wrote it down. Poetry is one of our earliest forms of ritual, of communion with the divine, and so I offer these words as such.

For Maggie

1.

As near as your heart can stand it
Can accept its existence

Without expanding beyond itself
Into Light

You
sending me off into rainbows and
Giant Taras made of cumulus clouds

You
turning away

You
beside me

Your rabbit, your dog

Your cat

Though blind can see

Your departure,
Accompanies you through darkness

You
A belly dancer!

These coins jangle at your belly

A monk sits in a Sacred Cave

A carpet, a chair and neighbors
Chanting

A teacher prepares to move into
Final meditation

The Sacred land awaits
Not far from here

Not so far after all.

2.

Off the islands
She waits in profound waters

These dreams of thousands of years

Remembers

These stories from the depths

Accompanies these boats to land

These Ancestors ride

The space between you and me

With your dark eye

An ancient coin of life

Turning to surf the waves

Traveling onto black sand

Here it takes two days for dreams to arrive,

Rushing across waters and over vast terrains

Here I am taking the train, feeling its metal flank

Leaving the suitcase at the other end

I get on

Traveling internally to reach it

Getting off again

Moving through sleek dining cars
Comfortable passengers

No time
Must find the suitcase

Can you describe it?
Is it the black one, the purple one, the long one?

Inside the house
The old apartment
At 45 East
The living room

There is an old lover
Arriving
To discuss with you
To receive a token, a remembrance
of time long past and yet ongoing

Eternal as passion sparks in the simple embrace.
Ah, yes

That's what it was, that's what it is.

But I'm still trying to get to you

A graphic, a pyramidal shape, a silver obelisk

This must be pointing the direction
To you
On your swift Journey

Beyond me.

While still in Auckland, New Zealand, I was asked to create a ceremony for the distribution of Maggie's ashes. I would not be able to attend the ceremony, but in this way I would be there; I would be represented. I created the ceremony and wrote it down, then sent it along as my envoy. I learned on my return from my performance tour, however, that my emailed message had not been received due to an Internet glitch.

Later, Maggie's friend Bella told me, amazingly, that the ritual I had created was almost exactly what friends and family also created and performed when they spread Maggie's ashes. Since then, the ceremony as I wrote it, not including the distribution of ashes, has been performed at different locations by several of us who were lucky enough to have known her.

We know now that Maggie's sisters are performing one of the most sacred rituals of all time for Maggie. They are circumambulating Mount Kailash in Tibet and distributing her ashes there.

Ceremony for Maggie's Ashes
To be conducted on Maggie's land in view of the Wahatoyas

Instruments: drums and flutes; also bring wands and feathers
Clothing: festive whites and colorful elements with beautiful scarves that float when dancers turn

The group makes a circle. All walk in procession to the chosen spot, chanting from the heart, and make a circle. Positioned at the four directions are four women; each holds a small urn of ashes.

"Om mani padme hum"[1] is chanted by all.

Each of the four women speaks in turn and turns around, and then sprinkles a few ashes. (I have indicated below a few elements that can be spoken for each direction, but the speaker can add what she or he sees or feels in that direction for Maggie.)

Successively, the women in the East, South, West and North speak: "The AIR listens, the FIRE listens, the WATER listens, the EARTH listens."

Each of the four women, in turn, then speaks and dances, turns around, and releases the ashes.

EAST—AIR: "The East receives you! AIR."
"The rising sun and butterflies, birds and winds, the rainbows crossing over…"
"Welcome Home, my daughter!"

SOUTH—FIRE: "The South receives you! FIRE."
"The joyful sounds of all things—the flame of passion, the fun and surprises of coyote, all the beloved animals of your life on this earth gathering…"
"Welcome Home, my daughter!"

WEST—WATER: "The West receives you! WATER."
"The dreams of bear and vision beyond sight…"
"Welcome Home, my daughter!"

NORTH—EARTH: "The North receives you! EARTH."
"The Benevolent Ancestors and White Buffalo Calf Woman, the truth and straight speaking of your heart…"
"Welcome home, my daughter!"

(At the center a dancer—or dancers— turns and chants and releases the remainder of the ashes to the sky and to the Earth.)

"All receive you in beauty, and you become one with all."

ALL say together:
"Maggie, you are the East.
Maggie, you are the South.
Maggie, you are the West.
Maggie, you are the North.
You are the earth beneath our feet."

"You are who we are.
We are who you are."
"As above, so below."

"In beauty we are one—one dream—one life—without end!"
"Gate Gate Para Gate Para Sam Gate Bhodi Svaha!"[2]

Procession departs, chanting "Om Mani Padme Hum."

[1] It is said that all the teachings of the Buddha are contained in this mantra: Om Mani Padme Hum. It cannot really be translated into a simple phrase or sentence. Tibetan Buddhists believe that saying the mantra (prayer), Om Mani Padme Hum, out loud or silently to oneself, invokes the powerful benevolent attention and blessings of Chenrezig, the embodiment of compassion.

[2] The Heart Sutra or The Great Heart of Wisdom Sutra. "Prajna" means "wisdom." "Paramita" means a crossing over, or going beyond. The Prajna Paramita is known as the most divine mantra. It has many translations. This is one:
"Gone, gone, gone beyond—gone beyond the beyond. May all be blessed!"

SECTION FOUR

Love in Action

 LOVE IN ACTION

After sufficient retrospection and circumspection, one is better prepared to take action and more assured that the action will be founded in wisdom and love.

One of the biggest ways that love impacts our lives is in the little things and through the little ones.

Oshun is a River Deity (Goddess). Often referred to as the Goddess of Love, some of the typical avenues of Oshun's manifestations are beauty, fertility, sensuality, healing, and social exchange. It is said that She is the one who is present at all gatherings, though you may not always recognize her.

One year I traveled to Nigeria for the Annual Oshun Festival. Thousands of people travel from near and far for the 16 days of ritual, ceremony, and festivities. To say that I (a daughter of the Great Mother Oshun) was elated or "on top of the world" at the fact that I was *there* for Her world-renowned annual fete would be a gross understatement!

At every festivity there were dangerously large crowds, and one could easily get swept along by the crowd and lost in the sea of Oshun devotees. I was being hosted by one of the high ranking dignitaries of Oshogbo (Osun's state). His family always accompanied and looked out for me. We received VIP treatment wherever we went and were regularly allowed to move beyond security posts and given admittance to "closed" ceremonial events and such.

I knew that on the culminating day of the festival there would be hoards and hoards of people making their way to the Oshun River. I asked to be taken to the river a few days before the main ceremonial festivities so that I could pay honor to the Sacred River, offering prayers and anointing myself with Her water. I had traveled there a few years prior (not during festival time, however) and, therefore, had an expectation of the beautiful vision that awaited me. When we passed the guards and were escorted down to the river after greeting (and being greeted at) the holy shrine of Oshun, to my shock and amazement there was trash strewn everywhere along the river's banks. I almost screamed! This could NOT be happening at Oshun's River... not at the Mother of Beauty and Loving Kindness!

Tears welled up in my eyes, as I glared up and down the river banks and in the apparently still waters at the uncountable small pieces of plastic. Honey is a popular representation of the sweetness of Oshun. Considered one of Her favorites, honey is therefore one of the most appreciated and popular offerings. During the days of the festival the marketplace vendors, as well as those along the side of the road, were selling small amounts of honey in tightly twisted pieces of plastic. It was simply unimaginable to me that devotees of Oshun would place plastic in any river, but certainly not in this most Sacred River. I was consumed with disbelief and the inner non-stop, repeating question—*who would do this?!*

Just then, a huge fish jumped straight up from the center of the river and appeared to stand suspended in midair, to be sure that I noticed it before it plopped back down, making as noisy a return as it had an appearance. And then I heard, *"There is Life in this river! Remember, there is more power in the unseen than in the seen!"* Oshun shut my mouth, broadened my consciousness, stretched my empathy, opened my heart, and magnified my humility in Her amazing act of Love. I understood that acts done from an honorable intention of Love trump any possible appearance of aesthetic or even ecological imbalance. No doubt, through other acts of love, the Sacred River would be relieved of any debris and restored to its obvious natural beauty.

Oshun's expression of love in action inspired me to coordinate a river-cleaning activity for the SACRED SPACE Youth. We participated in a nation-wide volunteerism effort by cleaning the Anacostia River (originally called Anaquash River) in "our own backyard" in Washington, DC. I remembered Oshun's teaching and shared with the youth that despite the HUGE amount of trash and debris that we were removing (glass and plastic bottles, tires, auto parts, clothes, etc.) the river was still Sacred and full of Life. At the end of the day as we offered rose petals to the river, we imagined how that river might have been hundreds of years ago when the Nanchotank Indians came there for their sacred ceremonies. My eyes and heart get full now with these thoughts and the teaching of the wisdom, power, and eternality of unseen love in action.

In this section, *Love In Action* celebrates the unlimited and formless way that love is. Love (if we are lucky) is minimally playful, enduring, transforming, instructive, wise, and activist by nature, and calm and cuddly all at once. In this section Love shows up in beautifully thought-provoking, heart-warming ways that call us to action, and to pause and reflect, as these women invite us into the heart, soul, and love of their lives.

The Golden Apple Award: A Ritual of Appreciation
Luisah Teish

Luisah Teish is a writer, performer, and ritual priestess. She serves as Olori (director) of Ile Orunmila Oshun (The House of Destiny and Love). She has authored six books of African and American spiritual culture notably, *Jambalaya: The Natural Woman's Book of Personal Charms* and *Practical Rituals, A Women's Spirituality Classic.*

Other credits include theatre, movie and television appearances and articles in 35 anthologies and magazines such as Essence, Ms., Shaman's Drum, and Yoga Journal. She offers online classes, spiritual consultations/rituals, keynotes/workshops and editorial assistance.

Sign her mailing list at: www.yeyeluisahteish.com, view her ritual performances at www.ileorunmilaoshun.com, also see luisahteish.writerfolio.com.

For many years I lived next door to a woman whom I'll call Sister Ocean. Sister Ocean seemed to birth a new baby about every 18 months or so. Her husband was a hard-working man; she was a good mother who worked part time when she could to supplement the family income. In addition, she found time to participate in the local voter registration drive and attended meetings that affected the community, such as Neighborhood Watch and the Parent Teacher Association.

One day while I was talking with her, she congratulated me on a performance I'd done at the local theater and lamented that her work lacked both recognition and glamour. The look on her face touched me. I saw a woman who, indeed, got up every day and performed tasks that would have driven me crazy. I began to think about the value and effect of recognition for work done. After discussing it with another priestess, we designed this simple but touching celebration called "The Golden Apple Award." Despite its name, what we created represents much more than an award. Done correctly, the celebration becomes a beautiful ritual, the high point of which is the actual giving of the award, wherein I believe the giver *and* the receiver are in touch with the Divine.

Go to your local craft or hobby shop and purchase the image of an apple. An apple candle would be my first choice, but these usually come in natural colors, such as red, green, or yellow. You may have to purchase a wooden apple, and then dip it in gold. If you are using an apple candle, purchase a yellow one and simply tie a thin, gold ribbon around it. You may also use gold napkins, napkin rings, or a gold cup and saucer. Gold, as you know, symbolizes excellence.

Produce a steaming hot apple pie. You may purchase it from your best bakery, but if you have good cooking skills, a home-baked pie adds to the significance of the celebration.

Steep a pot of the woman's favorite tea. I recommend an apple-cinnamon medley or something soothing like chamomile. I suggest getting a small jar of honey and a lemon, although these are optional, and arranging all of these things on a tray with a small bouquet of flowers.

Make or buy a necklace for the woman receiving the award. You can find beautiful and inexpensive necklaces made of apple seed, corn, and other natural objects at your local import store.

Most importantly, gather together at least two other woman friends. Choose an opportune moment, one when you are likely to catch the recipient of the award off guard. Knock on her door or meet her in the park, and present her with the Golden Apple Award.

In this presentation it is good to use language drawn from the metaphors of Eden. For example:

Hold the necklace over her head and say: "Today your sisters have gathered to honor you, as "Mother of All the Living." We honor the power of your body to birth and nurture. We recognize the gifts of your mind, your curiosity, and your creativity. The sweat of your brow bakes our daily bread and maintains the harvest home. We appreciate the blessing of your being, woman, and earth." Then place the necklace around her neck.

Now light the candle, if you purchased one, or give her the wooden apple, and say: "We see the bright light of spirit in your eyes, and we declare it Good."

Advise the award recipient to make a wish for herself. If this is being performed in the garden or park, encourage her to walk through the growing things as she recites her wish for herself. Make sure that she makes a wish for herself, not for the house, her children, the neighborhood, or the world, but *for her self*. The other women may want to whisper affirmations such as "Woman, thou art mother, woman, thou art earth."

By now she may be crying, laughing, or blushing. Relax! Sit down, eat the pie, drink the tea, and share stories of everyday triumphs.

This little celebration cost me less than 10 dollars. It increased my neighbor's sense of being appreciated, and all the participants had a nice evening together. Don't you know someone who deserves to receive the Golden Apple Award? If so, create this ritual of appreciation for her!

Love Never Dies:
Learning to Communicate with Your Ancestors
Sandra Rattley

Sandra Rattley, an oral historian, has conducted extensive field research in Africa and the Americas on African retentions and traditional African religions and culture. She has over 30 years of experience as a documentarian, and her production work has been recognized with Peabody Awards, the highest recognition in journalism, for Wade in the Water: African American Sacred Music Traditions and Making the Music. Both 26-part series were broadcast on National Public Radio. Rattley founded the African Learning Channel, a 24-hour social development channel broadcast in Africa via WorldSpace Satellite Radio. She also co-founded and is a founding member of numerous organizations, including the African Cultural Heritage Exchange (ACHE); Sacred Space: Where Indigenous Paths Meet; the Southern Africa Support Project; and the Spirit of Hope Campaign. Her mother's family, the Quanders, have traced their roots to Ghana, West Africa, and have been designated by the Smithsonian Institution as the oldest documented African family in the United States. Rattley is an initiated Yoruba priest, also known as Olufonde.

I am an initiated Yoruba priestess. The faith system I recognize and follow is called by many names in many places—it is known as Lucumi in Cuba, Condomble in Brazil, and Santeria in parts of the United States. At its source in Ile Ife, Nigeria, considered the Mecca of the Yoruba faith, practitioners call the system traditionalism, or traditional African religion. I prefer this designation. I like the idea of pursuing traditionalism, especially in the contemporary, hi-tech, and commercial terrain of U.S. society.

I have had a long and dramatic journey with this faith system, spanning close to 30 years. My pursuit began as an intellectual curiosity, fueled by a preoccupation with locating and experiencing African retentions in the Americas. I was particularly interested in knowing and understanding the indigenous African worldview—what it was that Africans and people of African descent believed and practiced prior to their contact with Europeans and prior to colonization. I also wanted to know what authentic practices could still be found intact. Repression of traditional practices occurred in the Americas from the Trans-Atlantic slave trade onward, and African religion was criminalized and combated by terror and violence. As a result, much of the information available about traditional ritual and spiritual practice has been kept secret, passed on orally and available only to those who complete a formal process of initiation.

I also am a journalist and oral historian by training who, beginning in the mid '70s, was lucky enough to travel to Africa frequently for work. In 1991, I made a very personal trip to Ghana to conduct genealogical research that I hoped would help me locate my relatives and my home village. My mother's family, the Quanders, have been recognized as the oldest documented African family in the United States. A will dated 1685, in which a British tobacco farmer in Calvert County, Maryland, indicated that slaves he owned—my relatives Henry and Margaret Pugg Quandoh among them— should be freed at his death, assigned my family this designation. Scouring through census data and conducting other time-consuming document searches, the Quander Historical Society uncovered clues that led me to Ghana.

A revelation of massive proportions and syncretism of the past, present, and future occurred for me on the other side of the Atlantic Ocean, along Ghana's Cape Coast in a fishing village called Dutch Komenda. There I was led to family members who bore a striking resemblance to my elder relatives in the States. And prophesy was fulfilled when Ghanaian family members indicated that not only was I the progeny of the former military protector and spiritual diviner of Komenda, whom, according to them, I physically resemble, but, in addition, his wandering spirit had returned home with me. It should have been no surprise that as I began my journey of spiritual development in earnest with involvement in the Yoruba faith system, my religious instructors indicated that my spiritual foundation and the engine for developing my spiritual intuition lay with establishing a connection and regular communication with my ancestors. Thus, my earliest experiences of personal ritual practice began with attempts to understand and establish a connection with my ancestors.

Regardless of your system of faith, or the extent to which you have specific knowledge of your ancestral lineage, clear benefits—spiritual clarity and protection—come from making and maintaining contact with your ancestors through ritual, prayers, and spiritual practices. Just contemplate and assume we all believe God is love and Spirit is the manifestation of love. Isn't it likely, then, that the energy you have exchanged and the relationships you have maintained with the people and family members you have loved and served—who have loved you passionately and unconditionally, who have done anything and everything to support and uplift you while here on this temporal plane—would remain intact and active in the past, present, and future?

Let me provide a testimony from my own experience of the indestructibility of this energetic connection of love. Almost 40 days to the exact day that my maternal grandmother made her transition, she appeared to me. My grandmother was the emotional and spiritual glue that held my family together. She loved her 16 grandchildren and many great-grandchildren equally and had demonstrated it in ways large and small throughout her nearly 100 years of life. That said, she and I had a particular bond. She served as my "daycare" until the age of five, because my mother was still in college. This was a major blessing for me; as a result, my grandmother became a constant presence in my formative years and taught me much, primarily by example. She infused my life with a moral and ethical center and an appreciation of the communal bond and interdependence of family.

On this particular evening, just as I was preparing for bed, my grandmother appeared to me in her rocking chair, the place she characteristically sat throughout her later life and the location of our many heart-to-heart talks. At the time of her death, my marriage was falling apart. I was frustrated, angry, and confused, externalizing my responses and blaming my mate. In her typical calm and reassuring manner, her spirit conducted a postmortem of my marriage, also surveying the relationship patterns of the women in my family, my intimate relationships and those of my female first cousins. In an analysis of my compulsive giving she concluded that my generosity was a cover for insecurity and my fear of not deserving love. She concluded her chat, which occurred at the foot of my bed, with advice: Reciprocity represents one of the fundamental laws of the universe, and that law had to guide my future relationships. In a profound statement that will resonate in my heart forever, that the cornerstone of love is self-love, she stated, "Baby, you don't have to do anything to make people love you. You are already worthy!"

This personal experience provides just one example of the benefits of ongoing communication with our loved ones, who serve as elevated spirits and upholders of the light. In the experience I just described, the "download" of information was soul-saving and life-changing, providing me a concrete example that just as she did in life, my grandmother continued to watch over me energetically in spirit, and continued to share her wisdom and extend her protection. A comparable blessing is available imminently to all of us if we open ourselves to the possibility.

Communication with ancestors seems to be a mainstay of most indigenous religious systems, but practitioners in systems that do not include ancestor ritualization as part of their spiritual commitment sometimes misunderstand the practice. In traditional African culture, ancestors are not worshipped, they are revered. Since spirit never dies, because love never dies, our ancestors are considered ever present. Thus, their presence is honored perpetually. The Yoruba are among a number of traditional African societies that express special reverence for their ancestors, a practice consistent with a foundational idea that society is circular, and that the living, dead, and unborn function as parts of one caring, cohesive, and interactive community.

I think people of all faith traditions are strengthened in their identity and confidence when they know their lineage and those who have preceded them. So I firmly believe and advocate that it is beneficial to maintain communication with those on whose shoulders we stand. If you wish to connect with your ancestral group, I think the best way to create a ritual for doing so simply involves beginning to focus time and attention on them. Quiet your mind, slow your thoughts, and focus your energy on those ancestors with whom you may have had a close bond, those whose wisdom you wish you could still access. Summon them, and ask for their intercession, their protection, their active presence in your life acting as a force for good. Part of the challenge of connecting involves listening—listening deeply with all your senses, not just your ears.

Numerous approaches to ancestor communication exist, but some are specific to certain faith-based systems. I am going to outline just one way you can initiate a regular practice to help you focus your energy and to solicit information and support from your ancestral group. First, establish a spot in your living space dedicated to your ancestors. This will be the place where you come to "talk," to ask for protection and advice from them. Select an area away from other people. Often people choose a corner of a room. Whether you choose a hallway or a closet, the location should be someplace quiet and fairly secluded. Do not choose a bathroom, or a room or space where you have any intimate contact or engage in sexual activity. Clean the space with regular cleaning products first and then with a light fragrance, such as Florida Water, which is a rose-scented water that should be easily accessible in a drugstore or store that sells religious objects, such as a botanica.

Do what you can to locate, collect, and acquire photos of those who have passed from your bloodline whom you admire and want to contact. You can place the photos directly on the floor or on a small table. If you want to establish an ancestor space with a mate or partner, photos of both family members should be set up in the dedicated space. If you are using a table, you might want to use some kind of cloth (preferably white) to cover it before you place photos or other items upon it. After cleaning the space and placing photos there, also present a glass of water, a seven-day white candle, and a vase of white flowers (real flowers—not plastic or silk). I recommend that you replace these items every seven days, preferably consistently on the same day of the week.

After you place the items on the floor or on the table, light the candle and then greet your ancestor group. You can greet specific ancestors whose pictures you have included by name, or those whom you miss or to whom you feel close. Be conscious of the fact that you have no way of knowing all those who have preceded you who want to act on your behalf. You may know some of them and some you may not. Therefore, it's best to be inclusive and to invite communication with all your ancestors, including those who are unknown to you. As you greet you ancestors, however, it is most important to mention that you are soliciting the presence, protection, and communication of only those spirits that are elevated and that have gravitated to the light.

After greeting your ancestors, thank them for their lives and for the examples they have set. Also, express the wish that, in whatever form and vibration of energy and spirit they are experiencing at this time, they are realizing the rewards of their lessons and accomplishments on the earthly plane and are feeling no pain, illness, sorrow, etc. Thank them for the things they have already done to support you. You should also express the desire to have them talk to you, communicate with you, be your guides, help you avert mishaps, losses, or accidents. Tell them that you want them to share their wisdom and counsel with you, especially now that they are on the other side of "the veil" and have a vantage point you don't enjoy. You should then share with them what is in your heart. Talk to your ancestors as if they are present, telling them what you are going through in your life, what you are feeling, and the challenges that require their help and intercession. When you ask for the intervention of your ancestors, ask for the "greatest possible good" to occur in the situation or circumstances you face, because sometimes the things we think we need are not the best things for us.

I also suggest that after you set up your space for ancestral reverence rituals, you become quiet for several days. In other words, minimize your social encounters and time in the world. Spend time at home alone, quiet, working on your communication with your ancestors, sitting in the space you have established. You can meditate there or you can talk to your ancestors and pray, by which I mean express affirmations for the things you want and ask for removal of external obstacles or for help improving qualities in yourself.

As you incorporate conversations with your ancestors into your regular schedule, you may get information or insights about other things you should add to the space. If one day you get an inspired idea that one of your ancestors wants a favorite dish or something in particular, prepare or acquire it and present it in your dedicated space.

In closing, let me share some advice that was given to a dear friend by a prominent spiritual leader. He advised that we humans should be "forceful" with our ancestors. This sage priest was not suggesting we engage in expressions of disrespect, but rather that we should not hesitate to give assignments to those who have passed on and are close to us and who want to support us. They are close, he suggested, precisely because they want to help us. So, we should let them.

As in all things spiritual, you must find your own way. Sometimes the way is hard to find and the information we get from the spirit realm is subtle or difficult to discern. Thus, this process of ancestral communication involves not just venerating our ancestors and those spirit forces who want to be active in our protection and support. This process also provides an opportunity for us to develop our spiritual intuition. My experience has demonstrated to me that what you get back from the ritual of communicating with the energy and spirit of ancestors is commensurate with what you put in. As you invest the time and energy, you see results.

My grandmother and others in my bloodline who have passed on, as well as others in my spirit circle, continue to appear to me. Sometimes I feel their presence and "hear" them when I am standing at my ancestor altar. Sometimes I get their messages in dreams, and sometimes in ritual. Mostly, their "feedback" seems like a part of my daily landscape. They are always with me. We are one community of love and support—the living, the dead, and the unborn—holding the past, present, and future intact as a tapestry of connectedness, keeping our lives intertwined forever. I invite their love. I know their love was a blessing in my life when I could see them. That reality has not changed because I cannot see them now. The love between us will never die.

Outshine the Sun

Gail Needleman

Gail Needleman teaches music at Holy Names University in Oakland, California. Her work as a writer, educator, and clinician addresses the essential role of music in the moral and spiritual development of children and the human values embodied in folk and traditional music. She leads workshops at national and international conferences exploring the deep roots of Anglo-American and African-American folk music. Needleman received the Parsons Fellowship from the Library of Congress for research in American folk music and co-created the American Folk Song Collection website, a pioneering online resource of American folk songs for teaching music to children (http://kodaly.hnu.edu). She is currently working on a book exploring music, nature, and the human spirit.

When the old songs die,
the great dreams are forgotten.

—American Indian saying

I. What the Children Know

This is a true story.

I hear the clatter of footsteps in the hall, the rising sound of small voices. Through the lunchroom door pours a river of children. Thirty-three kindergartners, a rainbow of colors and sizes, hopes and dreams; and something is clearly not right. The girls rush towards me, all talking at once. One girl is weeping. The boys stride to the opposite side of the room, surrounding one boy, who stands with arms crossed, his face grim.

The girls are anxious to tell me what has happened. It seems that the boy, Devon, has frightened the girl, Samantha, by telling her that he saw a monster in his back yard. The children are firm that "there's no such thing as a monster," but Devon "won't take it back."

It is picture day at school. The children are wearing their best clothes—tiny suits, tiny dresses, shiny shoes. The odd tale of the monster, the unusual fracturing of the class into girls and boys, the children dressed as miniature adults, give the sense of a ruptured world.

"Can we have the star?" Several voices sound as one, and the rest take up the cry. It is their favorite song. The first-grade teacher had heard them singing through the wall and said to me, "I'm so happy you're teaching them the old songs."

The children gather in a circle, seated on the red-painted concrete floor of the teachers' lunchroom that doubles as a music room. Still fidgeting in their hard shoes and fancy clothes, but visibly quieter and more settled than the moment before. I take a large gold cardboard star out of my bag.

Such a simple activity, our little play. One child walks around inside the circle, holding the star, trying to listen to the singing of the other children: "Listen for beautiful singing!" From the singing he or she chooses another child to give the star to, and the chosen child now takes the place in the center. Only one rule: A boy must give the star to a girl, a girl to a boy.

Star light, star bright,
First star I see tonight,
Wish I may, wish I might
Have the wish I wish tonight.

They never tire of the song.

Stillness enters the room as the children sing. As each child enters the circle, I see, feel his or her concentration, trying to listen, trying to hear the individual voices in the midst of the singing, trying to choose by listening. "Listen for the beautiful singing!"

"Star light, star bright..."

It is a tremendous effort for them. I feel them wishing, wishing.

"First star I see tonight..."

I feel they could go on like this forever. We are no longer in time. We are in the world of the stars, an ancient world, which is the world of our wishing, too.

When I first sang the song for the children, I asked them what they wished for. "World peace." "For people not to fight." What does it mean that what five-year-olds wish for is peace on earth?

"Wish I may, wish I might..."

Devon has the star. I watch as he walks slowly around the circle, the star clutched in front of his chest. His eyes flicker again and again to Samantha. For a moment he stops in front of her. He wants to give her the star. But the moment passes. He cannot cross over. Defeated, he hands the star to another girl and the play goes on.

"... have the wish I wish tonight."

And at last all the children have had a turn. It is the end. Silence.

Devon looks at me. "Can I have another turn?" I nod yes, and at once the children begin to sing. Devon walks around inside the circle, no longer uncertain. As the song ends, he stops, looks at Samantha and offers her the star.

The rift in the universe is healed, as the children knew it would be. On one side of the circle, I see Samantha helping Devon tie his shoe.

I can still feel the vibration of that moment, the pure feeling arising in me, the stunned and grateful witness to something great.

A friend of mine once called it the most central, most ancient place for human beings: to be seated in a circle, listening. Think how easily we gather there when given a chance, to sing or to listen to story or song or only to the sounds of a fire; to feel our companionship in the greatness of the night, our kinship to the earth and to each other, to the starry world above and the human world within. How joyfully we sing there, and how naturally fall silent.

II. What the Songs Carry

I open my email and find an invitation to a winter solstice celebration. I respond instinctively: "Shall I bring a song?" Yes, comes the answer: something we all can sing; something about the light.

Something about the light. I begin looking through songbooks, sheet music, recordings. Nothing seems right. These are good friends, serious people. Holding them in mind, everything seems either too shallow—the campfire rounds, the contemporary "ritual" songs with their vague New Age sentimentality—or too religious—out of a religious context, and for people of several religions, or none—or too difficult to learn quickly.

Ah, but there is a song. My colleague Anne and I had found it in the archives of the Library of Congress, among thousands of field recordings of American folk songs. These songs, mostly collected in the 1930s in rural

areas of America, are an astonishing and nearly unknown treasure, car-
riers of the lives and dreams, the suffering and the wisdom of countless
ancestors. Among the treasures we found there was a song sung by Huddie
Ledbetter—"Leadbelly"—and his wife, Martha:

> *Outshine the sun, O Lord, outshine the sun.*
> *Outshine the sun, O Lord, outshine the sun.*
> *O Martha, your name is called,*
> *I tell you, your name is called,*
> *At heaven's gate your name is called,*
> *Outshine the sun.*

Perfect.

I arrived at the house where the celebration was to take place. Someone had
made beautiful headdresses for us all to wear. A fire was burning on the
hearth. We shared the food we had brought. On slips of paper, each person
wrote what she wished to contend with in the coming year, and we cast
them into the fire.

Someone said: "It's a good time for a song." I spoke a little about how I had
found the song and sang the chorus a few times, the others gradually joining in. And then, more quickly than I had intended, I looked at one person
in the circle and began to sing:

> *Oh Hannah, your name is called,*
> *I tell you, your name is called,*
> *At heaven's gate your name is called,*
> *Outshine the sun.*

And all the rest sang with me on the chorus:

> *Outshine the sun, O Lord, outshine the sun.*
> *Outshine the sun, O Lord, outshine the sun.*

I looked at the next person in the circle and sang:

Oh Jamie, your name is called...

Somehow I had thought that the others would pick up on the verse and join me, but somehow that is not what happened. What happened was that I found myself in a *place*, and what was needed from me in that place was to look at each person in turn, and acknowledge that person, and call her name, call her to participate in something powerful that was now happening in the room.

Something passes between us when we sing a true song together. Something real, that cannot pass between us in any other way. And yet this was even more than that.

What is it in me, what is it in you that can outshine the sun?

When I came to my own place in the circle, I meant to skip over myself and sing to the person next to me, but, no—what happened was that the whole group started singing to me. And I felt a lightning bolt of joy pass through me, flinging my arms up in an ecstatic gesture—a gesture I had never made before—a movement I felt could have become a dance, or a song.

Then on around the circle I continued, singing to each person in turn, feeling the wonder and the dignity of each person in turn, and at the end the kind of silence that can only come after song; and it was over.

What had we stumbled upon? What kind of song was this?

A few weeks later, Anne and I are preparing for a workshop we are giving on songs we had discovered in our research. We don't yet have the recording of "Outshine the Sun" from the Library of Congress, and I am looking to see if I could find another recording of the song. And I find one—sung by Leadbelly—which includes the great American folklorist Alan Lomax interviewing him about the song:

Alan Lomax: You said that they sang certain songs for baptizing, Huddie; do you remember any of those baptizing songs?

Huddie Ledbetter (Leadbelly): Well now, let me see, do I?

AL: Think about when you were baptized.

HL: Well, when I was baptized… they sang…

AL: How did you feel? Talk about it…

HL: Well, I felt, you know, pretty happy…

AL: Was the water cold? Or—how did you think about things like that?

HL: Well, the water, it wasn't cold, because it was in the hot summertime, you know, and when you're baptized you've got on some old clothes, and your worst clothes, and you've got a handkerchief tied around your head— which I never did like to have no handkerchief or nothin' around my head—I like to wear a hat but I don't want no handkerchief or nothin' tied around there—But anyhow… it took me I think two men, the preacher and another man took me out and dunked me under the water. Well I didn't shout but some people, you know, go out and—especially women, when you dunk them under the water they're gonna come out shoutin'—Thank God!—and—So glad! Pray for me, sisters!—and all like that; but I just take it easy and come on out.

AL: Do you remember what they sang, Huddie?

HL: I'm tryin' to remember right now—I know they sang one song about "Outshine the Sun" and they sang that for me 'cause they wanted me to be shinin', so the preacher said, Now Brother Leadbelly, say you want to shine—so everybody began to sing:

> *Outshine the sun, O Lord, he's outshine the sun.*
> *Outshine the sun, O Lord, outshine the sun.*
> *Sister Sally, your name is called,*

Sister Sally, your name is called,
At heaven's gate your name is called,
Outshine the sun.

That's my mama's name, Sally, and he's called my mama 'cause I'se her son, to—

Outshine the sun, O Lord, to outshine the sun.
To outshine the sun, O Lord, to outshine the sun.
Brother Wesley, your name is called,
Well, I tell you, your name is called,
At heaven's gate your name is called,
Outshine the sun.

That's my father's name, 'cause I was his son and the only one—

To outshine the sun, O Lord, to outshine the sun.
To outshine the sun, O Lord, to outshine the sun.

Then they called me:

Brother Leadbelly, your name is called
Well, I tell you, your name is called
At heaven's gate your name is called,
Outshine the sun.
To outshine the sun, O Lord, to outshine the sun.
To outshine the sun, O Lord, to outshine the sun.

"They sang that for me 'cause they wanted me to be shinin'." A baptizing song. A ritual song. A song with deep, deep roots, calling the ancestors to witness, calling us to our inner divinity. That was what we had felt that winter solstice evening. That was the lightning bolt I had felt passing through me. I would have been one of those women who came out of the water shouting. All that was in the song. It was carried by the song.

III. What the Earth Needs from Us

"Omnis terra adoret te..."

"Let the whole earth adore thee and sing thy praises."

There was no place to rehearse indoors at the camp, so we were outside. It was midday, so we needed to be in the shade. And there were quite a number of us, so we needed a large space. And that is how I and about 20 other people had come to be standing in a circle among rosebushes, barefoot on the earth, singing a 14th century monastic song.

It was a lovely summer day, filled with sweet scents and gentle breezes, butterflies and birdsong; and as we sang these words, a new vision opened. Singing with others, feet on the earth, open to wind and sun and sky, feeling the presence of both time and eternity, we knew: *The earth sings through us.* We are the voice of the earth, no less than the wind and sea and singing bird.

This is the source of music's power to bring us together, to connect us to past and future, to express our deepest yearnings and sustain us in our greatest need; and behind all of this, to call us to a deeper question, a question that can connect us not only to each other but to something greater than ourselves, the stones and the stars, the earth and the sun, the mystery of life itself.

But it is not only for us—it is not only for us. The earth itself needs us to come together. Dare I say it? *The earth needs us to sing together.* The earth needs something that only comes into being when we enter into relationship. That is what ritual is for. That is what the children know when, to restore their wished-for peace on earth, they call for a song.

This is our obligation. And yes, it matters what we sing.

In Germany, on November 11, St. Martin's Day, the children parade at night, carrying lanterns and singing:

Laterne, Laterne,
Sonne, Mond und Sterne
Brenne auf, mein Licht
Brenne auf, mein Licht
Aber nur meine liebe Laterne nicht.

Lantern, Lantern,
Sun, moon and stars
Burn on, my light,
Burn on, my light
But don't let my precious lantern burn.

Starlight, sunlight, and the light within. Even a simple child's song can touch the great mystery, can help us to feel our place in the vastness of the universe, to experience our true calling as human beings. To be connected to bird and tree, open to earth and sky; to feel ourselves in the universe, part of everything existing. And from this sacred sense of ourselves, to find our voices together, which may also, if we listen—if we are very attentive— resonate with a greatness we cannot name.

Finding the Balance Between Personal and Professional Life: Rituals of a Scholar

Laura I. Rendón

Dr. Laura I. Rendón, a scholar/practitioner/activist, is interested in how educational institutions can recruit, retain, and graduate low-income, first-generation students. She also focuses her work on helping educators reconnect with their passion for teaching and learning in service of others and on the well-being of society. Rendón's most recent book, *Sentipensante (Sensing/Thinking) Pedagogy: Educating for Wholeness, Social Justice and Liberation,*[1] offers a transformative vision of education that emphasizes the harmonic, complementary relationship between the sentir of intuition and inner life, the pensar of intellectualism, and the pursuit of scholarship. Rendón is professor and former chair of the Department of Educational Leadership and Policy Studies at Iowa State University, College of Human Sciences. There she co-founded the nation's first social justice concentration in a doctoral higher education leadership program. Rendón was previously a fellow of the Fetzer Institute.

I am a scholar and a spiritual person. The two personas are not incompatible. Finding the rhythm and balance between the two represents the dance of my personal and professional life. With one part of my life I teach, conduct research, and theorize. With the other I look inward and take time to still my mind, become open to hearing the messages of my soul, be comfortable in my solitude, pray, love, and engage in social change. As I connect the two fundamental aspects of my being, traveling the path of integration helps me illuminate the sacred aspects of my professional and personal lives and uncover the highest blessings in all that I do.

Awareness: Discovering the Sacred in Academic Life

The act of being a scholar possesses a sacredness, though few scholars—likely only those who, through their research, develop a deep expertise in a particular field—can elaborate on the sacred nature of this profession. Few of us take the time to fully explore how our roles can involve something deeper and more purposeful than engaging in traditional practices of the academy, especially when we are expected to publish, teach, and participate in service to the profession.

I have had to work hard at developing a consciousness about the sacred for two reasons. First, the demands of scholarly life can feel overwhelming and leave little time for reflective practice. Second, my profession (like many others) often excludes and, in fact, trivializes and ridicules anything that smacks of spirituality. It has become easier for me to write about embracing the sacred now that I am a senior professor who has "paid my dues" in the academy. I have lived in the world of higher education for over 25 years as a professor and administrator. I have gone through the promotion and tenure process and been named full professor. Additionally, I have secured grants, been published in refereed journals, been awarded a prestigious endowed chair, and served as a department chair. Despite my long association with the world of higher education, I know scholars younger than I am embrace the sacred in their own ways but often keep their beliefs and practices private or "under the radar screen."

Like many other fields, higher education does not make it easy for scholars to be openly spiritual. Yet, I believe it is critical that academics charged with the role of creating new knowledge and working with students destined to become our new leaders reflect on the deeper meaning of what we do as scholars and to have a greater awareness of the heart of scholarly work. In addition, it is vitally important that scholars take time for ritual. Doing so allows us to develop habits of the mind and heart that can help us engage in our work and in our lives with a deeper meaning and purpose.

A scholar traditionally engages in three rituals in the academy: 1) researching; 2) teaching and learning; and 3) providing service to the teaching profession and scholarly communities. While these activities may not seem sacred at first glance, let me elaborate on how these rituals (for, indeed, they do constitute rituals), examined within the framework of a spiritual lens, contain elements of sacredness.

Uncovering and Illuminating Truth

One of a scholar's key roles involves conducting and publishing research. For many, gathering data and publishing findings represent worthy goals and an end to the process itself. Yet, the deeper meaning of doing research lies in the fact that, as investigators, we are engaged in uncovering and illuminating truth. A scholar approaching research with this perspective is likely to find both the intellectual excitement and the awe of his or her craft—to view discovery with wonder, and to be highly conscious of the responsibility associated with learning and sharing something that enlarges another's knowledge base, that broadens and deepens our understanding of phenomena. There is a moral and ethical responsibility to engaging in illuminating truth that speaks to doing no harm and to treating research subjects with respect and dignity as they, in turn, open their lives to us. The whole process of research, with its processes and procedures, has a ritualistic element, and the scholar or researcher can lose himself or herself in the process, opening the inter-human nature of the experience and illuminating the higher truths discovered.

Teaching and Learning

In addition to our work as researchers, scholars also teach. The relationship between teacher and student is a sacred one. The teacher/student union can inspire, transform, and cultivate deep insights as well as social consciousness and personal awareness. I believe each classroom constitutes a sacred space where teachers and students can engage in a rich, holistic learning experience that can be approached much like rituals. These include diverse forms of contemplative practice, such as meditation, use of music, photographs, poetry, and engagement in service learning.

The use of contemplative practices, which quiet the mind and engage the learner deeply in the material, provides an essential key to helping students acquire knowledge. This especially is true where the emphasis falls on acquiring facts as well as wisdom, where the focus is on the inner experience and the cultivation of self-awareness and sense of purpose.[2]

Providing Service to the Family of the World

Scholars also are expected to engage in service, to lend their expertise to professional and community organizations that benefit from their specialized knowledge. I view service as a sacred, even spiritual, endeavor, for at its highest level service involves making a difference in people's lives. This calls for scholars to be caring, compassionate humanitarians concerned not only with generating knowledge but with using that knowledge to make a positive contribution to the family of the world. I take on my acts of service as sacred rituals.

I have never seen my work as a scholar simply as a job in the academic profession; it transcends holding an intellectual position. For me, my work has always been about making a difference in the world. Making a difference in the lives of others is not only a civic duty, but also a sacred responsibility. Service gives scholars the opportunity to develop a "critical consciousness."[3] A scholar with a critical consciousness has the ability to recognize social and economic inequities and take action to remedy them.

I have never viewed the academy as detached from society. In our scholarly world, it is easy to watch television, read newspapers, or listen to the radio reporting about world crises (e.g., the threats of nuclear and biological warfare, devastating disasters such as tsunamis, hurricanes, and earthquakes, economic turmoil, world terrorism and genocide, and virus outbreaks) and disconnect from that which is not happening directly to us. Especially at this time, I believe that scholars must, to whatever extent possible, embody a life of love, compassion, and quest for peace and social justice.

Mindfulness: Personal Rituals of a Scholar

For a long time, my life had no real center. I went about my personal and professional life in a mindless, non-reflective, workaholic fashion. My main ritual was simple to explain: work, work, and more work. Over the past 10 years, I have adopted a more mindful lifestyle, which helped me turn inward.

Engaging in contemplative practice

Meditation and writing serve as my two most powerful contemplative activities. I have been trained in Transcendental Meditation (TM), which I try to practice on a daily basis. TM is a practice where one sits comfortably with eyes closed for 20 minutes twice a day, focusing on a mantra (a sacred sound, word, or syllable repeated during meditation or prayer). TM has helped me become more relaxed and to relieve stress, as well as to be more centered and fulfilled. I find that I am better able to deal with difficult situations and to see issues more broadly because of my meditation practice. I have also employed Maya teachings in a meditative fashion. I use the Mayan Oracle.[4] By meditating on these cards, I often am able to acquire breakthrough insights on a particular issue I am studying and analyzing.

Leading a life with multiple, competing demands, I admit that sometimes finding even five minutes to meditate can be difficult. Yet, even when I miss a day or two, I do my best to return to my practice. I travel often, and during these times I meditate while in my plane seat. When I meditate, my mind feels less foggy. This spiritual practice and ritual helps me take things less personally when I deal with difficult people as well.

Writing can be a powerful contemplative activity, too. I consider myself a writer, and writing always has been a part of my personal and professional life. I have journaled and written plays, books, and poetry. When I write, I feel creative, expressive, and free. For me, writing often serves as an outlet, especially in times of heartbreak. Writing also provides a venue to communicate what I theorize and the way I view the world. Each time I sit down to write, however, it feels like a spiritual activity, a ritual that allows me to move inward and to connect with myself and something sacred.

Giving and having a generous spirit

Mark Nepo wrote that the purpose of money is to make love work.[5] I have a yearly ritual that involves finding ways to give of my assets so they serve a greater good. I have established scholarships for low-income students. I have donated funds to political campaigns and to educational institutions. I have sent unexpected flowers to people I know. I have taken my students on professional travel with me, so they can benefit from attending conferences and networking with other professionals. To this day, I send money to my mother and sister in Texas; I know they need it more than I do.

I always have believed that the more you give, the more you receive; I believe the ritual of giving allows us to give and receive love. I will never forget a student to whom I gave a scholarship. His son had been struck by lightning, and he did not think he would be able to complete his education. He told me my scholarship made it possible for him to finish college and to care for his son, who had been paralyzed. I know that there are others who have benefited from my giving whom I will never meet. Yet, the idea is to give openly, without condition, and with love. I am blessed that I am able to make love work by sharing my assets.

Mentoring the next generation

At its highest level—the spiritual level—mentoring constitutes an act of love. I put my social activism into action in the field of education. I was born in poverty and literally went from the barrio to the academy, an extraordinary journey that transformed my life. I never will forget where I came from, and my role as a scholar includes giving back and making a difference in the lives of students who, like me, have hopes and dreams but often do not know how to realize them. I find it highly rewarding to work in the field of education, because here one can witness students' transformations. I teach in departments that work only with graduate students, those working on their master's or doctoral degrees. I see students from working-class backgrounds come to a place educationally that few, if any, members of their families have achieved before, and the experience is both exciting and deeply emotional. I will never forget a Latino doctoral student who successfully defended his dissertation with a photo of his deceased father in his shirt pocket. He wept as we embraced, and he told me how powerful that moment was for him.

I remember a Latina who chose me as her mentor. I took her on a trip to a professional conference with me, and paid her airfare. She told me how her family, including her parents, uncles, and aunts, all chipped in to help finance her trip. At the time, she was an undergraduate student traveling to a conference attended by doctoral students and professors. I was in awe watching her talk to professors that intimidated my doctoral students and working her way through receptions, taking the initiative to speak to people along the way. I asked her how she got the courage to speak to people with higher degrees whom she had never met. She told me she had to interact with them, because her family had invested so much in her. She simply had no choice but to make the effort to speak to those doctoral students and distinguished professors.

Every year I add to the circle of students I mentor. I take on this "job" as a sacred duty and a spiritual practice, a ritual that lends so much to both the mentor and the person being mentored. Without question, these students, men and women who represent diverse ethnic/racial backgrounds, embellish my personal and professional life in immeasurable ways.

Expressing gratitude

I have found that even in my darkest moments, my life contains blessings I sometimes overlook. Whenever possible, I make it a point to practice the ritual of expressing gratitude for small and large things in my life. I thank God and the universe for another day of life. I thank my ancestors for the guidance they have given me in my path. I give thanks to my family and friends, colleagues, and students who surround me with their caring and support. Also, since I travel to so many conferences and speaking engagements, I practice the ritual of giving thanks for the guidance I receive when communicating my ideas with others.

Taking time for rest and replenishment

For many years, I operated as a workaholic, working long hours, traveling extensively, and making little time for my own personal development and inner growth. I became a successful scholar, but I also paid the price for it. I suffered from chronic neck and shoulder pain and intestinal problems, and had my share of sleep deprivation. I was "successful," yet exhausted.

Finding time for rest, replenishment, and taking better care of my health through good nutrition and exercise represents a never-ending challenge for me, but I keep trying. I have found that taking time every year to do something that brings me back to my center proves very helpful. Thus, I've made this an annual ritual. For example, one year I took a few days off to experience Ayurvedic treatments to relieve stress, lose weight, and feel rejuvenated. I also learned TM. Another year, I engaged in a spiritual retreat with friends and colleagues in Mexico. This year I will attend a retreat with a circle of women that includes healing and empowering rituals.

I now recognize the compatible nature of being a scholar and a spiritual person who is able to embrace wholeness and connect the inner and outer life. This ideal way of being is not only realizable but also more authentic and rewarding.

Celebrating life

I made it a point to celebrate two important milestones in my life: my 50th and 60th birthdays. I invited friends, colleagues, and students to these events to share in my celebration of life and the transition to what Angeles Arrien calls the second half of life—"the ultimate initiation."[6] Arrien notes that in the second half of life "we encounter those new, unexpected, unfamiliar, and unknowable moments that remind us that we are a sacred mystery made manifest."[7] I decided that entering a new life as an elder should be celebrated. Mine were momentous rituals filled with love, enthusiasm, and spirit. We danced, sang, laughed, and cried, and we remembered our ancestors, those who had transitioned. I videotaped these events, rituals created to mark important occasions, which I know will remain in my heart for a very long time.

Praying

Prayer is the meditation of the heart. It stills us, offers comfort, and centers our beings. Sometimes I recite my favorite prayer, *The Lord's Prayer*, when I am getting ready to go to sleep or when I pray for my circle of friends and families, as well as those who have departed. I pray for guidance when I am not sure what path to take, when I experience heartbreak, and when life brings me difficult challenges. I pray briefly before giving a speech, asking that my words touch in a positive way everyone who can benefit from my ideas. These prayers constitute important, sacred rituals in my daily life.

I have learned that academics pray in their own way, yet their rituals differ little from those of people I know who aren't scholars. At a conference where I presented my work, a college administrator gave me a copy of a little book containing her prayers that she created and carried with her. She told me she used her little book of prayers every morning before she went to work. A friend of mine, also a college administrator, reads a booklet called *The Daily Word* every morning to gather inspiration for her day. I am blessed to have people pray for me. My mother prays for me every day, and I count on my families' prayers to keep me safe.

Honoring Our Deepest Truth

A scholarly life need not be sterile and dry. Scholars are thinkers; we are said to work best with our minds, but I believe we also can work with our hearts. Our work and our lives are sacred, and what we have to offer the world has the potential to inform, heal, and transform. Rituals, when viewed as heart work, serve to keep us present and alive, creating a state of mind that truly fosters our best work as scholars and our deepest truth as human beings.

Note: The author wishes to thank Riyad Shahjahan for his very helpful comments as this essay was being developed.

[1] Rendón, L. I. (2009). *Sentipensante Pedagogy: Educating for Wholeness, Social Justice and Liberation. Sterling,* VA: Stylus.

[2] Center for Contemplative Mind in Society (2007). *What are contemplative practices?* Retrieved January 5, 2007, from http://www.contemplativemind. org/practices/index.html.

[3] Freire, P. (1971). *Pedagogy of the Oppressed* (M. B. Ramos, Trans.). New York: Continuum.

[4] Spilsbury, A., & Bryner, M. (1992). *The Mayan Oracle.* Santa Fe, NM: Bear and Company.

[5] Nepo, M. (2000). *The Book of Awakening: Having the Life You Want by Being Present to the Life You Have.* Berkeley, CA: Conari Press.

[6] Arrien, A. (2005). *The Second Half of Life: Opening the Eight Gates of Wisdom.* Boulder, CO: Sounds True Incorporated.

[7] Arrien, A. *The Second Half of Life,* p. 4.

Putting Love into Action:
Rituals of Expansion, Involvement, and Activism

Riane Eisler

Riane Eisler, an eminent social scientist, attorney, and social activist, is best known as the author of the international bestseller, *The Chalice and The Blade: Our History, Our Future*, which has been translated into 23 languages, including most European languages, Chinese, Russian, Korean, Hebrew, Japanese, and Arabic. Her newest book, *The Real Wealth of Nations: Creating a Caring Economics*, has been hailed by Archbishop Desmond Tutu as "a template for the better world we have been so urgently seeking," by Gloria Steinem as "revolutionary," by Peter Senge as "desperately needed," and by Jane Goodall as "a call for action." Dr. Eisler serves as president of the Center for Partnership Studies, a keynote speaker at conferences worldwide, and a consultant to business and government on applications of the partnership model introduced in her work. Dr. Eisler can be contacted at center@ partnershipway.org. Visit her websites at www.rianeeisler.com and www. partnershipway.org.

Rituals of Daily Life

The first ritual I remember that was very meaningful to me was my mother lighting the Shabbat candles. I loved the way, in the Jewish tradition, the woman lights the candles and does this beautiful circle over the candles, making a circular motion with both her hands. The ritual is part of welcoming the bride, the Kallah, for the Shabbat. It was very lovely and I would watch my mother and listen as she said a prayer in Hebrew, which I didn't understand, of course. It was much later, when I was writing my books—especially when I wrote my book *Sacred Pleasure*, in which I was tracing the origins and the transformation of spirituality—that I realized that this is a rite that must go way, way back to a time when women were priestesses in the Hebrew tradition. This is a time that we don't hear about, but are beginning to learn about. I feel certain that the calling of the Kallah, the bride, must have had something to do with the celebration of the sacred marriage of the Goddess and the God, and of course we're not taught that. I write about that in *The Chalice and The Blade as well as in Sacred Pleasure*. To me, understanding what lay behind the Jewish tradition of women lighting the candles in this ritual was very important. When we think of religious rituals, they are mostly rituals that are performed by men, by priests, mullahs, rabbis. Some religions don't even allow women to be in the same space with men… for example, the Muslim religion or Orthodox Judaism. Yet, here was a ritual, performed by a woman, which clearly involved direct contact with the Divine. This ritual that welcomed the bride, the Kallah, the Divine Feminine for the Shabbat, was a part of daily life. So to me, rituals are really part of daily life.

Another ritual (you may not think of it as a ritual) that was part of daily life for me, which was done in those days when we still lived in Vienna, was when my mother used to bake challah, which is the Jewish twist egg bread, and the smell of that was so powerful, I think of it as a kind of incense. It was another wonderful ritual that was part of daily life that was done in preparation for the holy day of Shabbat. It was a ritual that enhanced our lives… and of course I loved that it smelled wonderful and tasted great.

I am certain that having grown up with my mother… a woman… performing these subtle but significant rituals has affected my life and work. I'm still very much a cultural Jew and I always will be. That means carrying on a tradition of caring work. It is not accidental that so many of the leaders in social justice movements have been Jews, because that has been our heritage, our ethical charge, if you will. I am no longer a religious Jew, although I have to say that when I hear that music, the music speaks to my soul. I have grandchildren now and I have one little grandson whose mother and father live near me, so every once in a while we go to synagogue together, and I love to have him hear the music and to experience the rituals. It is a reformed congregation and as a matter of fact, the Cantor is a woman, which is lovely. She sings beautifully, so I love that he is getting a little bit of that, and the music is so meaningful to me.

And I am delighted and excited that my lovely granddaughter, who alas does not live here, chose to have a batmitzva this year, and so proud of her. She was amazing the way she read from the Torah in Hebrew, and the beautiful speech she gave afterwards for her coming of age! It was indeed a beautiful ritual, and all of us, her brother and older sister, her cousin, her parents, and her grandparents were privileged to be part of it in the lovely garden behind her home.

For my own personal rituals, for me spirituality is putting love into action. It isn't so much meditation or prayer, although certainly there is great value in that. It is, as I said, in the Jewish tradition of service, of making ours a better world, not just ameliorating the pain and suffering caused by what, in my work, I call "domination systems." It's working not just on the symptoms but on changing the root causes and changing the beliefs and the institutions. For me the key question is what kinds of relations they support. Whether they are top-down rankings of domination, beginning with the ranking of one half of humanity over the other half, women under men, rankings which are foundational to domination systems—which is why regressives always want to push women back to their "traditional" place—or whether they are relations of mutuality, caring, and empathy and sensitivity and love. These are the kinds of relations supported by what I call partnership systems, where in both the family and the larger society human rights are fully respected. Here a key model for equality is the equal partnership of females and males, and here stereotypically feminine values and activities, such as nonviolence, caring, and care giving, are highly valued in both women and men. So for me, my work—my research, writing, speaking, activism—is a ritual too. It is a ritual of connecting with people, empowering people. I get many letters from people who say that my books and even my speeches have transformed their lives, and that, of course, is the greatest possible reward.

For me, walking on the beach is a ritual. Holding my husband's hand is a ritual. Reading a book with my grandchildren is a wonderful ritual. These are the rituals that provide a way of putting love into action to help make ours a better world… a way to be in touch with the beauty of ourselves as human beings and with the beauty of the world.

The Love of God

People often associate spirituality with the fear of God, with Divine retribution, instead of with the love of God and the joy of God. That is part of our heritage from times that oriented more closely to what I call the domination system. Because it is very appropriate, isn't it, for that kind of system to image the powers that govern the universe as these angry guys. Like the angry, punitive male head of household or the despotic ruler of the tribal state. These kinds of images of deity came out of people's experiences in times when the domination system was still more rigid, when top-down, despotic rule in both the family and tribe or state was considered normal and moral. We need to leave that behind, we need to leave that conception of deity behind. Imaging the deity as both mother and father, as both God and Goddess, is very important in the process of establishing a different, more positive and constructive conception of a more joyful and loving deity. After all, traditionally it has been the connection with the mother that's associated with love. That's why the Virgin Mary is so popular: She is still the mother of God, she is the great Goddess, though she has been demoted to become the only mortal figure in a very peculiar holy family where only the father and the son are Divine. For the mother of God to be the only mortal is ridiculous, of course. But it fits a domination system, doesn't it? Reinstating the Divine Feminine is very important. I also think supporting the movement of women to have an equal place in priesthoods in all major religions (Christianity, Judaism, Hinduism, Buddhism, Islam) is very important. If we are really talking about love and if we are really talking about justice, we have to look beyond the rhetoric to what's actually happening in the world's religions: the kinds of structures they have, the beliefs, policies, and practices they support.

Respect for human rights is essential to move to a more just and caring world. And it has to start with our intimate relations, with our gender relations, our parent-child relations...even our relations with ourselves. That is what my work is about. I wrote a book called *The Power of Partnership*, and it starts with how we relate to ourselves and ends with our spiritual relations. The subtitle is *Seven Relationships that Can Change Your Life*. There are the old tapes we carry, the old dominator tapes. But once we become aware of them, we can move forward, to partnership ways of living and loving.

Caring Economics

My first books re-examined old stories—which is very important, because we live by stories. Then I began to write more about action, about practical steps for moving forward. I look at old stories about "human nature" and human history in *The Chalice and The Blade* and *Sacred Pleasure*—because understanding our real history is essential. Then I wrote *Tomorrow's Children*, which is on education from K to 12, and *The Power of Partnership*, a new genre of self-help book. My newest book is *The Real Wealth of Nations, Creating A Caring Economics*, which is on changing economics.

When it comes to economics and wealth I think we have, again, this unconscious heritage of devaluing women and anything associated with women—like when people say to you, "It's just a women's issue," which is kind of ridiculous because we are half the population, actually the majority. When you analyze the values that drive present economic systems— and not just capitalism, but also what happened with communism—you see a devaluing of caring and care giving, of the soft, the stereotypically feminine, whether it resides in a woman or a man. This, too, is our heritage from more rigid dominator times, and it still profoundly affects what is or is not valued. For example, professions that entail caring work (which is stereotypically associated with women), such as childcare and elementary school teaching, get less pay than professions such as plumbing or engineering, which are stereotypically associated with men and do not involve care giving. I should add that the partnership system benefits both men and women. In fact, if you go to my website, rianeeisler.com, if you look under Impact, some of the strongest comments of people who said my work changed their lives have come from men.

We can't solve our economic problems unless we change our economic indicators, policies, and practices to give visibility and value to the most essential human work: the work of caring for people, starting in childhood, and caring for our Mother Earth. There's lots of talk about poverty, but we should be much more specific, because the poorest of the poor and the mass of the poor are women and children, worldwide. Seventy percent of those living in absolute poverty, which is starvation or near starvation, are female. Even in the United States, women over the age of 65 are twice as likely to be poor, according to U.S. census data, than men over the age of 65. Most of these women are, or were, caregivers. But that work is invisible, it isn't economically rewarded, they don't receive credit for it. In Norway the first seven years of caring for a child counts for social security credit.

Sweden has generous paid parental leave and high quality childcare. We have to see that all nations follow these examples of caring policies.

We have childcare tax credits, but we have no caregiver tax credits. The caregiver is invisible. So if we are really serious about changing poverty we have to give real value to the "women's work" of care giving, not only for the sake of women and children but for the economy. If we don't invest in caring for children, for example, we won't have what economists call the "high quality human capital" needed for the post-industrial knowledge economy. One of the key findings from my research is that what's good for women is good for the world and what's bad for women is bad for the world.

My work and my perspective on ritual have been referred to as "the ritual of expansion." Yes! Expand your knowledge. And then become involved. Get together with other women, look at the fact that we have such similar experiences—which means that the problems we each have are to a large extent social, not personal—and that, in itself, is an important ritual. Get involved with groups working for change, such as the Center for Partnership Studies (www.partnershipway.org). Working for change is the most effective ritual I can think of.

I love the phrase "the ritual of expansion," and would add ritual of involvement and ritual of activism, because that is how the world changes. There is only so much you can do on your own, but we can each be part of the change. That's what I think of as spiritual courage, the courage to stand up against injustice out of love. Spirituality in a domination system all too often is simply retreating from the pain of the world, like living in a cave. But partnership rather than dominator spirituality is going out there and being active as an agent for positive change. It's putting love into action.

Living In the Heart of a Movement: Incorporating the Divine Feminine for Personal and Global Transformation

Carolyn Rivers

Carolyn Rivers, founder and director of The Sophia Institute, is a teacher, visionary, and spiritual mentor. Her work centers on personal, interpersonal, and societal transformation that fosters wholeness, oneness, integration, sustainability, peace, compassionate community, and the emergence of feminine wisdom. Rivers has completed professional study with many of the leading transpersonal teachers and visionaries of our time, many of whom now serve as faculty of The Sophia Institute. She is writing a book about Mary Magdalene as a model of wholeness and another about Sophia and the transformation of self.

Sophia

Divine Love, Healing Light, Giver of Grace,
I offer you my gratitude
for your Love and your active Presence in my life.
Guide me and direct me.

Fill me with
Your Light, Love, and Wisdom.
Surround me in it.
Be with me in all that I
Think and say and do,
in all the ways that I relate and exist.
Direct me into Your Flow.

Lead me into Your way of Being
that is my way of Being,
into my work in the world
that is your work in the world,
to my truest Essence that is
Your Essence.

In all Love and Gratitude
I offer my prayer to You.

I created this prayer to Sophia out of my yearning to more deeply commune with her. It serves as one of my ways of connecting with Her in my own heart as my inner beloved.

I felt Sophia call to me just at the time in my life when I needed her most. I was profoundly moved when I first found her in Proverbs 8: "I was set up from eternity, and of old, before the earth was made—when he prepared the heavens I was there—when he balanced the foundations of the earth, I was with him." I was stunned by the realization that I'd never encountered this passage in any church I'd attended. I first discovered her through my research in the Wisdom books in the Canon, learning that Sophia in the ancient Greek means Divine Wisdom and was personified in the feminine. Once I'd found her, I was shocked to realize I'd never witnessed Sophia honored or celebrated, nor had I ever heard of her until that moment.

It became clear to me that the repression of Sophia mirrored the marginalization of women through the centuries. At a time, many years ago, when I began to recognize how my own life was impacted by this repression, I began what I now think of as my own journey to wholeness. Claiming the other half of the Divine Nature—the feminine side—seemed an essential part of this journey to me. Now, I understand that a Divine Wisdom works in the world, an evolutionary and emergent feminine consciousness that awakens us to our own divine nature, to what we're each called to do on the deepest levels, so we can make a difference in the world. The Divine Feminine is a co-creative wisdom found in the hearts of women and men alike. Relational, integrative, immensely healing, transformational, and centered in love, She calls us to midwife a much more conscious world. Women and men are awakening now to heal and evolve our world.

I began to search for Sophia in other places. When I discovered the Gnostic Gospels, I found her there more clearly. Through study, I found Sophia, the ancient Greek word for Divine Wisdom, in other religious traditions—as *Quan Yin* in Buddhism, as *Tara* in Tibetan Buddhism, as *Saraswati* in Hinduism. I created a composite of the Divine Feminine in my own heart from what I learned and encountered in each.

I began to call to Sophia daily through prayer, meditation, and my movement practices. I placed images of the Divine Feminine on my altar as a way of re-imaging her in my own psyche. She began appearing to me in my dreams.

While on a 10-day retreat in the high desert of Arizona, I dreamt that a tarot card appeared and on it was the face of Christ, but not like any face I'd ever seen. Yet, I was told it was Christ's face. Then, the same card turned, and it became the face of Mary. Again, this face did not look like the usual representation of Mary, but, rather, was a new and contemporary image of Mary. As I worked with the dream, I realized it was not the Virgin Mary but Mary Magdalene. This dream prefigured all that we were to later learn about Mary Magdalene. The dream spoke of integration and wholeness, of an emergent archetype of Divine Wisdom and of her active presence in my life.

Sophia appeared to me in a meditation as well. At first she came as a veiled woman, and then, as she turned her head to reveal herself to me, I saw my own face as her face. I felt startled and awed by this revelation, but I clearly understood that she was speaking to me of our union, opening me to a connection available to us all. I felt my life as a woman changing radically as I owned more and more of my own innate divine nature.

Finding Your Divine Self by Going Inward

The transformation I was experiencing began as an inner transformation, a need to go inward and discover my true self and find that connection between the outer and inner dimensions of who I am. It arose out of a great challenge I was facing, as it often does for many of us—a divorce, an illness, the loss of one's job, the death of a loved one—when it becomes clear that the path you've been on is no longer yours. For me, the challenge and resulting inner work came through divorce—my own "Dark Night of the Soul," which brought with it much pain and suffering and also healing, openings, revelations, and the awakening that comes out of doing deep inner work.

I discovered that much of what I had been taught about being a woman, both through my upbringing and societally, I could no longer put to use in my life. I could not intellectualize my way through this challenge, this passage into a new way of being; I had to follow my heart and the co-creative guidance I found there. I came to understand that I'd have to go inside and find a new way, my own way, born out of living my truth and tapping into what I was discovering as an emergent Feminine consciousness who values interdependence, relational thinking, collaboration, intuitive intelligence, compassionate community—all centered in love. I learned that I had to make this inward journey by following my inner knowing, gnosis, and listening for and following my guidance. I had to listen to the still, small voice that is the voice of my inner Beloved, or, in Jungian terms, the Self.

I found profound truth in the work of Dr. Carl Jung and the post-Jungian work of leading-edge visionaries and thinkers like Marion Woodman, Jean Shinoda Bolen, Paula Reeves, Helen Luke, Robert Johnson, and others, which attends to the Divine Feminine and to integration and wholeness. Their work gives us a transformative process to use. We know from Jungian teachings that all psychological and emotional difficulties come out of a lack of alignment between the local self, or ego, and the high Self, the central organizing archetype of the psyche (what some of us might call soul). Jung referred to the path of individuation as the process of opening to the indwelling spark of Sophia. Much of the personal work I have done has been through this Jungian approach.

I have chosen a path of heart. Divine Wisdom speaks to me in my heart through this still, small voice that resonates throughout my body as truth. I make this journey of self-discovery with no road maps; the guide is necessary, but the willingness to follow the guidance represents a choice. The tools I use include intuition, synchronicity, meditation, prayer, movement as sacred practice (yoga, t'ai chi, gigong, Eurhythmy, dance), attention to dreams, honoring the body as a temple, and listening to heart and mind. The journey requires that I relate, feel, have compassion, love, take enormous risks, excavate my shadow issues, heal, become whole, follow what calls me on a heart level. I must live from essential beingness, not from ego dominance; this became my daily mantra for years, and I return to it when I feel the need to do so.

The Path to Inner Guidance

For me, Sophia provides a direct path that centers on following inner guidance, gnosis, wisdom, and alignment with Divine Knowledge. In *The Power of Myth*, Joseph Campbell refers to our time as the "age of the Holy Spirit, who speaks directly to the individual." The Holy Spirit can be thought of as Sophia. I have come to believe that the ancient texts, often referred to as the Gnostic Gospels, were not found at Nag Hammadi by accident. They were found in our time, because at this time their teachings can be understood in a new way. Now, psychology and spirituality are finding some common ground, and these texts can be integrated by those who are willing to do their deep work. Together with the wisdom books of the Old Testament, the Gnostic texts give us a fuller understanding of the Divine nature. They also point us toward a Divine Wisdom and a path emerging in our time— the path of Sophia in divine union with God, in wholeness, guiding us co-creatively, available in our hearts continuously.

For years, I sought out and found teachers, visionaries, and healers with whom I could study, who were doing deeply authentic work. I implicitly trusted these highly spiritual and intellectual people, who served as mentors and guides to me. Being with them, usually in retreat, allowed me to step out of ordinary time into what I've come to think of as extraordinary time, time devoted to this highly transformational work. In retreat, I could move out of my head and into my heart.

I learned to anchor my days in meditation, prayer, and sacred movement. Each of these rituals served as integrative practices, linking mind, body, and spirit. They also often served to open my heart in gratitude and in an innate harmony with others and the world around me, as well as to inform the rest of my day as I worked in the world and lived with my family and friends.

Early on, I found an intimate circle of women, each of whom had committed to a similar, but unique, path for herself. We pledged to hold one another to our creative and spiritual edges, to attend to what we were holding in our hearts—to listen deeply to one another and offer feedback as requested from that place of deep presence. Our support of one another remains an essential part of my life.

Eventually, I was led to create The Sophia Institute and to invite many of those with whom I have worked to come there. The decision to create The Sophia Institute was born out of a deep heart calling to do so that came in fractal waves of knowing. First, it appeared as a yearning, then it gained greater clarity as I acknowledged and worked with this yearning, testing it, asking for dream confirmation, discussing it with my circle of friends and mentors, field testing it, and ultimately making plans to implement it. I believe inner work leads to outer action, to aligning with what one is called to be and to do to make a difference in the world.

Synchronicity represents one of my chief ways of knowing and receiving guidance. I'll never forget the day I was bumping along a dusty road in Bali on a pilgrimage led by renowned scholar and researcher of human capacities Jean Houston, who was mentored by Margaret Meade and Joseph Campbell. As we sat together, talking intuitively with one another, she said to me, "I see you creating a place that people can come to do their deep work. Are you considering it?" My heart leapt with her recognition of what I'd been holding in it—my vision of The Sophia Institute. Her words, her intuition, seemed like another sign pointing me in a particular direction.

Later, when I asked for dream guidance about my true work in the world, I received a powerful dream that came as a voice: "You are lifting the veil between the worlds." That served as an extraordinary confirmation for me that creating The Sophia Institute was right, and that leaving my career of 27 years just when I was at the top of my game was necessary if I were to follow this calling. It also felt like an enormous risk, but one worth taking.

Personal and World Transformation to Balance Energies

So much of what I'd been learning and to which I'd been opening became central to the work of The Sophia Institute. I am at that phase of my life where my life, work, and my being are intricately woven together. The transformation I was experiencing personally early on, however, is mirrored by that which is happening in the world now. I believe we are living in a time of great evolutionary shift guided by Divine Wisdom. The feminine impulse is coming into balance with the masculine and bringing with it a radical wisdom of the heart. Deeply purposeful, radically relevant and hopeful, it starts with personal transformation that ultimately leads to societal transformation as more and more of us awaken. Old patriarchal patterns—patterns of domination, aggression, and control—that no longer serve us are being transformed within ourselves and in our social structures. You can see evidence of this enormous change all around. We see it through economic cataclysm, wars in the Middle East and elsewhere, social issues centered around poverty and the marginalization of peoples and cultures (most particularly women and children), the devaluation of nature and our natural resources that has us on the edge of environmental disaster, and the exposure of corporate greed and issues of governmental influence. Yet, awareness gives us the opportunity to find solutions that cannot be born of the old mindset, as Einstein says, but only of a new, more wisdom-based mindset found in the hearts of women and men alike.

New patterns born of Divine Wisdom and centered in integration, wholeness, collaboration, partnership, oneness, and peace are emerging now. At the center of the great movements of our time—social justice (the women's movement and the civil rights movement), peace and reconciliation, the green movement—Divine Wisdom can be found, calling us to healing and "wholing" ourselves and our world, to partnership rather than domination, to "re-sacralizing" our relationship with nature, to honoring the sacred at the center of life.

Distinguishing between the patriarchal and the positive masculine impulse, we recognize that a union of conscious masculine and feminine energies is crucial to our wholeness and the advancement of egalitarian principles. We exist in a time when the reconciliation with the Feminine is necessary to bring about the transformation the world needs. We need leading-edge visionaries and teachers whose work reflects this vision. Their messages of wisdom, healing, integration, oneness, sustainability, peace, and the need for conscious feminine and masculine energy herald the arrival of new paradigms and fresh perspectives at the moment in our history when our very survival is at stake.

During a lecture, Sue Monk Kidd, The Sophia Institute's writer-in-residence, said, "Perhaps it is needless to say that there is a new spiritual consciousness breaking into the world. We could call it a Feminine Consciousness, even a Sacred Feminine consciousness. It has the potential to bring healing, balance, and a new paradigm of wholeness. It has the potential to do something that has never been done before: to open the immense common heart of the world. The particular genius of the Sacred Feminine is in its valuing of the wisdom of the heart, of interdependence, empathy, relational thinking, compassionate community, intuitive intelligence, peace, creativity, and the sacredness of the earth." I couldn't have said it better or agreed with her more.

Quite possibly, we live on the edge of a great evolutionary shift, a whole system transition, a leap-frogging into a new consciousness, and the chaotic phase our world currently is experiencing actually has purpose and potential. It has the capacity to heal us individually and to heal our world—to herald in a new way of living in harmony with all life on our planet and with the Earth itself, as well as to honor the sacred at the center of our lives.

Living a Path of Love: How to Become "God's Instrument" Through Committed Daily Practice

Lynne Twist

Lynne Twist, a global activist, fundraiser, speaker, consultant, and author of *The Soul of Money*, has dedicated her life to global initiatives that serve the best instincts in all of us. She has raised hundreds of millions of dollars and trained thousands of fundraisers to be more effective in their work. For more than three decades, she has held leadership positions with many global initiatives, including those to end world hunger; protect the world's rain forestss; empower indigenous peoples; improve health, economic, and political conditions for women and children; advance the scientific understanding of human consciousness; and create a sustainable future for all life.

When I consider what practices and rituals sustain or strengthen my connection with Spirit, I must first mention that I have quite an eclectic spiritual practice. I'm not a Buddhist, but I'm a student of the Buddha. I'm not Catholic, but I respect and honor the Catholic path. I was a Catholic for years, but I've drawn on the traditions that touched me in the past or that do so now. I learned from other priests and other paths, and I have expanded to a broader, more eclectic spiritual practice.

I worked closely with Mother Teresa for many years. She encouraged me to want to be "God's pencil." This required rediscovering myself as an instrument of something larger than life, larger than myself, which was a transforming experience for me. Mother Teresa's deep ethic was, and always will be, the power of love. She said the unadulterated love of one person can nullify the hatred of millions. When I heard her say that, it became clear to me that living a path of love constituted the best fit and the most appropriate spiritual path for me. Thus, all the things I draw on are really expressions of love.

My primary spiritual practice, by which I mean daily ritual, involves giving and receiving love in every human encounter. I just witnessed someone in the airport having a complete fit of anger. As I watched, I created an environment of loving kindness around him and the staff person at the ticket counter toward whom he was directing all of his anger. That kind of conscious action creates the theme for my spiritual practice; however, I think it permeates all that I do and the choices I make, not only spiritual practice but daily living as well.

Eclectic Spiritual Practice: an Example

To give you a better idea of my eclectic form of spiritual practice, and also how I add into this the spiritual practice of giving and receiving love, let me describe how I observe the ritual of Lent. I practice Lent, but not because I'm a Catholic or a Christian. I do so because I believe in spiritual practice, and I'm deeply inspired by Brother David Steindl-Rast, a senior Benedictine monk at Mount Saviour Monastery in Elmira, New York. They do a four-part practice every Lent, and I join them. In conjunction with Lent, I go to mass on Ash Wednesday and then I go to mass on Easter to start Lent, and complete it with honoring the tradition from which it all stems.

Each of the four parts of the Lenten practice is observed throughout the 40 days of Lent. First, you enter into a course of study. Second, you choose something you'll sacrifice for 40 days. Third, you consciously perform a daily act of service—one that you are not normally doing already. Fourth, you enter 40 days of additional spiritual practice.

Though I live permanently in San Francisco, one year I was living in Ecuador during Lent. Therefore, as my course of study each day I read either Pablo Neruda or Federico Garcia Lorca, both great poets and real giants in South American literature. Plus, through their writings they both offer spiritual teachings as well. That year, my sacrifice for 40 days was giving up wine, bread, and any form of dessert.

Also that year, my primary act of service during the 40 days of Lent involved touching, embracing, and having meaningful conversation with every homeless person or beggar who crossed my path. In South America, more often I encountered beggars. In my act of service to them, I was not to dismiss them, not to just give them money and make them go away, but actually to engage with them and embrace them, even if they were drunk, smelly, or dirty. I had to recognize their humanity and treat them with dignity. This, to me, involved giving love; in the process, I might also receive love, but that was not the purpose.

During Lent I also performed another act of service by picking up trash wherever I saw it along my path, whether it was my job to do it or not. (I actually do that regularly anyway, but I was more conscientious about doing it that year during Lent.) I also made additional financial contributions to things or organizations that touched me during this time period—sometimes very small, sometimes larger—but financially making sure my generosity was expanded during this period. In my mind, both of these activities are expressions of love. In the first case, I love my environment by caring for it. In the second, I offer love in the form of financial donation to those organizations or things that in some way gave to me.

My additional spiritual practice during Lent tends to be similar from year to year. It includes meditating more than normal—actually, every day. I practice journaling all the time as well, but during Lent I always do "gratitude journaling." At the end of the day I list the things for which I am grateful. On some days, I focus on a particular dimension or quality of life, like the color yellow, the music of nature, or the beauty of lights, writing in my journal about my gratitude for that and where that characteristic revealed itself to me.

During this period, I find I am more in touch with prayer. So, that's another practice I have all the time, a ritual I perform, but deepen, during Lent. Prayer represents a way of offering my love to Spirit. And I deepen my practice of yoga, another of my regular rituals or practices, during Lent.

That encompasses my four-part observance for Lent: study, sacrifice, service, and practice. Some of these rituals line up with basic Catholic and other Christian practices, but I add non-traditional elements as well.

I also observe Islamic religious practices during the month of Ramadan. I have a Muslim son and daughter-in-law and three Muslim grandchildren, and I find their Muslim traditions beautiful. Much like Lent, Ramadan is an annual religious observance that takes place for one month. During this holiday prayers, fasting, charity, and self-accountability especially are stressed. I fast from dawn till dusk with my son and his family each day of Ramadan; I say extra prayers, make extra contributions, and do extra service—some of the same things I do during Lent.

Random Acts of Kindness as a Spiritual Practice

Like a lot of people now, I also regularly practice random acts of kindness. For instance, sometimes when I'm on a toll bridge, I pay for the person behind me. (I live in San Francisco, where I travel over bridges all the time.) When I get to the tollbooth, I simply give twice as much and say, "I'd like to pay for the person behind me."

I also like to do that when there is a line at the movie theater. When I place my order, I'll pay for the fifth person behind me, so they don't know who did it. Or at Starbucks, I'll say to the cashier, "I'm giving you $20 for my $3.75 mocha, but I'd also like to pay for the fifth and/or sixth person behind me. Please, just tell them an angel would like to pay for their order today, if you could manage that."

I have lots of practices like that with money. These help people see that there's generosity everywhere and that they can be generous and practice random acts of kindness, too. Of course, generosity and random acts of kindness represent another way of expressing love in the world.

Rituals Based upon Conscious Action

Sometimes my spiritual practice takes the form of a conscious action or personal change based upon a belief. For instance, my desire to love the planet and other people, whether I know them or not, affects how I now adorn myself. I used to wear a beautiful gold Rolex watch, and I loved gold chains around my neck. I wore diamond studs in my ears. During that era in my life my husband and I were establishing ourselves as people who could afford those things. Now, however, I realize the suffering that goes into mining for gold, I know about the horrors of the diamond industry—I know what these businesses do to people and the earth. Gold and diamond jewelry is beautiful, and I don't judge anyone else for wearing it, but to me it now represents the suffering of many, many people and the desecration of the earth. Therefore, I don't wear it any longer. I realize that I don't enjoy adorning myself with people's pain and suffering.

However, I do like to adorn myself. So, I've replaced gold and diamonds with things created by people making their livelihood by turning some- thing natural, like cowry shells from Africa or seeds from the Amazon or objects from the forest—beautiful natural products that nature gives us without us having to desecrate her—or something old into beautiful jew- elry. My favorite adornments come from Bead for Life, a fantastic project in southern Uganda. Bead for Life (www.beadforlife.com) was started primarily by female heads of household who have AIDS and whose husbands abandoned them because of their illness. They all have children to support and do so through their work with Bead for Life.

These women have taken our U.S. magazines and catalogues—our excess trash, which is sent to them, and from the cover of *Vogue* or a page of *Newsweek* they create beads. They cut tall, very skinny strips of paper in the shape of a tall triangle, and they roll them around toothpicks. Then they dye them and lacquer them. Once they have dried, they take the toothpicks out, and they have created beautiful little beads. Out of our trash, they create "gold."

Bead for Life has become more than a million-dollar effort that's helped 13,000 Ugandan female heads of households out of poverty. A booming small industry in southern Uganda, it is now spreading to other parts of Africa. The jewelry is absolutely beautiful, and it's made with love. You can feel it when you wear it.

I support those types of activities or actions. I enjoy finding ways to support people who express their intense commitment to bringing their families out of poverty by making something that is natural to the earth or that takes trash and makes it into something unusual. I also see this support as a way of expressing love for these people. In my own small way, by purchasing their products, I send them love and support.

The Spiritual Sufficiency Practice

I'm very interested in supporting and promoting efforts that make me— and others—aware that we live in a world where we have enough, and I see this as another one of my spiritual practices. I sometimes say, "I dwell in the house of enough," and I consider my efforts to maintain that consciousness the spiritual practice of sufficiency. That's actually what I've written about in my book, *The Soul of Money*, and I promulgate that idea wherever I can.

Another personal practice I have is best stated by Aristotle's great quote, "I love going to the market and seeing all the things I don't need." In other words, I practice paying attention to what I don't need rather than to what I do need. And if I want to acquire something, I let something go. For example, if I decide I want to purchase something (a dress, a car, a book, a pot) I really don't need, which, with the exception of those things we need for survival—like food—constitute most of what we all purchase, I do the best I can to let something go of equal value or quality. I don't just let it go into the trash, but I let it go to someone who needs it. I taught this to my grandchildren, and we practice it as a family. My grandchildren know that if they want a new toy or game, they have to decide what they have of equal value and quality that they are willing to let go of and give it to someone else before receiving the new game.

Philanthropy as a Spiritual Practice

I believe that philanthropy can be a spiritual practice. It's about being generous, and in that way also supporting and loving other people. I think it's so important to practice generosity that my husband and I give our grandchildren the gift of generosity. We give them the ability to be generous, at the same time teaching them philanthropy as a spiritual practice.

On Thanksgiving, we give each grandchild either $50, $500, or $5,000, depending on their age, as well as the assignment, the opportunity, the invitation to give that money to three organizations in which they believe. They can choose any three projects, initiatives, or missions, and they also must volunteer in those three places between Thanksgiving and Christmas Eve. On Christmas day, they share the story of why they gave to those particular organizations, and they share the experience of volunteering and becoming a philanthropist for those causes.

I personally find it a wonderful practice to teach the ethics of philanthropy to the younger generation. It's so important for them to know that every person is a philanthropist, and they just need to exercise that muscle within themselves. The word philanthropy means "love of humankind." So, everyone alive is a philanthropist waiting to happen, and children are particularly eager to do that.

It's also important to see money in a spiritual light, and to handle it with a spiritual consciousness. It's such a huge part of our daily life. I teach my grandchildren about my spiritual approach to money as well. My little grandchildren have a piggy bank that has four slots in it: one that says "save," one that says "spend," one that says "invest," and one that says "contribute." When they do their chores or when they wash the car, instead of giving them a dollar bill, we give them four quarters, and they put one in "save," one in "spend," one in "invest," and one in "contribute." We do a lot of practices around raising financially fit children that understand that money is always a blessing—small amounts or large amounts, and that being responsible and ethical about money represents one of the great privileges of being a human being. Additionally, they need to realize, as do we all, that since money serves as the currency of the world, dealing with it in a conscious and spiritual manner strengthens their connection to people everywhere as well as to the Divine. Approaching financial matters spiritually, consciously, and responsibly represents a way of caretaking—loving.

Becoming—and Living—Your Commitments

Another simple practice or ritual we observe regularly in our family involves blessing our food before we eat. When we're together we do it out loud; when I'm by myself I do it silently. For instance, just before I began writing this piece, I went to Starbucks, and I did a little blessing over my soy mocha.

Again, this practice comes from my work with Mother Teresa. She taught me that if you live a committed life, your commitments move to the background and you become your word. A committed life is one in which your commitments wake you up in the morning, tell you what to wear, and tell you what to do—not your desires or your wants. When you live a committed life, you become your commitment—for example, to end world hunger or to bring forth an environmentally sustainable, spiritually fulfilling, socially just human presence on this planet—which is my work right now. My commitments, however, are totally woven into my spiritual beliefs and practices. Therefore, for me, they become a form of daily ritual.

When you realize you want to live your life as an instrument of something greater than "your life starring you," this knowledge empowers you and inspires you to take care of your body. It makes you want to take care of the temple, the instrument of love you've been given as an incarnated being. Thus, blessing food—even potato chips—may seem so silly, but it makes a huge difference to me, to my psychological state. And I think it probably makes a huge difference in my body.

For this reason, my family and I say grace over our food, but I have two favorite ones. The first is the Thich Nhat Hanh grace. Here is my version of it: "This food is the gift of the whole universe, the earth, the sky, and much hard work. May we transform any unskilled states of being and learn to eat with truth, respect, and moderation. May we take food that nourishes our bodies and prevents illness. We accept this food so that we may realize our path of wisdom, compassion, understanding, and love."

Another blessing we say regularly in my home comes from author John Robbins: "Infinite gratitude for all things past, infinite service to all things present, infinite responsibility to all things future. May all be fed. May all be seen. May all be heard. May all be loved."

Other ways in which my commitments and beliefs are woven into my spiritual practices on a daily basis can be seen in my approach to environmental issues. In my family, our environmental practices include reducing our water usage. We also recycle every possible thing. We never, ever take a plastic bag at the grocery store; we always use canvas. We drive a Prius, because it saves energy. We use public transportation wherever we can.

My family has a whole "green" ethic, as do people working in my field. It's so much fun to figure out ways to save energy. It's such a wonderful game. We offset our air travel with TerraPass or some other carbon offset program. Many websites offer ways to offset the negative impact of the use of jet fuel by planting tress or investing in alternative energy.

Additionally, my family is slowly, but surely, converting all of our investments into socially responsible investments. We're very carefully converting our investments so when our money is at work, it's at work on something in which we believe. My grandchildren all have accounts at the Rudolph Steiner Foundation, which is a socially responsible investment project. When they save money from the toys they *don't* buy (that we put in their four-compartment piggy bank), at the end of the year they either contribute to something or they put it in their Rudolph Steiner accounts.

Bringing Ritual into the Organizational World

As I work with different organizations and groups, I often bring ritual into their environment and into our process. For instance, in The Pachamama Alliance (www.pachamama.org), the organization in San Francisco and Quito, Ecuador, which my husband and I co-founded, all of us are very connected and deeply rooted in the practices of indigenous people. In that organization, we have a practice on the new moon for Pachamama ("Mother Earth, Father Sky, and all there is for all of time," a Kichwa word), which is a time of planting and nourishing the body, the earth, and the family. Each month at that time, those of us in the organization re-commit to our shared purpose. We send out a new moon communication to all of our followers suggesting ways in which they can lighten their footprints on the earth and re-allocate more resources towards conservation and less towards consumption. We also use shamanic practice to open every meeting, creating sacred space by lighting a candle, acknowledging and calling to the presence of the ancestors—the people and beings who have preceded us—and to the spirits of the place. We also call to the spirit of the meeting itself and to the spirit of the guides and unseen allies that we always ask to join us in our meetings and in our work, as well as to the beings yet to be born in whose name we do our work. We always close sacred space at the end of the meeting. This beautiful practice serves as part of our work.

At the Fetzer Institute, a philanthropic organization where I serve as a board member, I initiated a practice we do when we meet to approve grants. We stand in a circle after we've approved the allocation of those resources, and we bless the money. We bless it with our purpose. We declare the intention that the money will be a current, or a currency, that carries our love into the world, into the hands of our partners, into the projects, into the laboratories where we're conducting research. The Institute's mission is to reveal, inspire, and serve the global awakening that is turning the tide from fear and violence to love and forgiveness. So, we bless the money and give it our love, our intentionality, and ask that the money carry love into the world.

We also always bless the money that the Institute receives from its investments. We do a gratitude process each meeting to deeply treasure the increase in our endowment and money we've earned. We even bless the money we lose, for example, due to a downturn in the stock market, knowing that always the world of money is adjusting to the truth and integrity of life.

While much of what I do day to day may seem like ordinary living—recycling, investing, teaching my grandchildren about money, performing a random act of kindness now and then—for me these actions all stem from my deep spiritual beliefs and convictions. Thus, they all represent daily rituals and practices. I do them consciously and with an awareness of how they connect me to Spirit, to the Earth, and to other humans. I do them knowing that in the process I am giving, and also receiving, love. Hopefully, in the process I am fulfilling Mother Teresa's desire for me to become "God's pencil," or God's instrument here on Earth.

Lavender Dreams:
A Sleep-Enhancing Ritual for Purposeful Dreams

Ivy "Okolo Shadiah" Anderson Hylton

Ivy "Okolo Shadiah" Anderson Hylton has worked as an internationally known integrative behavioral healthcare administrator, recording artist, writer, inspirational speaker, psychotherapist, and spiritual healer for over 20 years. She has been blessed—and blesses others—with a voice whose distinctive presence captivates listeners, evokes emotions with them, and touches them at the depth of their souls. Hylton functions on the cutting edge of a new paradigm for psychological, physiological, and emotional healing, using a breakthrough concept in sound and vibration to teach, inspire, and transform. Her concerts, lectures, workshops, and retreats bring healing, releasing, cleansing, enlightenment, restoration, and moments of serenity, creating a sanctuary of wellness and love for those who attend. For more information on Hylton and her work, visit www.serenityhealingarts.com.

Dreams are actual experiences we have in the spiritual world. Thus, sleep time represents a sacred time for resting the spirit and getting in touch with the invisible realm of the soul. I describe the "soul" as a spiritual matrix pattern woven deeply into the DNA, nerve fibers, cellular tissue, and genes of each organ in the body, thereby creating a sacred communication process with the universal presence of Divine Creation and the purpose of life. The soul is pure consciousness and a state of being characterized by sensation, emotion, volition, and thought-mind.

Lucid ethereal dreaming is the manifestation of a conscious and super-sub-conscious state of mind. The lucidity of sleep consciousness comes from a process of comprehensive brain wave functioning, allowing for internal and external awareness simultaneously. Lucid dreaming is a more profound internal mind experience than "regular dreaming"; in fact, it is a cross between regular dreaming and daydreaming. Daydreaming occurs when waking consciousness turns its attention inwards, away from the outside world. Oftentimes, when we experience daydreaming, it can actually feel like a real-life phenomenon. In fact, most of us have had lucid dreams that can wake us from a deep sleep, leaving a feeling of an actual experience within the body. A consciousness wave of awareness is not detached from the real self, and the emotional-mental body (soul) never leaves us. Therefore, in the spiritual realm, soul constitutes lucid ethereal energy that can be manifested through dreams. Being in touch with our dreams helps us recognize a deeper reality of the self, which is knowing that we have levels of the personal self or mind that are consistently operating within us as multiple dimensions of reality, even when we are asleep.

To enhance your sleep time and support the forces of your mind and soul in manifesting clear and purposeful dreams, I created a ritual called Lavender Dreams. The ritual helps elicit powerful dreams. Paying close attention to the details of your Lavender Dreams will bless your life with powerful insights into your life purpose.

To begin creating your enhanced sleeping ritual, first select a time and day to conduct the ritual. This step is vital to your Lavender Dreams ritual, because the ritual involves the power of *purpose, intent*, and *focus*. Therefore, you would not perform this ritual in the spur of the moment. This ritual is designed to allow you time to nurture the process of sleeping and dreaming.

Next, you will need some special ritual items only used for your Lavender Dream time. You will need lavender candles. Select your candles specifically and carefully, because the nature of the candle-making has great significance to this ritual. When selecting the ideal candles, pay attention to the type of wax used to make the candle. Beeswax is preferred for this experience, but it is not absolutely required. Be sure the wax is colored inside of the candle as well as outside of it. For example, some candles are lavender on the outside but white on the inside. Lavender candles come in various colors, so be sure that the candles you choose are lavender/purple to the core. You will need enough candles to illuminate your bedroom and your bathroom.

Also pay attention to the candles' energy, since this plays a critical role in creating the perfect atmosphere for this ritual. When you see a potential candle for your Lavender Dreams ritual, hold the candle in the palms of your hands and close your eyes for a moment. Take a deep breath and focus your attention on the energy of the candle. Become aware of what sensations you get from the candle while holding it. Smell it, and take in the aroma as if you were smelling fresh lavender. You will know when you have found the right one. It will feel "right."

For safety, be sure always to enclose your candles in glass. That is the next step: selecting the glass covers for your candles. Be sure you select covers that speak to you and the décor of your bedroom.

Now, you need lavender sheets, pillowcases, and a comforter. It feels really wonderful to fall asleep on 400- or 600-thread sheets, so look carefully for the right sheets for this ritual. Next, you need to make lavender powder for the mattress and pillows. Put one cup of cornstarch in a bowl and drop 5–10 drops of lavender essential oil into the bowl; press the oil into the starch powder evenly. Sprinkle the powder onto your mattress and pillows before putting on the sheets and pillowcases.

This brings us to lavender sleepwear. Select loose and comfortable sleep-wear. For a special touch, have fresh lavender in a vase to brighten the bedroom and add the vibrational sounds of meditation music playing ever so softly in the background. (My meditation music works well for this.)

The last item that you need for this ritual is a dream journal, which should always be kept under your pillow for easy access. If you are serious about capturing your dreams, you will want to gently wake up and write your dream down, and then go right back to sleep. You will also want to pur-chase a purple pen.

Additionally, you will want some lavender bubble bath and a lavender-col-ored extra-large towel.

The time has come to conduct your Lavender Dreams ritual. Your bedroom should be illuminated with beautiful lavender and purple candles and glimmering reflections of their light beaming through the carefully select-ed glass covers. The aroma of freshly cut lavender and lavender-powdered sheets and pillowcases should waft through the room as well. While pray-ing for peace and serenity, place two or three drops of lavender essential oil in the four corners of your bedroom. Before beginning, you should have neatly prepared your bed and turned down the sheets, making it ready for you to enter into your Lavender Dream world. The dream journal should be carefully placed underneath your pillow for easy access during the night, with a special purple pen right next to it. Ivy's melodic healing music, or some other meditative music, should be playing softly in the background while you prepare a lavender bubble bath in the bathroom. The bathroom should also be illuminated with lavender candles, and a lavender-colored extra-large towel should be patiently waiting for you.

Start with a bath. Take your time in the bath ritual by directing your attention to your sleep time. Begin to think about your lavender dreams and sinking into your lavender-laced mattress and pillows for a peaceful slumber. Use this time to pray and to meditate on your soul's purpose in life and to gaze into the center of the candle flame flickering before you. Take in the messages that come to you, and when you are ready, gently get out of the tub and pat yourself dry.

Put on your lavender sleepwear and get into the bed, sitting in an upright position. Close your eyes and begin to take long, slow, deep breaths. Focus your attention on the center of your forehead, and begin to visualize a field of fresh lavender growing on a sand dune at the bottom of a 300-foot-high rock ridge next to a rolling ocean. Imagine the waves rushing in and out on the beach, splashing up against the rocks on the water's edge. See the stars flying high in the sky and draped with cotton clouds floating in and out from behind the moon. Imagine this image as if it were in your feeling world, and allow your mind to drift into nothingness... .

Begin slowly to bring your attention back into your bedroom, becoming aware of your surroundings. Move your fingers, toes, and fingers gently. Begin to circle your shoulders forward and then backwards. Move your head from side to side, and then slowly open your eyes, blinking them several times before opening them completely.

Now, you are ready for your sleep time... May you have Lavender Dreams that bless your life with purpose, clarity, and wholeness.

SECTION FIVE

BRAIDED PATHS

BRAIDED PATHS

Love moves us toward Oneness!

Acts of love are uniting . . . the glue for wholesome co-creation.

The Braided Path offers a clear route to Oneness.

The term "braided path," coined by Dr. Angeles Arrien, describes the place where I think and pray we are all headed. The braided path is the place where we comfortably accept, respect, and lovingly and peacefully interact with "the other"— different spiritual, cultural, and philosophical perspectives, realities, people. Admittedly, it is a place that I once avoided like the plague, disliked others for embracing, feared, refused to give serious or heartfelt consideration, and was dragged into while kicking and screaming the whole way . . . yet it is also the place that I witnessed my capacity to surrender into a greater truth of who I am and who we all are—Divine, Love, Oneness in manifestation, inextricably connected to God, the Creator, *all* of Its creation, and each other!

In Eckhart Tolle's evocation, his imaginative re-creation of the evolutionary path to the "New Earth" he suggests that we are on the brink of enlightenment, a flowering of human consciousness never before experienced. Tolle likens this time in our evolution to the emergence of the first flower, crystal, or bird in the plant, mineral and animal kingdoms respectively. I, too feel that a great and wondrous time is upon us. My evocation, my personal imaginative re-creation of our evolutionary and spiraling path to "unity" definitely supports and mirrors the outcome of Tolle's "flowering human consciousness". Before we achieve the flowering of our human consciousness or the unity and oneness that our hearts desire, it appears that we must first be able to navigate, pass through, and embrace the complex matrices of diversity along the "Braided Path". I imagine that perhaps, in the beginning, there was <u>one</u> Creative Force that created ALL life as we know it—our planet, our solar system, the galaxies—all energy and matter that exists anywhere. One day, from the One Mind/Heart/Spirit of that Creative Force, It—the Creator—decided to create humans who would be able to, like Itself, create ever evolving offspring and experiences that would be inextricably connected to (and as) them, as they (the humans) themselves were and would always be inextricably connected to (and as) the Creator.

The human mini-creators decided to *experiment* with the diversity in Creation that they, too, were a part of and that was everywhere apparent in the One's Creation. Why not, after all . . . they *had* been given Free Will. However, not having the capacity for Omniscience as did the One, the human mini-creators had not yet realized that the peace and harmony in the diversity of the Creation of the One was a key element to its attractiveness, its beauty. Each expression was valued and honored for its unique contribution to the whole. All of the species in the various kingdoms were quite comfortable with the multitude of individual expressions. There was no big upset with an oak being an oak, or an elm being an elm; a tulip a tulip, and a rose a rose; an amethyst an amethyst, and quartz a quartz; an eagle an eagle, and a dove a dove. The diversity, no doubt, added to the richness and beauty of the species and the kingdoms.

Without this highly developed understanding and appreciation, the human mini-creators' attempt at diversity was rife with un-evolved comparison, envy, jealousy, misunderstanding, dissention, and war. Attempts at diversity were becoming less and less diverse, with less and less potential for the true harmony, beauty, and equality that the highest aspects of diversity birth and sustain.

Over time, fortunately, some among the human mini-creators saw and thirsted for the great potential of harmony and the beauty of diversity that was available to be experienced by all. They chose to use their Free Will to dream-vision a time when *all of God's human mini-creators would re-member their inalienable rights of life, liberty, and the pursuit of happiness. . . and their power to create. The few began to refuse to wallow in a valley of despair (of their own creation) but, instead, to affirm that they still had a dream and to declare that Now is the time to make real the promise of Creation! Their righteous desires, selfless commitment, and the content of their character served as magnets for their cause. With their hope they were able to hew out of the mountain of despair a stone of hope. With their faith they were able to transform the jangling discords of divisiveness into a beauti-ful symphony of unity.

They inspired many others. One day the creative soil was rich enough for the root of their dream-vision to take hold . . . soon the roots spread ram-pantly and sprouted in many unsuspected hearts and places. The cry for unity could no longer be squelched; soon it could be heard from every village and every hamlet, every state and every city in every country. The time was at hand when all of God's creation, including the human mini-creators and all of their un-evolved mini-creations would join hands and hearts in true acceptance, respect, and peace, and all would live blissfully ever after in a harmonious world of countless beauty-generating differences!

All was well in the creation of the One and in the creation of Its human mini-creators as well!

The beauty of the diversity in the global common-unity is celebrated in this section as these women share the natural power of their interwoven paths. We are shown how braiding—ideologically, spiritually, ethnically, culturally, and physically, as well—is in itself an inevitable act of oneness that lovingly gathers the uniquely different and divergent parts back into the One.

When I can see me in you and you in me,

I can accept more of who you are while accepting more of me.

When I can accept more of me, I can accept more of others,

and so the braiding goes until all of the loose pieces are woven into one... again

*Note: Italicized text is inspired by and/or paraphrased from Dr. Martin Luther King, Jr.'s "I Have a Dream" speech.

All Things Water: The Importance of Ritual to Women

Ivanla Vanzant

Iyanla Vanzant is an author, Spiritual Life Coach, ordained minister, and Yoruba priestess. Using her powerful speaking and writing abilities, Iyanla fulfills her mission to educate women, especially those of color, and to help them create a better life for themselves and for their communities. She does this by assisting them in discovering the kingdom of God within. As founder and director of Inner Visions Institute of Spiritual Development, Iyanla shares her knowledge of universal principle and laws, Eastern and Western spiritual and religious traditions and teachings, and unconditional love as a way to motivate others to create a better life, a better community, and a better world.

Ritual includes anything you do that supports you in moving from moment to moment. People have all kinds of rituals that take them through the day, that connect one activity to another, that they do in the same manner almost habitually. For instance, how you brush your teeth every morning involves ritual. Do you brush before you shower, after you shower, or in the shower? If you do it the same way every day, that's a ritual.

One of my daily rituals involves the smell of coffee in my house in the morning. Sometimes I don't even drink the coffee, but I've got to smell it. When I was a child growing up, my mom would get up before everybody else and, after she did whatever she did (I wasn't awake, so I wasn't aware of her morning rituals), she would go into the kitchen and make the coffee. So, I woke up for the first 20 years of my life smelling coffee in the morning.

That let me know that mom was home, that everything was cool, and that the day was off to the right start—all because I could smell that coffee. Now I get up in the morning and, after I do my personal care, I come downstairs and put the coffee on. Sometimes I forget about it and don't even drink it, but I gotta smell it in my house. That's a ritual.

So rituals for me constitute a prescribed way, a regimented way, and a specific way of doing something that has meaning for the doer. Some rituals are spiritual or religious in nature and some are not. Not every ritual has to be about a spiritual practice, but every ritual does bring some level of energy to your spirit. Praying before you go to bed, for example, would represent a ritual that brings energy to your spirit. Saying grace before a meal is a ritual, but your process in the morning of getting from your bed to the shower to the kitchen to wherever, or from the bed to the prayer table to the shower to the kitchen, also constitutes a ritual. That sequence of how you move through those events is a ritual, and some of it may not be spiritual.

I, personally, believe women should have ritual, because any consistent and specific way of doing a particular thing ultimately becomes a habit. When we have a habit that supports and nurtures our spirit, when a woman has a specific way of doing things that support and nurture her spirit, it makes her a better woman. That's just how it is. By "better woman" I mean a more grounded woman, a more authentic woman, a more peaceful, focused, loving, first-for-herself and then-for-others woman. Most women I know have specific rituals that support them in being available to and for others. We buy groceries on certain days. We cook for the children at certain times. We go all out to make sure we handle our responsibilities for family and friends. We often miss the fact that it is equally important for every woman to have rituals and practices that support us in being grounded within and present for ourselves.

"Love me first" is a great motto for women in this new age, and it is for this reason alone that women should have rituals. We should be proud of those rituals, too, because our grandmothers had rituals and our great, great grandmothers had rituals, and our great, great, great, great grandmothers had rituals. Especially for us African women, those rituals were stolen from us on the slave boat. Probably the day those ancestral women were snatched from the woods and then put on the boats, that morning most of them participated in some kind of ritual. Returning to our personal ritual puts us back in alignment with the spirit of those women who came before us.

Water and Morning Prayer Rituals

I follow the Yoruba culture and traditions, which originated in Africa—chiefly in Benin, Nigeria. As a Yoruba, one of the first rituals you learned involved drawing water from the river. If you were a priest or you had any spiritual places or sacred implements in your home, you would first draw water from the common place in the earth, bring it back, and place it in the ritual corner in your temple or on your altar. Whether it was the river or the well or a tub outside, you would go there and draw water from that place. Water still plays an important part in my rituals.

The second ritual you learn involves speaking to God before anyone else each day. This remains true in Africa today. Before washing your mouth, to cleanse what we would think of as the remnants of the night that we don't want anyone to see or to smell, you begin to speak to your Creator with your mouth full of your "essence." The Spirit sees these remnants as the core and essence of our being. So, before you go to wash your mouth you go to your ancestral shrine, your prayer table, your altar, or simply to the earth or to the sun, and you begin to pray. I frequently tell students, "Make sure you pray before you answer the phone in the morning. The first person you speak to should not be the phone company or your friend. Let the first person you speak to in the morning be God." That's ritual, and I think that that's a practice that can support us in maintaining and developing a closer intimate relationship with our Creator. It's a ritual I use in my own life daily.

Working with the Divine Feminine, or Mother, Energy

I find other rituals and ritual elements sustaining as well. For example, I enjoy the feminine energy. I won't say "the goddess"; I'll say "the feminine energy of God" or "the feminine essence of God," and whether you call that the goddess or not doesn't matter to me. I personally call it "the Mother energy."

I've been an ordained New Thought minister for 19 years. Additionally, I've been a priest for 26 years, and I've been a functioning Yoruba practitioner since I was 13 years old and received my first set of Elekes, the sacred beaded necklaces that represent the different manifestations of Spirit or God in the Yoruba spiritual system. I received those more than 40-something years ago. I don't use the word goddess, because right now "goddess" has become a fad. I believe that She is real, and I believe we can tap into the essence of that energy, but we have to do it from a place of sincerity, honor, reverence, and respect, not because we think it's a thing to do over the weekend or it's going to get us a better boyfriend. So for me, to call it Mother energy or the Divine Feminine works just fine. My work as a Yoruba priest involves a close connection with the Mother energy, I have come to rely on and find sustenance in my relationship with the Divine Feminine.

The practices or rituals I use that reflect my attitude and relationship with the feminine energy of God include any and all things water. For instance, I turn bathing into a sacred practice, a sacred ritual. I do this with my incense and candles and what I put in the bath and what I do before the bath and what I do after the bath. If I just want to clean up my energy, my essence, I throw some Epsom salt and fresh-squeezed lemon juice in the bathtub. Or, I put some Ylang Ylang and fresh lemongrass in my bath water if I want to rest/relax, or I put some powdered milk in the bath. I also use some lavender and geranium oil for this purpose. I use MSM (Methylsulfonylmethane) to drain and detoxify, or if I want some energy. Bathing is a ritual; I wrote a lot about that in my book, *Yesterday I Cried*. For me, bathing is the ritual, and the tub is a sanctuary.

When in my office I also work with the feminine energy, the Divine Mother. In my office I have a small table in the corner where She sits. Actually, I have different images of the Mother. Additionally, I have water, candles, and certain music I use for Her—when I want to connect with Her or call on Her energy. Before I sit down to write, I go to Her. I will light Her candles and talk to Her about what we're doing for the day and welcome Her energy into my work space.

It's rare that I don't use this ritual when I work, but I notice a difference when I don't. It's harder for me to pull together the many thoughts that run through my mind. I've performed this ritual so often now that I can do it in my head. In other words, I don't have to actually go to the altar any more and light the candle; She's right next to my desk as soon as I begin thinking about wanting to perform the ritual. It's become a habit. So, if I'm writing something or creating something, I just look over and say, "Okay, mama, what are we going to do today?" Even if the candles aren't lit, because maybe that day I don't have any in my reach, it doesn't mean that I'm going to just ignore the process. I still perform the ritual in some manner, and no matter how I do so, the ritual accomplishes its purpose.

The external ritual allows us to focus the physical mind and eyes. Ultimately, you don't need the external ritual. To focus your physical senses, you only need to connect with God, Jesus, Orisa, whatever your name for Spirit, within yourself. People will say, "The Lord spoke to me." He didn't call them up on the telephone! He spoke in their spirits, to their spirits. They say, "I heard the Spirit say…" That experience comes from the habit of ritual.

The Importance of Blessing Your Head

For those searching spiritually, sincerely desiring to strengthen their rela-tionships with God, I recommend treating God like your lover. In the same way that you would get ready for a date—the same way you would prepare your home, your house, your bed, your self—you have to prepare yourself for your relationship with God. You really have to prepare yourself and be prepared in relationship, and in a good relationship you communicate with each other daily—you have to do this consistently.

I prepare myself for my relationship with God by blessing my head. I have blessed my head every morning for years and years and years. I use a ritual—a ceremony, if you will. I have water, and I put certain oils in my water. I leave that vessel of water on my altar with the Divine Feminine energies, and I change it once a week so I know that it's fresh. Sometimes, if I go to the river, I'll put river water in the vessel. (I don't put salt water on my head.) Sometimes I'll pray over a vessel of water, and I'll create my own Holy Water. I then bless, or anoint, my head with this water.

I do this ritual because I believe that without my head I can't do anything. Yoruba cosmology tells us that no man or woman can be blessed without the acceptance of his or her own Ori, the spiritual essence of the head, because if your head can't receive the blessings, the compliments, the information, the insight, then you won't be able to activate these things in your own life. Therefore, I always bless my head.

Years ago, when my book, *Acts of Faith*, blew up and became an entity unto itself, it didn't even have an author; it was just known as "the purple book." However, I was traveling a lot to promote the book, and I didn't take my ritual implements with me on my trips. I didn't think I could just create ceremony on my own. That's why I frequently say, "Thinking is hazardous to your healing." A distinction exists between thinking and knowing. We need to know; we don't need to think. While I was traveling here and there, I would go weeks at a time without blessing my head.

During that very critical point in my life when I wasn't blessing my head and I wasn't doing my daily prayer, stillness, and breathwork rituals and practices, I was approached by a major television studio to come and do my own television show. At the time I was doing a lot of work with Oprah Winfrey, and I wasn't clear about what I should be doing. I thought I could just jump right back into my ritual and get an answer. I thought I could begin my ritual practice of blessing my head, as well as the other practices, and find out from Spirit, "Do I stay, or do I go? Do I go, or do I stay?" I had a sense of knowing I should stay, but I wasn't clear about why these people were literally hounding me to do a show of my own.

So, *I* decided. Since I had not gotten a decision or information from a spiritual place, I would do seven days of prayer, and at the end of the seven days I would have an answer. I completed the seven days of prayer and, at the end, indeed, *I* had an answer. In other words, God or Spirit had not provided me with an answer that I understood, so I had to make up one on my own.

Many of us think we can get full-time rewards for part-time devotion. We don't do anything spiritual. We don't honor our connection and our relationship to God, and then when we want or need something, we go running back to God. We do three jumps on one foot, rub a crystal on our head, say a prayer, make an affirmation, and *voila*! We think we are connected. We always are connected to God, but are we in alignment with God?

You can liken this spiritual relationship to a relationship on the physical plane. If I had been in a relationship with a person and had disappeared for months, could I just go back to that person and ask for something without a conversation about where I was and what had happened? Heck, no! Why do we think we can do that to God? Why do we think we can do that to our guardian angels or to our spiritual guides? Not that they need that continuous relationship; they don't need it. We need it! We need the purging, the cleansing, the awareness, the acknowledgement, the forgiveness of ourselves in those weak moments that comes from that constant conversation and awareness of the connection to God and the spiritual realms.

Yes, I did the seven days of prayer, I did hear what I was supposed to do and I did what I heard. Subsequently, that decision led me into a place that offered me a powerful learning experience. I did my own television show with people who didn't share my vision, with people who didn't understand my work, and with people who didn't honor who I was—all in all a very different experience than the one I had had with Oprah, who did share my vision, understood my work, and honored me.

When that experience ended, I was able to look back and see how I had been out of spiritual alignment when I made that decision. Rituals and spiritual grounding keep us in alignment with spiritual principals, spiritual energy, spiritual law, and what's best for us. Had I been blessing my head and doing my daily ritual prior to making that decision, I don't know if things would have been any different, or even if I would have made a different decision. I do know I probably would have felt a lot better about the decision and its outcome, though.

It's important to mention and to recognize that the ritual is not the thing itself. The ritual, or the ceremonial way of doing things, first, purifies the consciousness and the energy. This brings us to a place of grounding, of center, and, again, of alignment. It's important for us to be grounded, centered, and aligned. It's important for us, it's not a requirement for God. Ritual creates for us a deeper focus.

So, if you're going to light the candle, burn the incense, play the music, do the breathwork, and do the prayer, that's seven minutes in which you've been focused (or 10 or 20 minutes, depending on what you're doing) on a particular intention. Whereas, if you just flop down on the bed and start saying, "Gimme, gimme," you don't necessarily have the grounding, the connection, the alignment, and the focus internally to achieve what you desire. Ritual, or ceremony, creates a peeling away of the outside layer so you can get to the core, the center of your being, for that is where your spiritual truth lies.

Principles Necessary for Practicing Ritual

To practice ritual, you need to stand in your authentic self. To do so, you need to put several principles to use in your life. The first of these is discipline. Discipline comes from doing. You can't pray yourself into a state of discipline. You've got to do the ritual, you've got to practice the ceremony over and over and over so it becomes an integral part of who you are. We need to embrace the principle of discipline.

To do this, you need what I call "inner and outer cooperation." As it relates to ritual, inner cooperation means that you want your mind cooperating with your heart; you want your heart cooperating with your mouth; you want your mouth cooperating with your body. You want a perfect alignment between those elements, so when you step into a sacred rite, when you step into a practice, when you step into the experience of a ritual, you have "inner cooperation." What's happening on the inside will impact and affect what's happening on the outside. If you're in alignment and you have inner cooperation, it's more likely that you can create that and experience that on the outside. Thus, cooperation constitutes a principle.

Authenticity also constitutes a principle you need. Very often we function from behind our masks—our people-pleasing, gotta-be-nice, don't-upset-people, don't-rock-the-boat masks. However, when you practice authenticity, and when you function from your authentic self, you do what is true, right, honorable, and loving in the moment—moment to moment to moment. You may go into an experience or situation and be perfectly aligned with it, perfectly onboard with it, and then you hear, see, or experience something in the process that makes you aware that something's off. The authentic expression in such a moment would be, "Wait a minute. Let's hold on. Something's wrong. Let us take a moment to get clear." That's an authentic expression. A masked expression would be, "Something doesn't feel right, but if I say something they're going to get mad at me, because I'm going to upset people." Or, "I can't say that!"

Truth also constitutes a necessary principle. When you express the truth of your authentic self, and you have inner cooperation, and at the same time you attempt to create outer cooperation, you are guided to tell the truth—moment by moment by moment—as you know it, as you feel it, as you experience it. Now, your truth may differ from other peoples' truth, but you at least stand in your truth and express your truth from a deeply grounded and authentic place within your being. Then, you strive toward cooperation. That said, sometimes you have to excuse yourself, because you can't be cooperative. Something in you may point to a dishonor, disrespect, or falsehood going on, and for you to be authentic and truthful and honorable, you can't *not* speak up. You must say something.

Discipline, authenticity, and truth all constitute principles we can practice. Indeed, we have to learn how to practice them all of the time, every day—ritualistically!

It is important for women to take the time and to give themselves the opportunity to become clear about and to embrace, acknowledge, and accept what works for them in their everyday living and in the rituals they adopt. We have become so programmed and committed to doing what's expected of us. For this reason, we sometimes go against our very own essence, nature, or spirit, to our own detriment, in an attempt not to upset anyone. It's imperative that we don't do this when taking on ritual and ceremony in our lives, or that we don't drop rituals and ceremonies from our lives in an effort to maintain status quo or to please others.

Living in the Aquarian Age

We live in a time when I think it is absolutely critical to get clear about what works for each of us, even if it means going against the status quo. The Aquarian Age is an age of oneness, an age of coming together, an age of humanitarianism, an age of the higher mind, an age of the Spirit, if you will. We live in a millennium experiencing the fallout of male dominance, competition, and aggression. This looks like a war, rising gas prices, corporate takeovers, and higher prices for everything.

In a metaphorical sense, the "king" was ruling, and left the kingdom a mess. Now, in this new age, this Aquarian Age, the "queen" takes on a bigger role. What does the queen do? The queen supports the king in maintaining the well-being of the kingdom. We haven't had a queen doing that in the recent past. The queen rules with fairness, truth, compassion, mercy, elegance, and honor. The queen makes just and balanced decisions even when those decisions are not popular.

In this time in which we find ourselves, we need that queen, that feminine, mothering energy. Too many mothers, by which I mean women, currently are experiencing the stress of the king's domination—not dominion but domination, the distinction being the hard-handed rule that comes with domination. Too many queens, too many mothers, are losing sons, losing breasts, losing lives to the stress, pain, and suffering caused by the king's domination. That masculine domination includes the masculine competition and aggression. Therefore, the essence and the energy we find ourselves existing in right now require the presence and the spirit of the feminine. It's a time for women to stand up, a time for women to be heard, a time for women to find their voices and use their voices. It's a time for women to express what's going on for them and in them.

I believe life goes from the micro (like the sperm and the egg) to the macro (the newborn child). That, to me, represents the process of life. You don't go from the macro (the outside) to the micro (inside); we go from the micro to the macro. If I look around the world, I look at the micro. When I do so, I see an overwhelming proliferation of single moms, which tells me that women are being both dishonored and dishonorable. I look at the growing number of AIDS and HIV patients, specifically among women of color, in the U.S. and in South Africa. It's a plague among women. I look at the rising number of breast cancer cases among women of all races, ages, colors, and nations. And I look at domestic violence and the number of women living in poverty. That's the micro.

Woman, the feminine, represents the heart. If we look at the heart, or the feminine, in a micro experience, we've got to make the connection with how that shows up in a macro experience as well. In other words, how is that showing up in the bigger world? What I see is that the heart (woman) is dying, besieged by a plague of disease. I see the heart left untended, unsupported, and unprotected. We are not providing for the heart. What is happening at the micro level is happening at the macro level. There we see that same consciousness, that same disregard, that same disrespect, that same dishonor of women.

To change that, we must support the queen. We must bring back the mother, the feminine energy. We must embody that within ourselves and through our rituals. We must take on the energy of the Aquarian Age.

As women, we have to strengthen ourselves through ritual, ceremony, gathering together, and connection with each other, as well as through our breath, our prayers, our speech. We must do this so we can begin to stand up for ourselves, within ourselves, in our authenticity, in protest of some of the things that are affecting us and humankind—life itself—at the micro level.

Drumming in the Day: A Personal Morning Ritual

Christine Stevens, MSW, MT-BC

Christine Stevens is a music therapist, the founder of UpBeat Drum Circles, and the author of *The Healing Drum Kit* and *The Art and Heart of Drum Circles*.

For more information, visit www.ubdrumcircles.com or email her at info@ubdrumcircles.com.

> *There is a temple in heaven that is only opened through song.*
>
> —*Talmud*

Some say the beginning is half of the whole. For this reason, how we start each day sets the tone for its unfolding song. Just as musicians tune up their instruments before a performance, the morning ritual provides a tuneup for the instrument of your soul. No wonder indigenous tribal cultures have morning rituals that often include musical expression.

Music is a gift as well as a creative, wordless expression of pure intention and heart, a Divine language of communication with Spirit and the birthright of each and every person alive. Just think of the first Muslim prayer sung to Allah before sunrise, the Buddhist monks chanting and lighting incense to greet the new day. Imagine the Sunday morning songs–hymns of the congregation gathering at a Christian church or of the Lakota Sioux chief drumming to the East to greet the day as the sun rises.

Greeting the Day in Music

Having experienced many different cultural morning rituals around the world, both collective and individual, I have always admired the fact that these rituals occurred without audience. A morning ritual is performed for the heart of Spirit—not for anyone else. I longed for this type of practice in my life. So, I asked Spirit in prayer to show me how to start my day.

The response came about five years ago during a trip halfway around the world to Korea. There I was guided to a morning ritual I've practiced ever since. I discovered that you do not need to know how to play an instrument to practice greeting the day in music. A musical morning ritual is about intention, not about musical ability. Just as a mother sings a lullaby to her baby, a morning ritual has nothing to do with performance. The mother does not need any musical training, because her song comes from the heart.

You, too, can bring the vibration of sound and music into your morning ritual. The story of my unfolding personalized morning ritual may help you see how.

A Tree That Drums

I was visiting my favorite place, the Chogesa Temple in Seoul, South Korea in Insadong, an old Buddhist neighborhood. Despite the beautiful interior of the temple, a tall tree in the courtyard outside the temple caught my attention. I carried a small flute in my backpack, so I decided to sit by the tree and play the flute. When I finished my improvised song, I felt a powerful message come through me. The tree symbolized the two main instruments I played—drum and flute. Both come from a tree. Both are made with the wood of a tree, but from opposite "poles" on the tree. The drum is made from the base of the tree; it is connected to the roots growing into the earth.

The flute comes from the branches that reach upward to the sky. I realized that the tree provided the bridge between heaven and earth, flute and drum, which are commonly paired together in sacred music around the world.

Later that year, at a Lakota sweat lodge much nearer to my home in California, I came to the next milestone on my journey to discovering how to greet the day in music. During this group purification ceremony, I received intuitive guidance for my personal morning ritual. I was guided to start by playing the drum in the morning to anchor and ground myself like the roots and base of the tree. Next, I could play my flute to reach upwards to the sky, heavens, and the uplifted spirit, just as the branches do on the tree.

I started the next morning to start the day facing East and playing each instrument, feeling the connection to the lower and higher parts of the tree. I found grounding with my roots into the earth through drumming, and the joy of the heavens uplifting me with my flute. So this musical, spiritual stretching became my morning yoga prayer that roots me and uplifts me simultaneously—a good metaphor for spiritual growth and a beautiful integration of the sonic polarity of flute (Heaven) and drum (Earth).

Here is a description of my morning ritual, inspired by the connection to Spirit created through the bridge of musical expression:

Drumming in the Day: 10–15 minutes

Materials: Sage, drum, and flute

Time: First thing in the morning (before speaking)

1. **Smudge**—First, smudge yourself with sage or your favorite morning scent. (Native Americans burn dried sage and use the smoke to clear the energy.) I use California white sage in an abalone shell and allow the smoke to wrap around me. You can also use sound to smudge yourself. Shaking a rattle will clear the energy.

2. **Drum**—The drum beat expresses the heart. Allow yourself to drum a heartbeat rhythm or a rhythm for gratitude. Imagine the trunk of a tree, your roots anchored in integrity, spirit, love, and creativity. If the mood strikes, you may feel like singing. I often sing the *Cherokee Morning Song* (by Walela), *Thank You for This Day* (by Karen Drucker), or a chant I wrote:

    > *I greet the day with music*
    >
    > *I greet the day with song*
    >
    > *I greet the day with music*
    >
    > *Won't you play along?*

    (Listen to a free download of this song at www.ubdrumcircles.com.)

3. **Flute**—Next, play the flute or use your voice and sing a wordless melody. Bringing in the breath, you can play a favorite melody or simply improvise. While playing or singing, envision reaching upward, achieving a higher vibration, touching the loftiest being possible through the branches of the tree. If you have special prayers or individuals for whom you want to pray, imagine placing those prayers—spoken or unspoken—into the flute before you play. Sing your prayers. Allow your breath to release the melodic sound wave that carries these prayers to Spirit. Allow the melody to come to a close. Release it, and let it go.

4. **Silence**—Take a moment to enjoy the creativity, energy, spirit, and vibration of this morning music. Sit still and honor the silence, the polarity of sound. Rest. Make space. Listen. When you're ready, conclude the ceremony.

Whether you choose to use this morning ritual or design your own, ask yourself a few questions to guide you on your way as you create a spiritual practice to start your day:

1. How do you start your day?

2. How much time can you devote to a morning ritual?

3. Can you attend a community ritual? (A community ritual puts you in a container for spiritual self-discovery.)

4. What gifts do you have to offer Spirit in the morning?

5. What is your intuition telling you? (Whether it's a direct statement, an overheard comment, a song playing when you walk into a store, or the whispers of the trees, listen.)

6. What do you need to release to allow this morning practice to emerge?

7. How can this practice continue to grow and unfold with greater creativity and uniqueness?

The following additional rituals might inspire your morning ritual, creating spiritual seeds for any day or any ceremony.

A Basket of Offerings—*Bali morning ritual*

In Bali, shamanic and earth-based practices have been woven together with Hindu Gods and Goddesses to create a fascinating culture of spiritual practice. Each day you see baskets made from strong leaves filled with rice and flower petals on the streets, at altars, near statues, and in homes. These offerings contain gifts to God that are put outside every morning just after breakfast, as well as at other times throughout the day, during rituals that include incense, water, flower petals, and a flower dipped in water three times. A shaman sings a mantra before an altar while offering the baskets. In this morning practice, the Balinese people begin by focusing on what you give more than what you get. You could easily create a basket, or buy one, and put rice and flower petals inside it (or something else) and make this offering part of your morning ritual, also stressing giving as well as getting.

Sonic smudge for a women's group

Rituals often begin with smudging, but you can incorporate music into the important cleansing start to a ceremony. For the past six years, I have met monthly with a group of women in the Los Angeles area for musical spiritual practice. Our group ritual always begins with what we call a *sonic smudge*. This provides a fantastic way to begin if you have people who are scent-sensitive and bothered by sage or cedar or incense; plus, a musical approach heightens our sensitivity to the vibrations of the person experiencing the smudge.

Instead of using sage or incense, for a sonic smudge we use soft rattles and bells as we gather around each person at the "gateway" of the ritual room. We also sing the person's name and make the sounds to cleanse her. It is an organic process that helps us tune in to each other as we enter the circle. We sing:

Enter the circle,

Enter the circle,

Enter the circle,

Leave everything behind you

Once we are in the circle and everyone has taken a seat on a pillow on the floor, we spend the first five minutes in silence. This echoes the importance of balance and the polarity of sound and silence. During this time, each woman can focus on her intention for that evening. We each share our intention and then manifest it in sound with the group's support by jamming with percussion instruments. Anyone could implement a similar ritual in her morning practice to replace traditional smudging and intention-setting.

Thank you to my teachers and tribes: Manny Council Pipe Sandoval, Kathy Hull, Connor Sauer, Peter Zinkala Oyate Catches, Jonathan Ellerby, Sonic Beauties, Long Dance, and Jean O'Sullivan.

A Path to Presence Outside of Time: Labyrinth as Ritual

Lauren Artress

Lauren Artress founded Verditas, the World-Wide Labyrinth Project, in 1996 and gave the organization the mission: to "pepper the planet with labyrinths." Artress states, "The labyrinth meets you where you are, gives you what you need, and connects you to an invisible web of relationships that open you to be of service to others and to the planet." Her work includes speaking on the contemporary spiritual issues with which we are confronted in our daily lives. An Episcopal priest, spiritual director, and licensed marriage and family therapist in California, she offers spiritual direction, life coaching, and brief psychotherapy in her home office. For more information, visit www.laurenartress.com.

Ritual is food to the spiritually hungry. Ritual has the potential to heal and warm; to glorify God and reify human devotion; to make objects and places sacred; to create community; to permeate the membrane between religion and peoplehood and bond one person in to the whole. Ritual physicalizes the spiritual and spiritualizes the physical.

—Letty Pogrebin, from her play, *Golda*

Imagine this: You are in San Francisco's Grace Cathedral at night during a labyrinth walk. If you have never been there, let your imagination borrow images from any experiences you have had in a gothic cathedral. See the stone floor, the vaulted arches, the stained-glass windows now darkened by night, and the long center aisle that leads down to the altar. Add a multitude of candles casting a soft, flickering light throughout while people gracefully, unselfconsciously walk the circuitous path of the inlaid stone labyrinth. (If you do not have any pictures in your mind as to what a labyrinth looks like, imagine a large circle, flat on the floor, with one path leading in a circuitous route from the outer edge into its eight-foot center.)

This particular Saturday night constitutes the highlight of a pilgrimage weekend. Forty people or so are walking the tapestry labyrinth, back in the time before we installed the final inlaid stone labyrinth. One of my favorite musical groups—Musica Divina—is accompanying the participants. Amid the soft glow of candlelight, some are walking without shoes, some prayerfully, some quietly weeping, some joyfully dancing. All are responding to the ancient primordial call to follow the labyrinth's spiral path to its center.

The theme for this weekend is "A Moment in Time: Meeting and Greetings on The Spiritual Path." To create a special "moment in time," we drop hundreds of fresh rose petals 92 feet down from the catwalk above onto the labyrinth below. They arrive like snowflakes, lightly twirling in the light. The participants see and feel them gently dropping on their noses, heads, hands, shoulders, cheeks, and the space in front of them. Some stop and look up to behold their beauty; others reach out to catch them before they touch the ground.

The music—because it follows the walkers, and does not lead them—dies out in a few moments of confusion. Then the string bass, piano, and voices all begin a twirling sound, mirroring the rose petals' tender dance downward. After a few moments, the walkers quietly and collectively chuckle as they resume their walk.

A woman stands frozen by the labyrinth, a single rose petal in her hand and tears streaming down her face. I notice her and decide not to intrude on her experience. Eventually her tears subside, and she sits down on the front steps of the cathedral with her one rose petal held preciously in her hand. Later, she says to me, "One year ago today I held another rose petal in my hand. It was from my husband's funeral wreath. What a year this has been, and now, receiving this rose petal, my year of grief has come to a close."

Hildegard of Bingen, the 12th-century Rhineland mystic, once said that when the inner and outer worlds are "wedded," then a meaningful moment occurs. When a bridge, a synapse, is created that melds the inner world with the happenings in the outer world—spontaneously, instantaneously—meaning becomes alive. The purpose of ritual is to create moments in time when the boundaries between the inner and outer experiences fuse and new insights—new revelations—speak to us in literal and symbolic, as well as metaphoric, ways. We hunger for these experiences, though our hunger often goes unnamed. Our inner spiritual compasses guide us to find the delight, the surprise, and the nourishment that these profound experiences offer.

However, ritual is not a friendly word. The first definition offered by most dictionaries originates from the 1950s psychoanalytic perspective and calls ritual "a series of meaningless acts." Other definitions refer to ritual as compulsive behaviors, such as hand washing, and to the tragedy of "ritual" abuse. Recently, however, the definition has broadened beyond these negative associations. Slowly, we are beginning to see that we need ritualistic ways of gathering together to stir the collective forces of bonding, community healing, and the power of presence in the moment.

Our liturgically based churches always use ritual in their morning worship. This often is associated—certainly among our young—with boredom and meaningless actions and words. Why? The spiritual practices employed by churches don't meld together the inner and the outer worlds to spark a raw experience of the Holy.

Liturgically oriented worship offers us what I call "Old Paradigm" ritual. The Old Paradigm is based upon what Diane Eck refers to as the "Old Smooth Stone" approach. These services offer a firmly set and trustworthy series of proceedings. The first part of the service is to teach the congregation historical and spiritual principles. There is a "collect," or call to prayer, that sets the intention for the service. Then, two or more scripture lessons are read with a recited or sung psalm and hymn in between. All this builds up to proclaiming the gospel, which is followed by the sermon and prayers of the people. With the completion of the education part, the second part, the communion, often called the Holy Eucharist, begins. The entire service ends with a dismissal, empowering people to go back out into the world "in peace to love and serve the Lord." This formula represents the Old Smooth Stone, well worn and often used. As long as everything happens as expected, the worshippers' minds can quiet, and they can find peace and comfort in the familiar cadence of the service. In this state of quiet mind, the ritual has the power to heal and glorify God as well as nurture spiritual insight, hold space for prayer, and "wed" the inner world to the outer world of experience.

Though the hoped-for outcome often is the same, New Paradigm ritual approaches the goal in the opposite manner. This ritual brings people into the present moment. You may be standing in a circle holding hands when an ambulance goes by. Instead of ignoring it as would be done in the Old Paradigm ritual, the leader folds it into the moment. For example, she may invite a few moments of silence directed in support of the person the ambulance is attempting to rescue. New Paradigm ritual helps everyone share the same moment in each and everyone's own unique way. Instead of moving through a series of established progressions, as in a liturgical service, it invites the people into the precious moment that the Divine has placed before them. New Paradigm ritual is more spontaneous, more reliant upon a leader, and often effective in smaller groups—up to 50 people.

The labyrinth lends itself nicely to New Paradigm ceremonies and rituals. By walking this highly structured, circuitous single path from the outside all the way to the center and out again, the mind quiets through the rhythm of the body's movements, which allows us the choice to open our hearts. Just as in the ritual at Grace Cathedral, a group of people can come together with heartfelt intentions to walk the labyrinth. One by one, walkers can meditate, pray, strengthen a commitment, and resolve a conflict within the embrace of a community. The fact that most meditative walking rituals are done in silence reinforces the power of the ritual.

Though there are many contemporary designs, my heart lies with the archetypal 11-circuit medieval labyrinth from Chartres Cathedral in France, which was inlaid in the stone floor in 1201. The design offers itself as a walking meditation, a path of prayer, a crucible for change, a tool of manifestation, a mirror of the soul, and a watering hole for the spirit. This pattern pre-dates the Cartesian split between the mind, body, and spirit and is encoded with meaning that we no longer comprehend. It is a map to a non-dualist form of consciousness that we need to recover. Truly, the labyrinth—especially the long-perfected archetypal design—represents a treasure to humankind just now being rediscovered. It orders chaos, quiets the mind, ignites the metaphoric mind, sharpens intuition, and gathers the collective wisdom of those walking it together.

Walking the labyrinth has become a ritual way of deepening and strengthening prayer and meditation practices. Embedded within the Chartres-style labyrinth lies the 14th-century mystic Teresa of Avila's Three-Fold Mystical Path—purgation, illumination, and union. More recently, we talk about the Three R's: releasing, receiving, and returning. As we walk into the labyrinth, we release our everyday cares to quiet the mind. It is an experience of emptying. When we reach the center, having emptied, we can receive whatever is there to receive: insight, a sense of peace, or the strength to carry out an intention. As we come fully into our own presence, we can sense the Presence of the Holy much more fully. When we are complete in the center, we follow the same path back out of the labyrinth. This is a time of reflection, resolution, and recommitment to live our lives to their full potential.

Using this simple three-fold pattern, meaningful rituals unfold. At Union Theological Seminary, I introduced the use of a labyrinth on Ash Wednesday. In the Christian tradition, on that day ashes are placed on a person's forehead as a sign of the fragility of life. As we do so, we say, "From dust thou art and to dust thou shall return." I set a kneeler in the center of the labyrinth, and each person who comes for ashes begins to reflectively, prayerfully walk the winding path to the center in preparation for receiving the ashes. Afterwards, they walk back out as another person comes in. In secular settings, this profound, yet simple ritual can be used in dedication ceremonies with new parents, or a care group initiating a care circle for a sick friend. In a hospice setting, where someone is facing the end of life, I would use the words, "You (person's name) are made from stardust and to stardust you shall return."

The labyrinth serves as a profound ritual tool for grief, both through meditative walking and in ceremony. Under ordinary circumstances, people who walk the labyrinth have a different experience each time they do so. Even if you return to the labyrinth a minute after your first walk, your inner terrain has changed because you have moved through thoughts and feelings that are now in the past. Grief—especially if it is fresh and close to the surface—can continue throughout two or even three walks, until the psyche is relieved of the pain and the well of tears runs dry for a time. The action of walking stirs the pockets of tears we hold back or cannot touch due to the demands of our ordinary days.

Bereavement groups frequently use the labyrinth ceremonially to move through the prolonged work of grieving. One group met and each member brought a photograph of his or her lost loved one. Each placed the photo somewhere on the labyrinth, and as the group walked together, they saw the faces and the warm, funny, precious moments of the loved ones others were grieving. They each knew they would soon come upon their own lost loved one as well. Another bereavement group wrote letters to the person each was grieving. Once all the members had reached the center, they sat and read them aloud to one another.

The labyrinth offers a profound ritual space. It lends itself to so many uses, because its outer edge becomes a strong boundary—a safe container for what is taking place within. It becomes a *temenos*, a Greek term for "sacred space." Even those who choose not to walk it often are profoundly moved by witnessing others using it.

The labyrinth can even serve as a theater in the round. Recently, I taught an advanced training for labyrinth facilitators. The participants have been teaching others about the labyrinth and how to use it for over two years and are well along the path of developing artful presentation skills. On our last evening together, we dedicated the labyrinth as the centerpiece for storytelling. Each person had to share a teaching story used in his or her work. The group members sat around the outer edge of the labyrinth and, when ready, each walked to the center of the labyrinth and shook a loud, sharp-sounding rattle to announce the beginning of the story. Then, when telling the story, the storyteller walked, not in any way following the path, around the labyrinth. At the end, each shook the rattle again to cut through the final moment and to make space energetically clear for the next story to be told.

Ritual is indeed food for the spiritually hungry. The labyrinth is a profound ritual and ceremonial tool. It opens the path to the Presence—God—outside of time. Amid the noise, chaos, and deep anxieties we experience while living on this fragile Earthly home, we need ways to call us back to ourselves, to the sacred, and to one another in community. Get thee to a labyrinth! I hope to meet you there.

The Universal Way: Incorporating More than One Tradition into Your Spiritual Life

Estella Yeung

Estella Yeung uses her healing gifts as a body worker trained in numerous modalities, including acupressure, hypnotherapy, and cranio-sacral therapy. She was born and raised in Hong Kong. Yeung's extensive travels and studies have given her diverse cultural and spiritual experiences. She currently lives in Minnesota and is the creator of a line of naturopathic body products.

I had an "eclectic" religious upbringing, which surely shaped my beliefs and openness to other religions. At an early age, I was exposed to different ways of worship and religious traditions, and later in life I chose to follow a spiritual path that spoke to my heart rather than to simply continue on in the spiritual or religious footsteps of my family members.

Both my maternal grandparents were born and raised in South America. Although my maternal grandmother looked Eurasian, she never revealed the truth of her ancestry. They were raised as Catholics. My siblings, cousins, and I all were baptized and raised in and attended Catholic schools. On the other side of the family, my father's parents were born and raised in Hong Kong. My grandpa was Taoist, and we followed just a few Taoist ways when visiting them. I was raised as Chinese with some Western influence.

While growing up in Hong Kong, some of my closest friends originally were from India. By the age of 12, I had been exposed to Buddhism and Hinduism and raised predominantly Catholic.

Diverse Experiences

Everything I have done and experienced in my life makes me who I am today. This includes my upbringing in Hong Kong and the process of Sunday school, confirmation, and confession. Learning languages, working in and exploring Europe for nine years, living in the Bay Area of California for 11 years, and rediscovering the Chinese way of health and healing have all added to my present approach to holistic healing and health. Through learning about acupressure, herbs, Tui Na, Reiki, cranio-sacral therapy, and hypnotherapy, I have broadened my practice exponentially.

For the last 15 years I have been blessed to have met people who have influenced my whole way of praying and living. Through their humor and belief in spiritual practice unbound by modality or dogma, I have learned that my spirituality is personal and cannot be dictated by any one correct form. At this point in my journey, I feel protected, guided, and as if I am not alone.

I feel fortunate to have been able to follow the Dakota ways of life to strengthen my connection to Spirit. I have worshipped with a Dakota community since 1993 and have become closer to this community since I moved to Minnesota in 1995. I am extremely grateful that they have allowed me, a non-Indian, to join their community and I am amazed at how they have welcomed me with open hearts.

This spiritual path spoke to me. Despite all I had been taught by my own family and ancestors, I resonated with the ways of the Native Americans, with their rituals and prayers and way of life. I didn't give up my Chinese ways, but rather adopted Dakota ways as a means of adding to my spiritual practice. As for Catholicism's ways, in which I had been raised, I never felt fully connected to the message. I found it boring, repetitive, and contradictory. It made me feel guilty and ashamed. It made sense to me to pray in the chapel, but I didn't understand the reason for mass. I continued with these practices until I found a path I wished to follow which made sense to me spiritually.

Prayer and Mindfulness

The Chinese way and the Dakota way both lie very close to my heart. I've never forgotten where I came from—Hong Kong. I'm constantly comparing and learning, and always feel a sense of gratitude for all who have touched and influenced my life, especially the Chinese and Dakota cultures. The more I learn, the more I realize and sense the similarities of the two. The spiritual ways of these two cultures are parallel in many ways, such as the burning of incense and smudging, offering food to the ancestors and preparing a spirit dish, and the teachings of the Taoist symbols and the Medicine Wheel. I am passionate about integrating and using both cultures in my everyday life.

I do this by implementing rituals from both cultures into my daily life. For example, in the morning, I generally need to have some quiet time alone. This involves taking a few mindful breaths and stretching. In times of hardship or stress, I say a prayer and place a tobacco offering on the earth, really focusing and praying hard on the issue at hand. This has been especially helpful when friends have asked for prayer.

There are times when I sing a few songs while I am walking, swimming, or even driving, as a form of prayer or meditation. I quite enjoy finding creative ways to pray, meditate, and give thanks by trying to listen and to feel whether it is the right time and place to do so. How do I know when the time is right for prayer or ritual and what I feel I should do? It's not easy to identify the clues. I just know in my heart that it is time. For instance, when I feel stressed or before I take a trip, I say a quick prayer. These are just simple everyday life things I do.

The Dakota way has taught me how to pray and really look at myself. Their tradition teaches you about praying from the heart, not from the head. As a child, I found it comforting to pray in a chapel because that's where I started my religious experience. I don't pray there anymore, but as a child attending Catholic school, chapel was available and praying there felt good. That continued during my time in Europe too. In times of need, I would just sit in the chapel.

I have very recently returned from a seven-day Buddhist silent retreat. There, while involved in a Chinese spiritual practice, the silence, meditation, and kindness gifted me with the reawakening of the realization that prayer has nothing to do with a right or wrong way of performing this ritual. Speaking to or with God has to do with prayers of sincerity, compassion, love, and kindness. Prayer is the universal language of the heart. Gifts and teachings await us if we can just slow down enough from our everyday life and listen. We can then be mindful and listen to our hearts in order to communicate in a 'heartistic' manner.

Prayer is about finding that peacefulness and mindfulness, whether we call it meditation or something else. It's about finding that quiet space. And we can do this anywhere—in nature while taking a walk or sitting by water, or while driving a car. During the retreat, we talked to the instructors about how we were feeling and the issues with which we were having trouble. They told us not to worry or get frustrated with ourselves if we couldn't focus and quiet our minds. They said, "Even if you can find 15 minutes of stillness within the 45 minutes of silent meditation practice, that's okay; just go there with an open heart." Other people shared the issues with which they were struggling and what worked for them. I listened and thought, "If people just share a little bit of how they reach their quiet place, that's all we need to help us get to our own place." By sharing our struggles and our solutions, we support each other, connecting on a deeper level.

Honoring the Ancestors

Whether we are aware of it or not, our ancestors are with us. One of my biggest lessons is to remember to give thanks for all the help I have received from my ancestors and friends. When I was younger, I just asked for things, but I never offered enough thanks for the gifts I received (physically, emotionally, or spiritually). Generally, I now put a dish of food out for the ancestors and friends before I eat. I then pray a little and maybe sing a song. I had seen and experienced this ritual as a child, and later in my life "offerings to the ones who came before us" became an important ritual in my own life. Remembering my ancestors, thanking them, and respecting them—these provide essential tools for staying connected to Spirit.

I think about my ancestors and feel grateful for their influence on my life often, especially in times of struggle. For example, I like to go to thrift stores. I always find really great stuff. One time, while searching for a Pendleton blanket and a piece of deer hide, I just walked into a store and there they were! I thought to myself, "One of my ancestors must be a bargain hunter, and that's why I find really good stuff." I was amazed at the ease with which I was directed to these items and I offered thanks to my ancestors for their gentle guidance. Another part of spirituality involves finding that peace within where I can communicate with my ancestors. I can talk to them, and sometimes I can hear them speak to me.

Our Collective Connectedness

The Native Americans talk about how we're all related. One of the elders shared that all cultures had sweat lodges at one time but stopped using this ritual and lost this tradition. I think about the saunas in Scandinavian countries, the Japanese and Roman steam baths, and the many other ways different people around the world cleanse and heal with water. In addition, many cultures use incense and smudge as a way to cleanse energy fields. I was at a conference this past spring and a Mexican lady used rosemary to smudge in order to cleanse people's personal energy fields. That same evening, someone used bay leaves as a cleanser and wiped people down with it.

I'm just fascinated by the similarities between the Chinese and Native American cultures. I enjoy seeing how each form of spirituality has a spark of the same belief, ritual, or practice, joining these differing spiritual traditions. And I relish in my amazement of each one speaking to my heart in my daily life, combining them in ways that guide me in finding the most meaningful or powerful personal path. Although I have chosen not to practice any of my Catholic education, I can't deny that it influenced me in becoming the spiritual being I am today. In the same way, my life in Hong Kong, my Chinese upbringing, and my exposure to Buddhism have all put me on the spiritual path I walk today. On a very deep level, the Dakota teachings have allowed me to incorporate all previous paths into my present spiritual journey. In this sense, I have created a unique, multifaceted, and multicultural spiritual experience that helps me to maintain balance in my daily life.

A Path of Passion: Peace Walking As Ritual

Audri Scott Williams

Audri Scott Williams, the vision keeper for the Trail of Dreams World Peace Walk, is a woman dedicated to upholding the ancient wisdom teachings of love, wisdom, compassion, and forgiveness. She holds a master's degree in liberal arts (indigenous science) from Naropa University and a bachelor of arts in criminology, with post-graduate studies at Harvard University, the University of Maryland, and American University. She has traveled as a representative of the Worldwide Indigenous Science Network and participated in programs in Benin and Kenya with Prometra International, an organization with a mission to preserve and promote traditional healing and medicine. Williams formerly served as dean of instruction at the School for Spiritual Awakening at the Institute for Divine Wisdom in Atlanta, Georgia, and for the past 16 years she has been the executive director of the Spirit of Truth Foundation in Washington, DC and Atlanta, Georgia. She walks with the authority of the modern-day shaman and bears the responsibility of bridging earth wisdom and the world. For more information, visit www.audriscottwilliams.com.

In 1999, walking became an integral part of my life. Little did I know at the time that I would spend a substantial part of the next 10 years walking for healing and social change. In fact, *walking* constitutes the most powerful and rewarding ritual I do on a daily basis.

At the invitation and with the support of friends in the metro Washington, DC area, where I lived at the time, I traveled to Wales in the summer of 1999 to witness the coming together of the World Peace Flame. Something magical surrounded this journey. First of all, my finances were tight, yet I was compelled to purchase a pair of walking boots—my first ever. When my friend Anne and I arrived in Wales, we settled into the guesthouse where we would sleep during the next few days. From the guesthouse we would take a nearly 45-minute walk every day to the Life Foundation, an ashram in Snowdonia. Each day was filled with excitement about the flames being flown in from five continents around the world. They would be joined into one in Snowdonia.

The evening following the ceremony when all of the flames were joined and became one World Peace Flame, Anne and I walked back to the guesthouse together by the light of a full moon—and I mean a *full* moon. Since little light pollution exists in that part of the country, when the sun goes down you cannot see your hand in front of your face, which made the light of the moon that night a giant, compelling spotlight in the night sky.

As we slowly walked, occasionally sharing our excitement about the event we had just witnessed, I began to see into my future. As though I were watching a movie, I saw a vision of myself returning to the U.S. and preparing to take an ancestral journey by walking from Pennsylvania to Georgia. I would call this journey the "Trail of Dreams" walk. I would take this walk for the purpose of healing the energy of our ancestors, brought to America during the Atlantic slave trade, and our Native American ancestors, tragically displaced from their lands during the Trail of Tears. I would call the walk the Trail of Dreams, because in my vision I was told that by taking this journey I would "return the dreaming to the children."

On April 21, 2000, a team of walkers—Karen Watson, Anne Devine, Ricardo Myrick, and Nefertiti Allen, with the support of Sylvester Williams and Elizabeth Neal—joined me to walk through the Appalachian

Mountains from Pennsylvania to Georgia. Now, 10 years after I purchased my first pair of hiking boots, I am still walking for healing and global transformation.

On October 21, 2005, the Trail of Dreams World Peace Walkers—Natalie Scott Williams, Karen Watson, Tony Shina, Chandelle Binns, Lessie Pat Randal, who were later joined by Rahfiya Carrion and Zenobia Mustafa— set out once again on another Trail of Dreams walkabout. This time the mission was to walk around the world for three and a half years to affect change leading to world peace. Engaging in a walk such as the Trail of Dreams World Peace Walk meant letting go of everything we thought the walk should be and letting the power of the Creator, the ancestors (our own and the ancestors of the lands we walked through), our angels, and our guides lead the way.

This required learning certain skills to stay on the path: giving and receiving unconditional love; deep listening; rituals to keep the energy around us clear; patience; staying in the moment; moving one step at a time; embracing all experiences and observations as essential; knowing; courage; joy; and bearing witness to life.

I'd like to take this opportunity to translate our process of becoming "peace walkers" on the Trail of Dreams World Peace Walk into daily rituals that can be useful to you. Let me begin with what the word "peace" has come to mean as we walk around the world, in and out of diverse communities and geographic surroundings where language and customs are often beyond our knowing. It means:

Passionately Engaged Affecting Compassion Everywhere.

I keep this in mind as a walking meditation as I move through the world. You can do the same as you move through your daily life or as you take on a walking practice.

Early in the walk, we learned seven basic "steps" to inner peace that continue to aid us as we walk for peace:

1. Establish a healthy relationship with self.

Walking requires time with self. Use this time to feel rather than to "think." Feel your way into knowing the spaces and places within where healing and restoration are needed.

2. Develop a spiritual practice.

Having a spiritual practice keeps us connected to a "Source" greater than ourselves. It grounds us in our potential. It enables us to walk with open eyes that witness awesome moments only a power greater than us could have created.

3. Spend at least 20 minutes a day in nature.

Nature heals. Nature fills us with her breath, the very breath of life. In nature we can breathe deeply, inhaling oxygen and exhaling carbon dioxide in a beautiful process of life-giving exchange. Nature reminds us that we are a part of a great unfolding story of Creation. Spending time in nature allows us the opportunity to develop a greater sense of awareness of life. When we begin a walk, we may find that we miss a lot, but as we continue and become attuned to what is around us, we begin to see with greater detail— flowers that nestle in a quarry of rocks, birds that sing and whistle as we pass, deer looking in our direction as we take a break for water, the orange glowing mushroom on the side of a tree, the rainbow that forms a complete circle in the sky.

4. Build supportive relationships.

Relationships are sacred, and the ultimate success of our life work comes down to the relationships we build that mutually support our life work. To many indigenous cultures of Turtle Island, North America, all relationships are considered sacred. In many North American native tribal folk tales, the turtle or tortoise offered her back to all of the land creatures when the earth was underwater. Without the Big Turtle, the earth would never have been formed. Taking the time to build and sustain relationships, even when those relationships end up looking different than we envisioned them in the beginning (e.g., couples who break up), is essential.

5. Help somebody.

We can all offer ourselves in service to others, and if we all did this, we could transform the world immediately into a place of harmony and balance. All the great masters that walked this earth did so with a mission to serve humanity. We all need help sometimes and will never forget those who reached out to us. So, be a blessing to others; practice unconditional love in all that you do. Be in service to help someone, not simply when it feels convenient but when the need is present.

6. Enroll in a program or activity that expands your awareness of self.

We often find ourselves stuck in old routines that seldom provide us the opportunity to grow, to experience ourselves in new territory, to have different experiences. Fear generally keeps us from venturing down a path of self-discovery—fear of the unknown, even fear of what others may say, fear of losing what we have, or fear of changing who we perceive ourselves to be. I encourage everyone to include in your practices programs and activities that enable you to learn more about yourself in relationship to the world around you.

7. Develop the strength and courage to follow your passions, even if at times you must walk alone.

Follow the path of your passions. What makes you resonate joy? What activity makes you completely feel you are doing what you came here to do? When you are fully engulfed in an activity, what is it that makes you feel good about yourself? So many of us lose sight of our passions, our joy, as the "stuff" of life becomes pressing. We forget the dreams that awaken us to our potential. We don't remember that we are all powerful and, instead, we settle for getting by. Our dreams have a way of rising up when we least expect it, begging for an opportunity to become our reality. Know that following the path of your passion will lead you down a path of many twists and turns. If you have the courage to go the distance—even through the times you may have to walk alone, may be misunderstood, may be talked about—you will discover the gift of your passion and make a difference in the world. In fact, you may discover what so many dream of but never realize—the true meaning of life.

Peace Walking as Ritual

A peace walk is different than an ordinary walk for exercise. Therefore, I do not recommend walking with portable music devices, such as iPods and MP3 players; they distract from the purpose of the walk. Besides, blocking out sights and sounds could make you miss something important.

Before you begin your peace walk, here is a checklist of items you'll need and things you'll want to do to make sure your walk is comfortable and safe:

1. Have appropriate, loose fitting clothes.

2. Make sure you take plenty of water.

3. Wear a hat or sun visor where appropriate and sun screen/block.

4. Wear protective sunglasses if you are sensitive to sunlight.

5. Wear appropriate shoes and socks (next to water, your most important consideration).

6. Take time to stretch your muscles.

Peace walking requires that you be fully engaged in the act of walking. I suggest you do your peace walk early in the morning when the sun is just beginning to rise. It does not matter if you are preparing for a 15-minute peace walk or a longer one. However, be sure that prior to walking, you take a few minutes to engage in a daily practice of meditation and thanks-giving. During this time, set a clear intention for your walk. These represent important elements in the peace walking process.

My daily ritual generally begins with prayers and chanting. Fragrances can enhance your meditation experience. Light incense. (Nag champa, frankin-cense, and sandalwood are among my favorites.) When using incense, don't purchase cheap incense, because it seldom has the true fragrance and often leaves an after-smell that may not be appealing.

You also can mix various oils in water and use a spray bottle to enhance the atmosphere and cleanse the energy in the room where you are praying and meditating. Spraying essential oils in the room also creates an environment that feels peaceful and sacred. (Some of my favorite oils are lotus, sandal-wood, lavender, and musk.)

Light a candle to serve as a focal point. This can prove helpful during those times when your mind begins to wander. The flame on the candle serves to bring your mind back in focus.

Following prayers and meditation, take a moment to journal things that come to you during your meditation—thoughts, ideas, points of clarity regarding something that may have been on your mind.

Having completed your morning pre-walk ritual and stretches, you now are ready to begin your walk. Make your walk as sacred as your medita-tion room. Find a broken branch on the path and turn it into your walking stick. Make it personal by varnishing it, adding feathers and beads, carving a sacred message on it, or even attaching a prayer bundle to it. Along the way you may see stones or feathers that call to you. Before you pick any-thing up, take a moment and place something personal on the ground in exchange, making an offering to Mother Earth; then, if it feels right, pick up the items that call out to you. Let these become a part of your medicine bag or altar. Remember the cyclical nature of things; when the time comes and the stones are ready to go to someone else or back to Mother Earth, release them lovingly.

A peace walk is similar to mindfulness walking, or a walking meditation, in that it doesn't matter how fast you walk. Your awareness during the walk matters most. Begin by putting a smile on your face, remembering to be grateful for the fact that you are alive and faced with the opportunity of a new beginning as you step into this new day. As you take that first step, inhale the early morning air… deeply, slowly inhale and exhale, several times. Be passionate as you begin to walk!

As you find your pace, begin to notice everything around you—the trees, the birds, bodies of water or simple puddles, the ground, any plants, unusual sounds, and smells. When you see people passing by, engage them by looking at them, smiling, and saying "good morning." If you come across something like a flower or a patch of grass, trees, or a body of water that interests you, stop and look more closely—take it all in, and give thanks; then resume your walk. Continue on like this until you have completed your walk.

As you come to the end of your Peace Walk, restate your intention for the walk and affirm yourself as one big ball of pure potential flowing in total harmony with Creation. Remember, you affect the world around you with your joy and gratitude; your radiance shines everywhere.

Incorporating walking as a daily practice has many benefits:

Body: Good cardiovascular exercise; consistent walking is excellent for toning the body and is generally good for total fitness.

Mental & Emotional: Quiets the mind; allows you to see things more clearly; connects you to the beauty of nature and the rhythm of the earth.

Spiritual: Creates a sense of connectedness to Source and to hearing that "small voice" within.

By taking on a peace walking practice, you are now Passionately Engaged Affecting Compassion Everywhere. You are peace walking. Give thanks, and enjoy your day!

Ocean Ceremony
Shri Natha Devi Premananda, Mataji

Shri Natha Devi Premananda, Mataji, Respected Spiritual Mother and founder of Eagle Wings of Enlightenment Center, has served as an instrument of light in South Los Angeles since 1985. Mataji is dedicated to the upliftment of World Peace and Non-violence. She teaches compassion, forgiveness, love, non-violence, and universal wisdom. Since 1985, she has helped many people over the years through various ancient ceremonies, teaching them to respect the Mother Earth and all people. For her humble, selfless service, she has received awards worldwide such as the Ambassador of Goodwill, International Ambassador for Peace, and recognition from the White House.

Mataji states, "Universal Oneness–the common thread that weaves all traditions together is Love, we all have come to serve each other."
ewoec@earthlink.net

In the summer of 1986, I went to the Pacific Ocean with seven offerings. While I was sitting and meditating on the beach, a beautiful being approached. She was floating off of the Pacific Ocean and coming directly toward me. She spoke these words, *"I am out of Africa. I am Yemaya. I live in the waters in Africa. I followed my children from Africa when they were forced onto slave ships that crossed the Middle Passage Way to North America. I have been with them since their arrival, during slavery and remain with them today."*

She had come with a message about making offerings to the water. She said that when I would come to make offerings to the water, she would be there every full moon. She requested that the women wear all white in honor of our ancestors who had lost their lives in the waters and on the land. She said that all of the ancestors and Mother Earth would receive a healing. She said we should come in the morning time before the sun comes up. After listening to her message and being blessed in her presence, I presented the seven offerings of honey, fruit, rice, kosher wine, yogurt, milk, and corn-meal. Those were the original seven offerings made on behalf of all of our relations. These offerings represent the wholeness of life.

In the beginning, I would journey to the ocean alone to make offerings. I later invited other women to join me in the Full Moon Ocean Ceremony for the healing of body, mind and spirit. We would make the offerings together. In 1988, more women heard about the ocean ceremony and more began to come. The numbers would range from seven women to sometimes over sixty. Over the years, Mother Yemaya gave the instructions to increase the offerings from seven to nine , nine to eleven, and eleven to thirteen. Our prayers always include a call for peace to prevail throughout the Earth; healing of all races; harmony between all the elementals; and our global elevation to become better caretakers of Mother Earth. We also pray to become more conscientious of our actions towards Mother Nature; the four-legged, the winged-ones,the creepy-crawlers, and the two-legged.

In the early '90s, I met an indigenous grandmother from the Chumash Nation. She told me that when she was a little girl she would go to the Los Angeles river and make offerings and prayers with her mother. She said that it was a good thing that I was taking the women to the ocean, and that she would be there with us in spirit. She also encouraged us to continue to make offerings monthly, for this would bring healing among nature and families and promote unity within the community. This journey to the ocean monthly has become a way of life. We have gone to the ocean for over 30 years consecutively, with an unbroken commitment to pray for all people and the world.

The purpose of the ceremony is to bring about the greater healing that is needed among women from around the world. When the women are healed, so will the men become healed. This was the message that was given when I made the first offerings to the ocean. Because of the prayers and the unconditional love that is poured from the hearts of the women who make the offerings, our ancestors benefit and *all peoples from different walks of life* benefit. The whole Earth benefits from the up above, the down below, the east, the south, the west, and the north. The flowing waters represent consciousness and movement. This flowing liquid light, is not only in the ocean, but is inside of our bodies. The winds take the offerings to the ocean and, at the same time, we are also feeding the water inside our bodies that touches divine consciousness throughout the universe.

Oneness of the great water is embedded in our consciousness as each offering is made with love and prayer. In connecting with the Great Spirit through prayers and the offerings, it helps us to remember our sacredness with all creation. It inspires us to become more expansive, caring and open hearted; and it encourages us to take better care of Mother Nature.

Mother Yemaya teaches us about peace, generosity, harmony, honoring, balance, integrity, and respect. Her spiritual presence touches us from within as we meditate upon the vastness of the ocean. It gives us the sense of unlimited possibilities with each prayer that is being offered.

<u>Mother Yemaya's Message at 7:54 p.m. PST, November 28. 2009</u>

"My children of Earth, you have violated the waters. Not only have you polluted them, but you have violated the waters. Mother Nature has extended her boundaries to all on Earth. Now is the time for no more violations. The caverns within her bodies of water have become damaged over millions and millions of years. These things have happened through the sonic boom that has caused a tremendous side effect deep within the core of the Earth Mother. The fish are losing their capability to travel in their normal pattern. The great sea monsters are angry because the food that they eat mostly has been destroyed. The whales have been eating toxic waste and they are suffering from hearing impairment. From the tiniest fish to the biggest fish, the food supply is shrinking. The king of the ocean is disturbed because their homes have become damaged. Many of the beings and creatures are becoming dislocated inside the waters because the frequencies have been tampered with which causes them to lose their way back to their original destinations. Their reproduction systems are becoming obstructed because they are missing their mating calls. The seamen are taking too many fish to eat upon at one time. They keep asking for more, but this cannot be satisfied. The sonic booms in the waters have tampered with the frequency that has offset their pattern. Mother Nature is gathering a strong force inside of herself that will cause great movement in the waters of the Earth. She has become restless. The time is now to assist in shifting the consciousness of human beings on Earth through love, caring, compassion and consideration for life forms other than human. There is no turning back for the floors of the ocean are becoming damaged by too many sonic booms. (Not sure if the message ends here or continues. I'm assuming it continues since there are no closed quote marks. However, open quote marks are needed in at beginning of each subsequent paragraph of Yemaya's message.

"In making the offerings, it becomes a gesture of love toward all creatures and beings. At the same time, the two-legged are the ones to take care and not cause problems with Mother Nature. There is a destiny that is in store for all of us. This destiny will reach its highest level of regeneration through Mother Nature, for it is not for man to make decisions on how Mother Nature is to regenerate herself. It is for man to pray and feed nature as nature also feeds him, with love. For the time is coming when man must accept his full duty throughout Mother Earth as a caretaker, not as one who takes and takes and takes and does not leave anything behind. In ancient times, man understood the law of nature. Whenever, he went to pick something to eat, he always left something behind. In turn, his daily sustenance would have been met.

"The women who have been going to the water to make the offerings on behalf of all two-legged are remembering the ancient ways. For this way keeps the balance and the harmony throughout the universe. It restores peace in the hearts of the two-legged who may not have it. It opens up new ideas for it will flow from the up above and touch every cell throughout the body… It flows into the Earth and comes back up again through the feet, the legs, the heart, and the head and joins once again with the Creator in consciousness. When they feed the waters and stand inside, they will connect with the Creator. They will be in oneness with the Divine remembrance, and the things they need to know in the life will be there for them. For this is the walk of the two-legged: *To remember how in ancient times man did not take without giving back.*"

May all women be touched by Mother Yemaya's message to make offerings to all the bodies of water throughout the seven continents. It is our time to give back to our Mother Earth with gratitude and remembrance that we are all related. The time is now to demonstrate our compassion through pure actions by allowing ourselves to go to the water and pray for all people, your community, and the world. May the Great Spirit bless all people to remember that they are the Sacred. May we all live in harmony and unity with our brothers and sisters. As Mother Yemaya said many moons ago–"*When the women are healed so will the men be healed.*" That message is ringing loud throughout the Earth at this time. Women all around the world are protesting for their rights. This is why Mother Yemaya calls for all the women of the Earth to make their prayers and offerings at the water. Healing is inevitable. Sooner or later, it will manifest itself. May all women from all walks of life go to the water and pray for all people, your community, and the world. Mother Yemaya welcomes you! Aho!

Ceremony of Self-Marriage

Rev. Uki MacIsaac

Rev. Uki MacIsaac, MA, is an internationally acclaimed speaker, intuitive counselor, and ordained minister who was born and raised in Stuttgart, Germany. Through her unique gift of clairvoyance, she empowers her clients to integrate their spiritual purpose and live a fuller, more meaningful life. The experience of overcoming life-threatening illnesses more than once inspired MacIsaac to make her mission teaching, healing, and inspiring others to heal themselves by connecting to the power of Spirit within. For more information on MacIsaac's work, visit www.ukimacisaac.com.

As a non-denominational minister, I often am asked to perform wedding ceremonies. I love to be the officiant at a time that represents such a milestone in a couple's commitment to each other. A lot of planning and preparation goes into the creation of that special day. Many future brides plan their big day to the minutest detail, spending tremendous energy and a lot of money on creating the perfect wedding. Family and friends may come from afar for this one special occasion. It is an emotional moment when the couple speak their vows to each other. They commit to honoring and supporting the other through thick and thin, in good as well as in challenging times. Unless the bride and groom are mired in the illusion of some perfect, infallible mate, they know their beloved has some faults and flaws. They trust that the love they feel for each other will allow them to ride the current of life with all its expected and unexpected turns.

So why is it that we are so willing to be fully supportive and loving of our partners in marriage, but we don't extend that same loving kindness to ourselves? Why are women, especially, often so nurturing to others but merciless toward themselves and critical of their own perceived shortcomings? I have asked myself these questions often, and I also have come to understand that sometimes it is better to stop analyzing and to just take action in the direction of the desired goal. A ceremony of self-marriage provides an important action step towards quieting the voice of the inner critic, calming the heart and offering greater harmony within.

To some, this may sound like a self-obsessed or vain proposal. Let me explain why I believe this ceremony does not represent an ego-based parade but rather an important expression of healthy self-love.

Why We Need a Ceremony of Self-Marriage

We live in intense times. The evolution of our souls progresses at such a rapid pace that we sometimes feel breathless and uncomfortable. The study of sacred geometry and wave phenomena reveals that increased vibration affects matter; familiar structures give way to chaotic energy before new structures and patterns of a higher complexity establish themselves. Along these same lines, many of us feel old definitions of self and the roles we play in partnership, family, business, and community are changing quickly. A new self announces itself gently, but the old self, the ego, clings to the known and does not want to relinquish control.

Moving through such times of transition can feel unsettling, as I recently experienced in my own life. Even at an older age, we experience growing pains. I have found that "shadow" aspects of self—character traits or behaviors I denied or did not accept as my reality—emerged quite strongly at these times. The unhappy, unhealthy trinity of blame, shame, and guilt raised their ugly heads, despite my many years of deep soul-healing work. Every unloved, unhealed voice inside my mind wanted my attention like a spoiled, yet deeply unhappy child. I compared my insides to other people's outsides, and in that comparison I was always "less than." Memories of painful events that occurred over 25 years ago emerged. I had not forgiven myself for my failings—perceived or real—at that time. I came to identify these voices as expressions of the ego mind, and it was impossible to silence them. The only lasting change came from a place of inner acceptance of all that I am and from a gently loving voice—the voice of my true self.

The true self, or Higher Self, voice never comes from a place of blaming or accusing. It doesn't come from arguing but rather from accepting. A gentle, quiet voice, it resides in the heart or the belly; it cannot be heard through the thunder of the thinking, ego-based mind. The true self is child-like, innocent, unafraid of trying. It gently knocks on the doors of the rational self, not knowing if it will ever be heard. Sometimes the doors open just a crack, and the child slips through, eager to discover and explore.

What if this little fearful ego mind wants to melt into the loving arms of the Higher Self? What if the Higher Self can embrace that ego mind and create a greater union, greater harmony, greater love between the two? For this to happen, the initiative must come from the mortal, limited self. Maybe all the resistance and fighting that the ego mind creates leads to the point of surrender—and surrender opens the door to what lies on the other side: the infinite love of the divine self, the true self. The more I can surrender to the grace and the wisdom of the God/Goddess within, the more I can become the vessel for the Divine as expressed through me, with me. I am not speaking about a God high up the heavens, far above the joys and tribulations of human beings; I am addressing the Divine that is our true essence, the "Spirit having a human experience."

Self-Marriage Makes Room for a "Real" Partner

If you feel concerned that a ceremony of self-marriage does not leave room in your life for a "real" partner, don't worry. We can give only what we have. If we don't know how to be our own best friend and unconditional support, how can we be that to someone else? Most would agree that acceptance and embracing of all aspects of self are almost a requirement for a healthy, happy, and lasting relationship. To me, intimacy means being fully present: body, mind and spirit. It means an open heart and the willingness to give and to receive. How can we be intimate with each other if we are not comfortable with our own selves? As we affirm our heart's truth in spite of the voices of the ego mind, we also affirm our wholeness, our divine blueprint of perfection. The ceremony of self-marriage opens the door to healing and to alignment with divine plan.

Creating Your Self-Marriage Day

Imagine a wedding celebration with no other partner than the one you will surely live with for the rest of your life. (No divorce until your last breath!) Imagine a sacred union that brings together all aspects of self—both the likeable and the not-so-likeable traits—wedding the inner masculine to the inner feminine expression, the receptive and the assertive, the warrior and the fearful child, the creative and the wise parts within. It brings into divine harmony that which has been separated by limiting beliefs and life's tough lessons, but which, in actuality, has always been whole and complete. The conditioned mind simply cannot comprehend the truth of our being. Only in rare moments, such as during meditation and ceremony, do the limits of the egoic mind expand to allow for our light and love to shine as beloved children of Source, Creator, God, Goddess, Nature—whatever you wish to call your Higher Power.

The ceremony of self-marriage also is not limited to gender, race, or religious beliefs. It does not discriminate, only unifies. It does not matter whether you are single or divorced, in a relationship or hoping to be in one soon, a woman or a man, straight or gay, young or old. None of this matters. As long as you are willing to make a commitment to your wholeness and "holiness," in a very undogmatic sense of the word, this ritual may serve you.

By engaging in the ceremony, you simply make a sacred commitment. You promise to be fully present with you through thick and thin, in sickness and in health. Whether the wording of the vow to yourself is simple or elegant, short or elaborate, the importance lies in your intent, in your heart energy, as you speak your truth.

Here are some of the words that ring true for me. Imagine your Higher Self speaking these words to the self you identify with most of the time, the ego self.

"(Name), I love you so much! I will stand by you no matter what. I won't let you down, no matter what life shall bring. I am here for you. I stand by you. I support you. I honor you and respect you. From this moment forward, I promise to hold up a sacred mirror of unconditional love, especially in moments of fear or doubt. I celebrate the love and the light that you are. I will be your faithful companion on this Earth journey and beyond. I am so grateful for who you are. We now are one, inseparable, whole and holy, forever."

Speaking your vows as you look into a mirror sends a powerful message to your heart, anchoring the importance of the promise you make. If your soul expands more fully in a beautiful place in nature, by all means, go with that choice. We are connected to and reflected in all of creation, so it does not matter if you pronounce your sacred vows to the you that is the ocean, the you that is the earth, the you that is the sky, or the you in the mirror.

As in a more traditional wedding ceremony, you may wish to set the stage for your ceremony of self-marriage. The subconscious mind relates to images, symbols, and special objects that hold value to us. A ring often symbolizes unity, unending love, and the circle of life. Special clothing, maybe a new dress and shoes, fresh flowers, and a bottle of bubbly assist in creating a festive setting for this celebration. Play your favorite music, light a candle; allow your heart to be playful and have fun.

The signing of a wedding certificate serves as an important step towards sealing the marriage. When we put things in writing and sign our name to a document, we commit to the content of the document. Ask an artist friend to create a marriage certificate for you, or make your own, on special paper and in a pretty font. You can even get fancy and imprint a fake seal. The sky, or rather, your imagination is the limit!

Another important decision in preparing for the ceremony is the choice of being alone or in a group of supportive friends. I can imagine a whole circle of like-minded people speaking their vows of self-marriage, one by one, while the others hold the space with their intent and support. It is important, though, to choose only people who resonate with the ceremony, so that the energy remains consistent and uplifting. You don't need to invite skeptics on your special day!

When my husband and I prepared for our wedding, we wanted to speak our very own personal vows to each other. Looking for inspiration in books and on the Internet, we were surprised to find that many of the published vows, traditional or New Age, did not resonate with us. Finally the right words emerged. We spoke them to each other not only at the wedding ceremony but many times after that. I actually have a copy of those vows always with me on a small slip of paper in my wallet. There have been times when I pulled that slip out and read them aloud. I needed to remind him and re-mind myself, maybe at a time when we were not communicating so clearly or when feelings were hurt, of our commitment. Speaking those vows again shifted us completely back into the space of honoring and listening and loving each other.

I offer you our words to use in your ceremony of self-marriage, slightly modified from the original vow. We did not come up with the words entirely on our own, but I am not able to give credit to the many sources that inspired us.

"I, (name), ask you to be my partner and my friend. I announce and declare that I will give you my deepest friendship and love, not only when your moments are high, but when they are low. Not only when you remember clearly who you are, but when you forget—not only when you are acting with love, but when you are not. I promise that I will always see the light of Divinity within you. I ask to be with you forever in a holy partnership of the soul, that we may be and do the work of Spirit, sharing our gifts with all those whose lives we touch."

This example illustrates the importance of living the vow, not simply speaking it once. As in any marriage, living in full partnership with our Higher Self means moments of bliss and moments of challenge. Any relationship has its ups and downs, times when one partner wants to control and dominate, demanding to have his or her way. For some time, the balance can tip toward one end or another, but that does not mean that the relationship is doomed. Maybe it just needs to be brought into balance again. The voice of fear inside tends to be noisy and insistent, but the voice of courage and hope also exists. When I can acknowledge the voice of fear and accept, rather than fight it, I am able to shift the balance of my inner self back to center. Maybe fear and courage, rather than being opposites, exist on a continuum of thoughts and emotions where each constitutes one end, polarities on a delicate scale. Repeating your vows to yourself at times of challenge helps shift the dial on that scale just a little towards the positive end of the perceived polarity, towards acceptance and loving what is.

In a healthy partnership, we can serve as sacred mirrors to each other, as promised in the vows, and we can be that same sacred mirror to ourselves. When my perception becomes clouded by health challenges, financial hardships, or perceived or real threats, then that sacred mirror allows me to gently slide into the greater expression of self. I take a deep breath and tell myself: "I know I am not alone in this. I have vowed to support myself lovingly through all aspects of life. I am here for myself in unconditional love and support. I allow the voices of my critical mind to subside and surrender to the loving voice of my higher self. I am at peace."

The commitment to speak your vows in a special ceremony and to live them to the best of your ability, reminding yourself frequently why you spoke them in the first place and what you promised to yourself, represents an important step towards greater self-love and self-acceptance. As in any marriage, it is not enough to have a one-time, glamorous event and sign a piece of paper. That paper might be legally binding, but the document alone obviously does not make for a successful, long-lasting union. Relationship, with self or others, requires awareness of our thoughts and feelings, clear communication, the ability to speak our truth, and forgiveness and embracing what is.

If every day, just before you moved into your daily routine, you took a moment of quiet to recite your vows to yourself, silently or aloud, this one ritual would set the tone for your whole day. It would connect you with your Higher Self in your thoughts, words, and actions. This practice is not about being perfect but about awareness and conscious intent. Being more fully present within ourselves allows us to be more fully present with others.

Creating a ceremony of self-marriage, or simply speaking your vows of unconditional love and support to yourself, represents much more than an ego-serving exercise.

Ego is a very powerful influence in our lives. A strong motivator in the emotional and physical body, it shapes our presence and experience in the real world every day. And yet the ego often "lives" in fear of being dismissed, disregarded, destroyed. Honoring the ego, giving it a place and a higher purpose, brings its actions into alignment and partnership with the intention of our Higher Self. This is not ego-serving: instead, it enrolls the ego in a loving partnership with the Higher Self to fulfill Divine purpose.

When we fully accept and embrace all that we are, we shine our light into the world with greater clarity and beauty. In the holy union of all aspects of self, we are whole again. Inviting more light into our souls allows us to perceive and honor the light in all others, bringing full embodiment to the truth that loving ourselves is the first step to loving others. May you find your own truth and light by being open to the celebration of the God within. To place this thought within a different context, remember the famous lines of a Chinese proverb:

> *"If there is light in the soul,*
>
> *There will be beauty in the person.*
>
> *If there is beauty in the person,*
>
> *There will be harmony in the house.*
>
> *If there is harmony in the house,*
>
> *There will be order in the nation.*
>
> *If there is order in the nation,*
>
> *There will be peace in the world."*

The Way of the Healer: Pay Attention to What Has Heart and Meaning

Angeles Arrien

*Dr. Angeles Arrien was an extraordinary anthropologist, author, and corporate consultant. She lectured and conducted workshops worldwide, showing the bridge between cultural anthropology, psychology, and comparative religions. Her work reveals how indigenous wisdoms are relevant to our families, professional lives, and our relationship to the Earth.

The archetype of the Healer is a universal mythic structure that all human beings experience. Among indigenous cultures the Healer supports the principle of *paying attention to what has heart and meaning.* Healers in all major traditions recognize that the power of love is the most potent healing force available to all human beings. Effective Healers from any culture are those who extend the arms of love: acknowledgment, acceptance, recognition, validation, and gratitude.

People the world over consistently acknowledge each other in four ways. We acknowledge each other's skills; each other's character qualities; each other's appearance; and the impact we make on each other. Wherever we receive the least acknowledgment is where we may carry a belief of inadequacy or low self-esteem.

Healers in any tradition are inherently skilled in the art of acknowledgment. They fully recognize that the greatest remorse is love unexpressed. Probably the most powerful contemporary example of a person who demonstrates the healing power of extending love was Mother Teresa. In shamanic traditions she would have been called a medicine woman.

AN INTRODUCTION TO THE BRAIDED WAY

Angeles Arrien

Braided Way Healing Arts, is derived from a quotation from **Dr. Angeles Arrien, Cultural Anthropologist**, "We must learn to walk the braided way and bridge the different worlds."

THE BRAIDED WAY… Where diversity is respected and, out of our synergetic joining, capacities for communication and people skills are enhanced. The authors in this anthology have addressed the themes of interdependence, new models, and skills that bring attention to and expression of self-esteem, integrity, and enjoyment. Our challenge is to foster creativity that supports cooperative economics for the purpose of creating a global society that values diversity and universal common grounds. We have reviewed the trends and research and we have many resources mobilized to the direction where we are all mutually challenged, recognized and supported to create a New World Order.

Working Together ~ Diversity as Opportunity

What is The Braided Way

The Braided Way is a Spiritual path that weaves the world's many beautiful traditions that serve true seekers in knowing the Divine. The Braided Way has no special dogma other than welcoming the exploration of traditions that teach peace, love and inclusion. The Braided Way is not a melting pot of world religions into one philosophy. Instead, the metaphor of the braid represent our many wonderous paths, intertwined together, creating an unbreakable cord of human connection.

The Braided Way does not dictate which traditions one explores. For example, a person who identifies primarily as Catholic may also engage in Loving Kindness meditation from the Buddhist tradition. The Agnostic may want to explore Shamanic journeying while the Secularist embraces the medical benefits of a meditation circle. The freedom inherent in The Braided Way honors the journey we are all on together. Aho! Amen! Namaste! (**thebraidedway.org**)

BRAIDED WAY—Faces and Voices of Spiritual Practice

The Braided Way is a framework to see every faith tradition as a strand, braided into a larger whole of spiritual awareness. In the Braided Way, combining spiritual practice from various faiths allow us to explore sacred experience and wonder in forms that resonate with our personal spiritual needs and sacred intuitions. In today's culture, many people shun religious dogma, but yearn for spiritual connection. The Braided Way allows the ceremonies and practices of multiple faiths to be available without the confinements of cultural dogma. (**braidedway.org**)

WISDOM QUOTES FROM ANGELES

*"As Maya Angelou said, 'I've learned that people will forget
what you said, people will forget what you did,
but people will never forget how you made them feel."*

*"We must learn to walk the braided way
and bridge the different worlds."*

*"The visionary is the one who brings his or her voice into the
world and who refuses to edit, rehearse, perform, or hide.
It is the visionary who knows that the power of creativity
is aligned with authenticity."*

ACKNOWLEDGMENTS

Amshatar (Ololodi) Monroe

Amshatar (Ololodi) Monroe is an Initiated Priest, Founder of Sacred Space Where Indigenous Paths Meet, a Ceremonialist, and a Sacred-Events Coordinator. For more than 40 years, she has been a professional "gatherer" of people from divergent paths and an advocate for indigenous culture, earth-based spirituality and oneness consciousness.

Later her work began to shift and respond to the beckoning of the Divine Feminine. Amshatar midwifed Women of Spirit an organization that facilitates retreats, conferences, tele-seminars, classes and other gatherings to invoke, engage, and ignite the unifying principles of the Divine Feminine, honoring nature, difference, oneness, love, compassion and peace.

My sincere appreciation and heartfelt gratitude to the many who encouraged and helped in the birthing of this collective volume ... Women of Spirit share Rituals Divine. Thank You, Thank You, Thank You!

I give an abundance of gratitude to both Dr. Angeles Arrien and Iya N"Ifa Farinola Efunyale (a.k.a Mother Taylor), for there strong encouragement for me to write a book on ritual! That had just been a minimal thought in my mind—It was a challenge, however, for which I became deeply grateful and appreciative for their love and wisdom.

I extend my deep gratitude to my treasured and longtime friends and colleagues who encouraged me to 'keep on pushing'! ... So, keep on pushing I shall!

THE POWER OF PRAYER!

Dearest and Beloved Kimberly, Kanika and Teja, my longtime, loving, lifetime sister prayer queens. I still treasure our break-of-dawn morning prayers. Thanks to each of you, I am blessed to have dedicated and sincere prayer-queens who catch my back when needed and who lift my prayers when I weaken. Know that my prayers and presence, though not always in the flesh, are ALWAYS with you in Spirit. Eternal Blessings my beloved prayer queens!

To my deep sadness five awesome women contributors to *Women of Spirit share Rituals Divine* made their transition prior to the final touches of the book. Though they are no longer with us physically, they and their contributions are certainly with us in spirit. May they each: Angeles Arrien, Iya N'Ifa Farinola Efunyale (Mother Taylor), Barbara Daniel Cox, Nana Yaa Densua, and Sobonfu Somé know unquestionably that they are eternally loved, remembered and blessed!

DEEP GRATITUDE TO MY LONGTIME FRIENDS & COLLEAGUES!

"I AM SO BLESSED"... Lyrics & Recording By KAREN DRUCKER

I am so blessed, I am so blessed, I am so grateful for all that I have! I am so blessed, I am so blessed, I am so grateful (to have YOU in my life) ... I AM SOOO BLESSED!

Wow ... I am SO blessed with my encouraging and supportive friends and loved ones ... Thank You All!

Arnae Batson your research skills are still sharp I'm sure! I often think about the research you did on the museums for the Women of Spirit project. Much Gratitude! Omilade I'm so thankful for your wisdom, patience and GREAT suggestions! Omosade, she who offers much to many! Thank you for always being willingly helpful! Sangodare and Alexis Gumbs, Thank you so very much for your helpful guidance, and yes, I'm still trying to catch up with your 'how to' wisdom, smile!

Asantewaa, my long time friend and supporter, you always extend your willingness to provide support when needed. I thank you immensely for your consistent loving kindness! Andrea Sharpe (aka Honey Chile) is the big hearted one who is always willing to share her wisdom and give a helping hand when needed ... thank you so very much..."Honey Chile"! Alison and Mama Skeete you are always offering uplifting thoughts and wise suggestions, deep gratitude and appreciation to both of these big-hearted angels! Gwen Whitfield and Fannie Jo Tate, two friends that I have known like sisters sense we were in kindergarten thru high school together in Washington, DC, I give thanks! God bless my DC crew who also have my back when needed and for whom I will always do the same, I give thanks for ... Lona Alias, Veronica Thompson, Latore Whitaker, Romas Maith are also my DC friends forever! My Atlanta sister-friends also mean so much to me, we always share our love and support with any project that any of us are working on! Doctor Rashon, Aba Bailey, Dionne Turner, Lydia Floyd, Janice Clemons, Nadia Ramadan, Remi Burns, Niyonu Benson, Andi Anderson, Saabirah Bashir and my other Atlanta sisters...LOVE to You All!; The very wonderful EJ and SaraLu and my new Jazmin Hankins Winston Salem friend too are wonderful women of wisdom! I hope you will meet each other soon come.

WOW... How blessed I am, and we each are, to have such AWESOME Kind, Loving and Wise Lifetime Friends Forever!

JANELL WALDEN AGYEMAN ... is Founder and President of Next Steps Literary Services, and is an Editorial and Publishing Consultant! Her work is awesome and her knowledge exquisite! What a gift to have her on our team!!!

Cindy Radford, a longtime friend and wise financial, professional wizard! Her willingness to manage the accounting for this project is a HUGE gift of support! I am so thankful for your generous openheartedness. Thank You Cindy. May your blessings always be abundant.

EDITORS EXTRAORDINARE
Nina Amir, Megan Scribner, Linda Horton each are exquisite nonfiction developmental editors extraordinaire! What a blessing they each brought to the project! Deep gratitude! If you have need for an editing expert, I highly recommend either of these awesome and exceedingly knowledgeable editors!

INSIDE GRAPHIC DESIGN
Alice@Infographcreative.com
Alice Sanders, owner and designer of InfoGraph Creative. Her inside design work for this project was impeccable. Deep Gratitude!

BOOK COVER AND WEBSITE DESIGN
Contact@SoulIndigo.com
Thank you **Mark "Feijao" Milligan II** for your exquisite creativity and your patience with my multiple requests to make minor changes!

BCP DIGITAL@yahoo.com
Paul Coates, I am so glad that your name surprisingly came up during a brief conversations while I was visiting in D.C.! I knew then that I would reconnect with you and your work before I left D.C. How perfect!

FETZER INSTITUTE ~ *"It's Been Such a Long Time, Since I Saw YOU! How long has it been? A dated Song by* New Birth"
Hafsat Abiola, Paul Boumbulian, Agbanyero Chukwudebe, Mirsad Jacevic, Sue Keister, Robert Kenny, Kathleen Kostelny, Elise Miller, Laura Rendon, Alison Sander, Saki Santorelli, Lisa White, Eugene Callender (I pray he is peacefully continuing his work of service to the masses in heaven!), **Sharon Ball, Thomas Inui, Linda Lantieri, Carmella B'han, Mary Corrigan, Wayne Muller, Jacob Needleman, Mel King, Meg Wheatley, Arthur Zajonc, Mark Nepo, Dave and Carole Schwinn, Marlene Arnold, Marianna Cacciatore, and Marian David** ... Wow!

All of you, *every-one of you* made a *huge* impact on my life. Yes, Angie in her wise and loving ways nurtured most of us in one way or another. I am finally completing a task that Angie encouraged me to embrace *years ago ... a book on rituals ...* Only Angie!

Our time together with each of us under the magical wisdom of Angie was transforming. Those were indeed, for me, "the good ole days". I pray that all is wonderful and well with each of you and yours, now and forever!

Additionally, I want to use this opportunity to thank you all for your loving kindness and your powerful impact on my life. Because of each of YOU...and Angie of course, I am joyfully looking forward to completing the book, "**WOMEN of SPIRIT share RITUALS DIVINE**". Of the forty female contributors in the book, I'm happy to say that Laura Rendon, Linda Lantieri, Lynne Twist, Meg Wheatley, Carole Schwinn, Gail Needleman and Pat Harbour ... all of whom are Fetzer contributors in the book...yeah team!

Of most importance… Deep Gratitude to my Daughter (Esharan Monroe-Johnson) and Son-In-Love (Kelvis Johnson) who were of immense technical support. THANK YOU, THANK YOU, THANK YOU! Thank God that my granddaughters can navigate on computers. I have often sought them out for help, with what to any of the four of them, seemed miniscule to them and HUGE to me! My love and appreciation to my girls Amaya (age 14), Mikayla (age 13), Niyae (age 10), Eliah (age 8) ... and our new baby boy, Kairo (age 5 ½ months)… He Rules! What a blessing!.

I pray that you will find lots to be moved by and much to embrace! ENJOY **Women of Spirit share Rituals Divine!**

I am living in the field of Infinite, Unlimited and Unlimitable Possibilities!!!

Amshatar (Ololodi) Monroe

101020-200-2-60W